Tany Trowbridge

Women and
Culture Series

*The Women and Culture Series is dedicated to books that illuminate the lives, roles, achievements, and status of women, past or present.*

# MARRIAGE, CLASS AND COLOUR
# IN NINETEENTH-CENTURY CUBA

# MARRIAGE, CLASS AND COLOUR IN NINETEENTH-CENTURY CUBA

## A Study of Racial Attitudes and Sexual Values in a Slave Society

Verena Martinez-Alier

ANN ARBOR
THE UNIVERSITY OF MICHIGAN PRESS

Published in the United States of America by
The University of Michigan Press
Manufactured in the United States of America

1992  1991  1990  1989    4  3  2


LIBRARY OF CONGRESS CATALOGING-IN-PUBLICATION DATA

Stolcke, Verena.
    Marriage, class, and colour in nineteenth-century Cuba: a study
of racial attitudes and sexual values in a slave society / Verena
Martinez-Alier. — 2nd ed.
        p.   cm.
    Bibliography: p.
    Includes index.
    ISBN 0-472-06405-3 (alk. paper)
    1. Interracial marriage — Cuba — History — 19th century.   2. Social
classes — Cuba — History — 19th century.   3. Cuba — Social conditions.
I. Title.
HQ1031.S77   1989
306.84'6'09729109034 — dc20                                          89-32475
                                                                          CIP

# CONTENTS

v

## Contents

# PREFACE

When I first went to Cuba in 1967 my intention was to study its present-day family organization. I wanted to test the various hypotheses developed by sociologists and social anthropologists on family structure in other parts of the Caribbean and examine the extent to which the 1959 revolution had already brought about changes in the Cuban family. For bureaucratic reasons, however, I was only able to spend two months in the field in a small, predominantly coloured coffee-growing village in the Sierra Maestra. This brief stay allowed me to gain an overall impression of the villagers' family organization – the prevalence of stable consensual unions – but was clearly insufficient to understand its complexities, and much less to assess the impact of the revolution, although there were many indications that it had already affected family values in some ways. Thus I was often asked by the villagers, and in particular by the women, whether I had been sent by the revolutionary government in connection with the 'collective marriage' campaign, which had already reached other parts of the island and whose aim it was to give those couples who had so far lived in concubinage the opportunity to marry formally. While the women seemed to welcome this measure, men appeared to be more evasive. Also, the local political secretary, one of the judges of the local people's court, and the secretary of the peasant association pointed out repeatedly that as high-ranking members of the community they would have to get formally married at some point.

Before this short field-work trip and while waiting in Havana for an opportunity to return to the village, which in the end never materialized, I searched the National Archive in Havana for historical material on the family. The largest sections of the Archive, namely the Fondo de Gobierno Superior Civil, the Fondo de Gobierno General and the Fondo de Asuntos Políticos, are catalogued by subject matters. The heading 'marriage', particularly in the Fondo del Gobierno Superior Civil, proved to be a mine of information on marriage practice and policy in nineteenth-century Cuba. Supplemented by more scanty material from other sections, these data constitute the bulk of the information underlying this study.

vii

Another voluminous section, uncatalogued as yet, the Fondo de Miscelánea, yielded most of the material on elopement and seduction.
Already in the early stages of checking and extracting these materials,
the relevance of nineteenth-century Cuban marriage policy and practice
for an understanding of the twentieth century became apparent. Thus
I spent the rest of my stay of a year in the Archive, checking secondary
sources at the Biblioteca Nacional 'José Martí'. Subsequently, I also
spent some time in Spain at the Archivo Histórico Nacional of Madrid
and at the Archivo General de Indias in Seville, but as the judicial questions
in connection with marriage were for the most part the concern of the
Cuban judiciary, the material in the Spanish archives is scarce.

I am much indebted to the people of the Cuban National Archive
for their guidance to the various sections and for their never-ending
patience in locating the documents for me, and also to Julio LeRiverend,
its head, who made it possible for me to work there. I also want to thank
José Luciano Franco, Juan Pérez de la Riva, Jorge Ibarra, Magnus Mörner
and Ravindra Jain for the fruitful discussions we had on critical points
of the study and for guiding me to useful materials and secondary
sources.

This book is based upon a D. Phil. thesis submitted to the University
of Oxford. Both for editorial reasons and for the sake of readability a
substantial part of the evidence contained in the thesis has been omitted
here. Anyone who should want to consult the thesis can find it at the
Bodleian Library in Oxford. I am very grateful to the two examiners of
the thesis, Tulio Halperín and John Campbell, for their encouragement
to turn the thesis into a book, and in particular to Sidney W. Mintz for
subjecting it to careful scrutiny and offering many useful comments. I
owe special thanks to Malcolm Deas for his humorous criticism and
helpful advice on how to thin out a dense thesis. And I want to acknowledge the help of the Bodleian Library and in particular Colin Steele
in acquiring valuable secondary sources hitherto unavailable in Great
Britain.

My particular gratitude goes to Peter Rivière who taught me social
anthropology and who supervised the thesis, for his continual encouragement and his many useful suggestions. Paradoxical though it may seem,
considering the view on marriage proposed in this study, I have a husband.
It is to him that I owe my greatest debt. His patience in coping with the
various domestic crises that arose throughout my work did much in
providing the peace of mind the work required. Our many fruitful
quarrels clarified many points which would otherwise have remained

obscured. As he grew increasingly fascinated with the subject he gracefully undertook for once to play second fiddle, and became a most useful research assistant.

St Antony's College, Oxford
*February 1973*

V. M.-A.

# ABBREVIATIONS

| | |
|---|---|
| ANC | Archivo Nacional de Cuba, Havana |
| GSC | Gobierno Superior Civil |
| GG | Gobierno General |
| AP | Asuntos Políticos |
| CA | Consejo de Administración |
| Misc. | Miscelánea |
| AHNM | Archivo Histórico Nacional, Madrid |
| AGI | Archivo General de Indias, Seville |
| ACEM | Archivo del Consejo de Estado, Madrid |
| CDFS | Richard Konetzke (ed.), *Colección de documentos para la historia de la formación social de Hispanoamérica, 1493–1810* (3 vols, Madrid, 1953–62). |
| Leg. | Legajo – a box or bundle of documents |

# INTRODUCTION
# TO THE SECOND EDITION

Books are like people; they age, although some do it better than others and some even mature before their time. When I wrote this book in the early seventies its central thesis, the dynamic interaction between racial prejudice and gender hierarchy in the reproduction of a slave society (and, for that matter, of class society), had not yet become part of the agenda of feminist scholars' investigations of women's subordination. Only very recently have feminist anthropologists proposed a more unified analysis of gender relations and kinship systems. This newer approach stresses the social construction of gender and kinship relationships by processes of social reproduction, by contrast with earlier naturalist interpretations that attributed women's subordinate condition to the burden of maternity or to their relegation to the private sphere, which was conceived as naturally distinct from the public sphere.[1]

Recent work on marriage patterns and kin relationships among blacks in the Caribbean has focused, in turn, on the slave family, challenging earlier notions of family disorganisation under the harsh conditions of slavery. This revision has generated a more differentiated understanding of the possibilities slaves had to form domestic units and to maintain kin ties, though it also entails the risk of minimizing the coercitive nature of slavery.[2]

---

1. J. Fishburne Collier and S. Junko Yanagisako, eds., *Gender and Kinship: Essays Toward a Unified Analysis* (Stanford: Stanford University Press, 1987). I thank Jane Collier and Rebecca J. Scott especially for their kindness in reading this introduction and for their very useful comments.

2. V. Stolcke, "The Slavery Period and Its Influence on Household Structure and the Family: Jamaica, Cuba and Brazil," paper presented at the Seminar on Changing Family Structure and Life Courses in LDCs, Honolulu, 5–7 January 1987, forthcoming in a conference volume by Oxford University Press. Attention should also be drawn to some more recent studies of prenuptial conflicts and marriage patterns in colonial Latin America such as P. Seed, *To Love, Honor, and Obey in Colonial Mexico, Conflicts*

Finally, matrifocality, one of the central issues in this book, has also been the object of new investigation. R. T. Smith has analysed the interaction of race with class and gender inequalities in contemporary creole class society with a dual marriage system.[3] The specific meanings of matrifocal domestic units depending on whether they result from interracial or interclass sexual relations or from intraclass unions, to which I only alude, have, however, not yet been clearly distinguished.[4]

Simultaneously, racism has again raised its ugly head in Western industrial societies. In the seventies, capitalist societies experienced the end of the postwar economic boom. A growing concern over the decline of birth rates in Europe (especially in both Germanies and France but more recently also in Spain) found expression in a natalist discourse and public policies designed to induce women to return to the home. This trend went hand in hand with a deepening antagonism toward so-called non-European immigrant labour and progressively more restrictive immigration policies with clear racist overtones, even in the industrialized countries without a past in slavery. In the United States the turn to the right has reinforced the image of women as wives and mothers and, on the other hand, supported restrictive social policies that have contributed to the feminization of poverty and a recent increase in racism in a progressively more competitive society. At the same time, the debt crisis in Latin America has produced a noticeable increase in female-headed households there.[5] Despite these economic, political, and analytical developments, the interaction among racial discrimination, gender relations, and class formation remains unclear.[6]

It may be appropriate on the occasion of republication of this book to spell out and qualify some of the implications of my own analysis

*over Marriage Choice, 1574–1821* (Stanford: Stanford University Press, 1988), and R. Gutiérrez, "Marriage, Sex, and the Family: Social Change in Colonial New Mexico, 1690–1846," Ph.d. diss, University of Wisconsin-Madison, 1976.

3. R. T. Smith, "Hierarchy and the Dual Marriage System in West Indian Society," in Collier and Junko Yanagisako 1987.

4. For such a differentiation see Stolcke 1987.

5. J. Massiah, *Women as Heads of Households in the Caribbean: Family Structure and Feminine Status* (Unesco, 1983); M. A. Lycette and W. P. McGreevey, eds., *Women and Poverty in the Third World* (Baltimore: Johns Hopkins University Press, 1983); V. Stolcke, *Coffee Planters, Workers and Wives: Class Conflict and Gender Relations on Sao Paulo Plantations, 1850–1980* (London: Macmillan/St. Antony's College, Oxford, 1988).

6. Katherine Burdekin in her fascinating dystopia *Swastika Night*, published in London in 1940 under the male pseudonym Murray Constantine, set out the interplay among race, class, and gender most clearly. Academic scholarship, however, was slow to develop these themes.

in this respect and to draw some parallels with modern class society in general.

## RACE AND GENDER UNDER SLAVERY

The interracial marriage prohibition introduced in Cuba in the early nineteenth century exemplifies the essentially jural political nature of the dichotomy between public and private spheres sustained by liberal political philosophy. Marriage patterns, family structure, and kin relationships, far from being natural facts, were sociopolitical constructs responding to the political interests of the colonial government coupled with the ingrained racism characteristic of a slave society. But nineteenth-century Cuba was not a closed caste society, as some authors would have it. On the contrary, the liberal ethos of individual achievement and freedom, manifest in the though-limited opportunities available to negotiate a compensation of racial status by economic performance and in the role love played in the choice of marriage partners had also left its mark. In particular white parents' and the government's attitudes toward interracial marriage revealed a tension between this liberal ethos and the imperatives of racial purity. I thus interpreted nineteenth-century Cuba as a class society whose mechanisms of sociopolitical reproduction were informed by an ideological conflation of heredity and inheritance, that is, of the genetic transmission of racial purity and the legal and economic perpetuation of social privilege and rank.

The principal victims of this normative tension between the tenets of racial segregation and of individual freedom of choice were, in different ways, black women and men as well as white women. The prevailing social hierarchy was legitimated in racial, that is, in putatively genetic, terms. Aspirations to social preeminence and recognition demanded racial purity. Phenotype was thus ideologically collapsed with genotype and social status. White upper-class women and their families were controlled by the males of their families and protected from racial "pollution" through marriage or, worse, sex with a black male. Such control was necessary because the ideal of love as a prerequisite for marriage constituted a permanent potential challenge to the opposite ideal of racial purity in a multiracial society.

At first sight it might appear that white women were the double victims of their biology, being potentially mothers and under the circumstances responsible for maintaining family "purity." As the old proverb has it, *mater semper certa est*. Only women could introduce half-castes into the family whereas white males could easily deny their paternity, as they indeed most frequently did in nineteenth-century Cuba with regard to the offspring of their sexual unions with black women.

Still, biological facts acquire social significance only within wider systems of meaning. Gender subordination is socially conditioned, as it were, in three successive steps that link class, race, and sex. The elites, in their endeavour to safeguard their social cum racial preeminence, endowed otherwise neutral sexual differences between women and men with specific sociopolitical meanings that then found expression in the form of gender hierarchies. As I show in this book, in Cuba the emphasis on white women's sexual cum racial purity derived its distinct meaning for family purity and social status from the wider social-racial hierarchy. Male control of women's sexuality and the latter's consequent subordination was the result of the central role they played in reproducing family preeminence based so importantly on racial purity. In this sense, white women were conceived as wives and mothers in an instrumental way.

By contrast, black or, as they were also called, coloured, women were the prey of white men in sexual liaisons that were very rarely legitimated through marriage. Legal marriage was the appropriate form of union among social-racial equals, while interracial unions, that is, unions among partners who were regarded as social-racial unequals, usually resulted in more or less stable concubinage and/or matrifocal domestic units.

I have argued that the numerical predominance of men in the white population was one of the reasons for the occurrence of interracial and usually relatively stable concubinage. The Catholic church's largely unsuccessful campaigns to consecrate these unions through marriage indicate that these were more than sporadic sexual relations, and that the white men involved were generally single, though married white men also exploited coloured women sexually.

Higman has recently challenged the view that seeks the grounds for interracial sex in white demography, suggesting instead that it was the sex ratio among slaves that, at least in Jamaica, accounted for the incidence of miscegenation. Higman's focus, however, is on interracial sex, while mine is on forms of interracial cohabitation. According to Higman, the greater the excess of slave women over slave men—a pattern that was especially pronounced in the towns—the larger the coloured slave population. In the urban areas female slaves formed the largest group, although white and free coloured males were also present in considerable numbers. Since fewer slave mates were available, Higman argues, black women were more ready to accept white men.

He argues then that the sexual choices of white men cannot be attributed solely to a lack of white women since white sex ratios were relatively balanced in the towns. Coloured males, for their part, tended to have female black slave partners because they lost out in competition for free coloured females to the whites.[7] This thesis may be extended also to the behaviour of free coloured women. But while Higman denies a demographic imperative for white men's sexual exploits with black and coloured women, he also implicitly presupposes coloured women's willingness to enter into sexual liaisons with whites despite their perils, endorsing, unintentionally, the disdainful Cuban proverb *"no hay tamarindo dulce ni mulata señorita"* (there is no sweet tamarind fruit as there is no virgin mulatto woman). I would agree that among the coloured population a desire for whitening did exist, as described, for example, in Cirilo Villaverde's novel *Cecilia Valdés*. This desire, of course, is reflected and recorded in the petitions for permission for interracial marriage that I cite in my study. It was one expression of the powerful effect of white racial prejudice in a society in which other ways of self-assertion were largely closed to the black community. Still, it may also be that these sources led me to underestimate the extent of resistance to white men's sexual advances by black and mulatto women, a phenomenon that is much more difficult to assess historically. Individual, informal opposition to racial oppression of this kind would hardly appear in the records. Cirilo Villaverde, in fact, in a way blames Cecilia Valdés for her misfortune even though he also shows her white lover's typical betrayal. Marriage was a symbol of social status because it was reserved for social equals. The promise of marriage by a white man, reinforced by possible material advantages, might have persuaded some coloured women to initiate a sexual relationship but others were surely not taken in by that. The persistence of a black population, despite the incidence of extramarital miscegenation, suggests that a substantial proportion of blacks chose partners from within what was defined as their own racial group.

### RACE AND GENDER IN MODERN CLASS SOCIETY

In nineteenth-century Cuba the reproduction and reinforcement of class inequality through the interplay of racial discrimination and gender hierarchy should be clear. I would argue, moreover, that in a more

---

7. B. W. Higman, *Slave Population and Economy in Jamaica, 1807-1834* (Cambridge: Cambridge University Press, 1976), pp. 143 ff.

subtle, less obvious way similar ideological and political processes are at work in all class societies, although there has occurred a shift in meaning that affects the way the image of women is construed. From being instrumentally defined as the reproducers of social status, whose actions and freedom need controlling by men, women have come to be conceived as essentially different from men in their primary functions as mothers. This does not mean that women cease to be regarded as the reproducers of social status. This shift, which is in line with growing individualism, only obscures further this structural function.

In modern class society, racism, understood as the ideological construction of social inequalities in racial (that is, naturalist) terms, always lurks under the surface to become explicit at times of socioeconomic polarization. To demonstrate this, one needs to take a closer look at the modern liberal universalist notion of the free, self-determining, autonomous, and responsible individual. This notion began to acquire its modern meaning in Western society during the Enlightenment along with a conceptualization of social inequalities in biological, natural terms. This paradox between a conceptualization of the individual as free and hence responsible for his achievements and social inequalities perceived as ascribed at birth was consolidated in the nineteenth century. The crucial issue became how to reconcile alleged freedom and equality of all men (but not women despite the generic use of the term *man*) with deepening social inequalities. Racial classifications in Western societies from the eighteenth century onward collapsed phenotype and genotype with sociocultural status, being applied not only to the "savages" abroad but also to social inferiors at home.

Developing scientific naturalism in the nineteenth century provided these contradictory notions with a pseudoscientific basis in such doctrines as social Darwinism, Spencerism, and Lamarckism, eugenics, and more recently, sociobiology. Striking in the nineteenth-century debate over the place of man in nature is the deep and persistent tension between men's quest to conquer and "master" nature, on the one hand, and the tendency to naturalize social man, on the other.[8] Because de-

---

8. R. Young, "The Historiographic and Ideological Contexts of the Nineteenth Century Debate on Man's Place in Nature," in *Changing Perspectives in the History of Science*, ed. M. Teich and R. Young (Dordrecht, Holland: Boston D. Reidel Publishing Co., 1973); V. Stolcke, "Women's Labours: The Naturalisation of Social Inequality and Women's Subordination," in *Of Marriage and the Market*, ed. K. Young, C. Wolkowitz, and R. McCullagh (London: CSE Books, 1981). It should be noted that racism does not require visible phenotypical differences to prevail, as the persecution and extermination of the Jews in Nazi Germany made tragically clear.

veloping bourgeois society espoused an ethos of equal opportunities for all people regarded as born equal and free but generated growing social inequalities, if the self-determining individual by his or her social inferiority seemed to prove incapable of making the most of the opportunities society appeared to offer them, this must then be due to some essential, inherent, natural defect that by being natural was hereditary. Their genetic endowment rather than society was to be blamed for this inferiority—an effective way both of obscuring the socioeconomic and political roots of social inequality and of enticing them at the same time to keep trying.

These doctrines of biologically grounded class inequality, on account of their naturalist base, also reinforced a notion of individualized biological parenthood that finds expression, for example, in our Western understanding of the parent-child bond as a "blood tie," in the strong desire, especially of men, to perpetuate their genes through the generations, and in the image of women as by their biology destined to motherhood and domesticity at the service of the male. In a highly competitive society in which, by contrast with nineteenth-century Cuba, achievement and function acquired growing importance in determining a person's social status, gender ceased to be one among other criteria such as, for example, family origin, and has been construed as the single most important principle of social differentiation. Women, especially in advanced industrial societies, tend to be defined now, on account of their ascribed function as mothers, as the essential, incommensurable, genetic others. While in slave society white women played the important role of, as it were, mediating racial purity and social preeminence, in modern achievement-oriented class society they have become, on account of their "natural" function as mothers, monogamous, subordinate, and dependent on men in themselves. This conceptualization has in some cases been reinforced in response to women's growing demands for social equality in recent decades.[9] This is only one instance of the pervasive tendency in class society to confuse differences with inequality and, conversely, to make equality dependent on sameness.

Still, despite a primarily male concern with transmitting their genes, Western kinship systems continue to be thought of as bilateral, a child

---

9. This shift in women's image is particularly clear in the most recent variety of scientific naturalism, namely sociobiology. According to this doctrine females are by nature monogamous vessels for profligate males' genes. See, for example, E. O. Wilson, *On Human Nature* (Cambridge: Harvard University Press, 1978).

deriving his/her "essence" from both parents. Hence, if social position is seen as expressing genetic endowment, then for those claiming social preeminence, class endogamy and the use of women's reproductive capacity in the interest of social purity continue to be crucial to ensure this preeminence. Even if this biological conceptualization of social inequality in class society may not always rest on visible phenotypical characteristics, and there is a conspicuous reluctance to call this naturalization of social processes racism, the interaction between racism, women's subordination, and class inequality should be clear also in this case.

As I pointed out above, gender relations are socially constructed in interaction with kinship systems that are equally socially construed as a function of the wider sociopolitical context in which they are embedded. The recent obsession with declining birth rates in some European countries and the natalism that this concern generated is only one more instance of racism that reinforces women's maternal role. Yet, if falling birth rates threaten, as some conservative politicians in these countries argue, the viability of the welfare states, one solution would surely be to open their frontiers to the poor millions of the Third World, but then they are generally not white.

The differentiating "racial" characteristics on which racial prejudice is based vary historically in a double sense. They depend on a country's racialist tradition and on the concrete contemporary sociopolitical cleavages that racism serves to legitimate. In the United States, for example, the "visibility" of racial distinctions—a legacy from slavery—endows race with a degree of autonomy as a source of discrimination that obscures class as its ultimate root. By contrast, because class is recognized as the dominant structural principle in European capitalist societies and the processes of naturalization of social inequality I have described above may be "invisible," since they do not necessarily rest on external phenotypical differences, racism and its consequences for the conceptualization of gender roles and the maintenance of class relations may be harder to perceive.

My own concern with and understanding of racism derives from my biographical background as a German and my research on nineteenth-century Cuban slave society. The concrete historical roots of racism in either case are clearly distinct. I would, nonetheless, argue that there is no qualitative difference between them. In Nazi Germany, as in nineteenth-century Cuba, racialist ideologies and policies developed to legitimate segregationist practices because an ethos of individual achievement and freedom did prevail that threatened to challenge the socioeconomic system of domination. The idioms in which racism is expressed may vary, as well as does the severity of its consequences, but the message is always the same, namely that in an unequal socioeconomic system pertinent differences are chosen to mark/make a dehumanizing difference. It is my hope that the analysis of the interplay of racial prejudice and sexual values in nineteenth-century Cuba offered in this book may also contribute to the awareness of renewed racism in contemporary class society.

Verena Stolcke (Martinez-Alier)
Stanford, February 1989

# INTRODUCTION

I shall be concerned primarily with marriage as a focal point for an assessment of nineteenth-century Cuban society. Yet, rather than taking the normal events as a basis for investigation, I have used the well-documented deviations from the norm as provided in the administrative and judicial proceedings of cases where parents oppose a given marriage, of cases where this opposition is overcome by means of elopement, and of cases of interracial marriage. These deviations from ideal behaviour, while by no means everyday occurrences, nevertheless highlight the conflicts obtaining in the system and make its norms all the more apparent.

From the dominant sector's point of view, marriage in nineteenth-century Cuba was ideally isogamic, i.e. like married like. In 1776 the enlightened Charles III had passed the Royal Pragmatic on marriage which by severely restricting freedom of marriage lent legal support to the aspirations of social exclusiveness. While surely most sons and daughters followed the dictates of their elders in their choice of spouse, nevertheless there were also instances where this was not so. These dissidents had two paths open to them. They could either appeal to the authorities to have parental dissent overruled, or they could resort to elopement. In the latter case, the ensuing dishonour of the daughter often compelled parents to reconsider their posture and grant their approval after all. Yet, certain limits were set to the effectiveness of the elopement. When the social distance between the partners exceeded the tolerated maximum, considerations of family prestige came to prevail over the regard for a daughter's moral integrity. At this stage marriage was no longer the appropriate form of redress. It was then deemed preferable to take the daughter back into the home and have the culprit prosecuted.

The elopement, which derived its effectiveness from the high regard for virginity and chastity, reveals the interrelatedness of female honour and family honour and the connection of both with the social hierarchy. This hierarchy is maintained through the high regard for virginity and chastity, which thus appears as a structural rather than cultural feature

I

of the system. In this way an alternative hypothesis is suggested with regard to the concepts of honour and shame studied by some anthropologists in the Mediterranean area.[1] Moreover, this interpretation will also shed some light on the much-debated question of the allegedly particular forms of family organization obtaining in the Caribbean area, as well as on marriage in general.[2]

As will become evident from the analysis of the marriage pattern, the basic line of cleavage dividing Cuban nineteenth-century society was race, to the extent that legislation was passed regulating and restricting interracial marriage. The acute racial consciousness of all sectors of the society becomes manifest in the analysis of interracial marriage and of marriage among free coloured people (marriage among slaves will be dealt with only in passing). It will be argued that in nineteenth-century Cuba racial perception was a direct consequence of the degree to which slavery and its exigencies had affected the total social structure. Slavery appears as a system of forced labour but also of social organization, and of class and racial discipline. At every point the coloured person, whether slave or free, was forced to shape his behaviour in accordance with the actions and expectations of the dominant white sector, who, in turn, also had to adjust to the presence of the non-whites.

The nature of slavery and racism in the Spanish and Portuguese colonies vis-à-vis the British West Indies and the American South has been much debated. In the studies of Tannenbaum, Elkins and most recently Klein[3] the relative mildness of servitude and harmony of race relations in Latin America is emphasized. The present monograph challenges once more this optimistic view by showing that, as Mintz has pointed out, slavery cannot be regarded as a uniform social phenomenon, but its character depends importantly on the differing levels of economic development within those countries and colonies which employed it.[4]

A comparison of eighteenth- and nineteenth-century Cuba fully supports this point. Up to 1760 and despite the clandestine trading activities of Cuban sugar producers, the development of the Cuban sugar industry had been severely stunted by metropolitan restrictions on trade. Yet, with the taking of Havana by the British in 1762, these restrictions were lifted and would not be reimposed even after their departure eleven months later, and an estimated five to ten thousand slaves were introduced. Thus the scene was set for the Cuban sugar boom which by the end of the century would make the island the first producer for the world market, a development which was decisively aided by the Haitian revolution and the decline of the British West Indies. The number of sugar mills rose from 93 in 1760 to 227 in 1792. And in the same period the production of sugar increased roughly fourfold.[5]

Vital to the growth of this plantation economy was the availability of labour; and in the absence of free labour this meant slave labour. As Moreno Fraginals writes, 'there is a parallel increase of sugar and slaves on the Island'.[6] He estimates that between 1765 and 1790 an annual average of 2,000 slaves were brought into Cuba. The effect this 'great awakening'[7] had on all sectors of Cuban society is shown in Table 1.

TABLE 1. *Population of Cuba by colour and status, 1774–1899*[8]

| Year: | Whites | Free coloureds | Slaves |
|---|---|---|---|
| 1774 | 96,440 | 30,847 | 44,333 |
| 1792 | 133,550 | 54,152 | 84,590 |
| 1817 | 239,445 | 114,077 | 199,198 |
| 1827 | 311,051 | 106,494 | 286,942 |
| 1846 | 425,767 | 149,226 | 323,759 |
| 1862 | 757,610 | 221,417 | 368,550 |
| 1877 | 1,023,394 | 272,478 | 199,094 |
| 1887 | 1,102,889 | 528,789 | — |
| 1899 | 1,067,354 | 505,443 | — |

There was a remarkable increase in the slave population – it should be noted that the census figures are probably underestimated, since a treaty between England and Spain in 1817 had declared the slave trade illegal. But there was also a marked rise in the free coloured sector. Clearly, the possibilities available for slaves to obtain their freedom and the social abilities enjoyed or disabilities suffered by freedmen are crucial factors in an evaluation of the nature of a slave society. Klein maintains that 'the religiously inspired policy of manumission was probably the chief source for freedmen over the long run',[9] and that freedmen largely enjoyed the same prerogatives as their white counterparts in an 'integrated community' in which colour or physical appearance played a secondary role to socio-economic criteria of stratification. The proportion of freedmen in the coloured population was admittedly higher in nineteenth-century Cuba than in Virginia – with which Klein compares Cuba – but this may well be due largely to the natural demographic increase of the free coloured community which had emerged under the more favourable conditions obtaining in the previous century. Klein does not attempt to trace in detail the source of this increase. Perhaps Knight, by attributing the increase of the free coloured population chiefly to natural growth, comes closer to the truth than Klein.[10] Undoubtedly manumissions took place, but it would be interesting to know the age and sex of those manumitted: for to manumit women or old people could relieve a master of a burden rather than being an indication of his magnanimity towards his slaves.

As this study will show, in Cuba legal and social discrimination of the free coloured community increased rather than diminished. Klein, disregarding the fundamental change undergone by slavery as a system of production in Cuba at the turn of the eighteenth century, asserts that 'the 1806 free-marriage decree [ended] the last vestiges of caste arrangements',[11] while, as we shall see, it was precisely this decree, interpreted with increasing vigour throughout the nineteenth century, which provided the basis of official segregation in marriage between whites and free coloureds.

However, opinion in nineteenth-century Cuba was far from unanimous on the subject of slavery and racism. The Catholic Church did not attack slavery as such, but in its zeal to promote marriage and combat such excrescences of slavery as interracial concubinage it challenged the social order which produced it. Although the growing secularization of the State, as well as the overriding political and economic interests of the secular powers undermined the Church's efforts to impose its egalitarian ideology on a politico-economic system that was characterized by marked inequalities, its influence must not be disregarded.

Opinion also varied widely about the effectiveness and advisability of slave labour among the sugar interests themselves. In the 1830s a fission in the planters' interests occurred. In view of the growing demand for slave labour and the difficulties in obtaining it, and of improvements in technology, a progressive wing of planters emerged who felt acutely irritated by their growing economic dependence on the slave dealers, and as a consequence advocated the gradual abolition of slavery and its replacement by free labour. However, their position was severely weakened on the one hand by the progressive infiltration of the ranks of the planters by the slave dealers themselves on account of the indebtedness of the former and the acquisition of plantations by the latter, and on the other by the guarantees the existence of slavery was felt to provide for the hegemony of the colonial power. In view of the Haitian experience large segments of the Cuban population, both *criollo* (native Cuban) and *peninsulares* (Spaniards), saw only one alternative for Cuba: to be

4

either Spanish or 'African'. Consequently, those desiring independence from Spain saw the end of slavery, and (in view of the impossibility of expelling the African element) the progressive whitening of the population through intermarriage, as the first steps towards their goal.

The instigators of the first war of independence of 1868–78 abolished slavery on their estates for clearly tactical reasons. This war saw the emergence in the ranks of the rebel army of a number of coloured officers, most prominent among them Antonio Maceo, which again seemed to prove right those who had warned of the danger of Africanization. Eventually the Cubans were defeated and Spain succeeded in imposing its rule for another twenty years. As for slavery, although opinion was so deeply divided on this issue, it was effectively abolished only in 1880, despite the extremely liberal interlude in Spain (1868–73). Significantly the law prohibiting interracial marriage was abrogated a year later.

D. B. Davis[12] has shown that in British America slavery was the source of tensions and fears similar to those in nineteenth-century Cuba and that the similarities between the Latin American and the British American varieties of slavery and racism are greater than the differences. Without intending to join the debate at this point, it might be suggested that an explanation for the unquestionable difference in the race relations of the *post-emancipation period* in the United States and Latin America might be found in the varying nature of the process of emancipation in the two cases rather than in the character of slavery. In the Cuban case emancipation of the slaves by the white Cubans was felt to be a precondition for their own emancipation from Spain and therefore was in their own interest. In the American South, however, it was a measure imposed from outside after defeat and against at least partial resistance. Ibarra in his analysis of independentist ideology[13] has indicated that in nineteenth-century Cuba the racial question and the national question were very much the same one. Cuba's national identity, and independence, could only be achieved through racial integration. As shown in the present study, the fluctuations in the interracial marriage policy support Ibarra's interpretation.

This study will also throw some light on the relationship between racism and slavery. As will be seen, in nineteenth-century Cuba it was not physical appearance as such that caused prejudice and discrimination, but what physical appearance stood for, i.e. an individual's occupational role in an economic system based on the exploitation of one group by another. Significant in this connection is the fact that negroid phenotype as opposed to caucasian phenotype, rather than differences like those between tall and short people, for instance, formed the basis for discrimination, and that when phenotype no longer sufficed, legal colour was resorted to instead. Thus, with regard to the Cuban context a case might well be made for explaining racism as a pretext for economic exploitation, rather than psycho-analytically, or in terms of any innate tendency of people to form groups, the more so as a connection can be detected between changing economic needs and intensity of discrimination.

Nineteenth-century Cuba cannot be treated as a historical and geographical isolate. Political factors outside Cuba were significant in shaping interracial marriage policy. The cultural tradition of Spain which during three centuries had espoused 'purity of blood' as the essential requisite of Spanishness must also be taken into consideration. Racism antedates slavery in the Americas and, as W. Jordan[14] has proposed, the question would be to explain why African negroes (and not for instance the American Indians) were enslaved in the first place. To establish, therefore, a direct causal link between slavery as a highly exploitative system of production and racism would be too simple.[15]

It should be emphasized that throughout this study I will mainly be discussing racial discrimination rather than racial prejudice. While slavery produces discriminatory practices, the absence of such practices does not necessarily imply the absence of prejudice. Moreover, the persistence of some racial consciousness in Cuba not only after the abolition of slavery but even after the 1959 revolution with its egalitarian doctrine throws doubt on such an interpretation, even if one accounted for some measure of time lag due to socialization. I would suggest rather that race stands often as a symbol for other differences – the division of labour in nineteenth-century Cuba, religion in fifteenth- to eighteenth-century Spain – or in other words that strains and tensions in society that may be the result of a variety of factors are often justified and rationalized in terms of racial distinctions. By showing the symbolic nature of race this study also goes to challenge the view of Hoetink and Gilberto Freyre who attempt to explain the alleged difference between the two American variants of race relations in terms of a culturally determined difference in the 'somatic norm image' or 'miscibility' of citizens of the respective colonial powers.[16]

But whatever the origins of racism, the division of society along racial lines has often implied coercion on the part of the dominant sector and rebellion on the part of the dominated. By contrasting this essentially conflictive situation with the Hindu caste system I shall question the approach of those sociologists who have studied American race relations in terms of caste. They treat race as a distinct criterion of social stratification and endow it with a false permanence, and they disregard the significant difference in the ideological framework of the two contexts. In Cuba, hierarchy and the norm of isogamic marriage often clashed with the value of equality and the norm of freedom of choice in marriage.

This monograph is basically anthropological in intention and only secondarily historical. An important difference between the approach of the social historian and that of the social anthropologist lies not so much in that the former derives his material from the study of documentary evidence while the latter obtains his data from participant observation – in this respect my material is identical with that of the historian – nor in their methods of analysis, but in that the historian must periodize while the social anthropologist may consider social phenomena synchronically. Some sections of my analysis are static in this sense. In investigating the reasons for parental dissent and the elopement as a device for overcoming such dissent, my intention is to construct a model of the relationship between social inequality and sexual values. But when I study interracial marriage policy up to 1881 some punctuations of history become apparent. For instance, it was precisely in 1864, as a consequence of the emancipation of slaves in the Southern United States, that the restrictions on interracial marriage were enforced with increasing rigour in Cuba.

What happened after 1881 is scarcely covered in this study. Since elopement as a means to win over reluctant parents continued to be used in the twentieth century, an analysis of the corresponding judicial proceedings and the reasons for dissent given in them, which in some respects are likely to differ from those adduced in the nineteenth century, would, on the one hand, disclose the criteria of social stratification in force in this later period, and, on the other, allow us to determine by comparison the type and direction of change. Finally, after the 1959 revolution, while virginity is still valued – which I find functional in a stratified society but not in an egalitarian one – and while, therefore, elopement with a view to marriage is still resorted to, it is probable that a check of the court cases would reveal a decline in the frequency of elopement. However, this study of marriage and class in twentieth-century Cuba must be left for the future.

# PART 1. INTERRACIAL MARRIAGE

'in a very fundamental way, we all of us distinguish those who are of our kind from those who are not of our kind by asking ourselves the question, "Do we intermarry with them?"'

E. R. Leach, 'Characterization of caste and class systems' in A. de Reuck and J. Knight (eds.), *Caste and Race: Comparative Approaches* (London, 1967), p. 19.

# CHAPTER I

# INTERMARRIAGE AND FAMILY
# HONOUR

## INTERMARRIAGE IN LAW

In 1776 the Spanish Crown enacted a Pragmática Sanción aimed at preventing unequal marriages resulting from the allegedly ill-understood freedom of marriage. Parental consent to marriage was made a formal requirement for those under twenty-five years of age and/or living under parental tutelage. Parental dissent was deemed justified when it was thought the proposed marriage would 'gravely offend family honour and jeopardize the integrity of the State'.[1]

In 1778 the Royal Pragmatic on marriage was extended to the overseas possessions in view of the 'same or greater harm done there by such unequal marriages on account of their size and the diversity of classes and castes of their inhabitants', and 'the very severe damage done by the absolute and indisciplined freedom with which these passionate and incapable youngsters of both sexes betroth themselves'.[2] The penalty for infraction of the law was disinheritance. Nevertheless, its enforcement in the colonies seems to have met with considerable difficulties. The clergy inquired repeatedly about cases where couples were willing to forfeit their inheritance and where 'reasons of conscience' were pleaded as a ground for marriage. In the colonies the threat of disinheritance was surely not a very effective one. Many who had migrated to America had done so because there was nothing to be had at home, and the property they had been able to acquire there was often rather meagre: 'the number of poor parents . . . being large, their sons mind very little about losing the hope of inheriting from them', commented one official.[3]

In 1803 a new decree was passed setting the age of consent at twenty-three for men and twenty-five for women. Parents or their substitutes were the arbiters on whether a proposed marriage was acceptable or not. Only in cases of dispute did the civil authorities intervene.

One such case occurred in Cuba in 1791. The girl in question was white; she was the 'sacrilegious' daughter of a priest and wanted to

II

marry a *pardo* (mulatto). Her sister was opposed to the marriage, on account of the 'difference in colours and consequent stains on the family'.[4] The Cuban authorities had accepted the reason of dissent as justified. The girl, however, appealed. The case was then taken to the King, whose advisers overruled the initial decision on the grounds that the couple had already had offspring and the girl's illegitimate origin offset her suitor's inferior colour. Nevertheless, it was emphasized that this ruling 'should not set an example for others'.[5]

According to these laws those of age, unless they belonged to the nobility, enjoyed absolute freedom of marriage. However, they did so only in theory. In 1804 the marriage of a white man of fifty to a *parda* with whom he had lived in concubinage for many years and who had born him several children was opposed by his brother. The attorney general of the Crown ruled that 'marriages between white and negroes or mulattos descending from them, who have their origin either closely or remotely in slaves, should not be allowed for they tarnish the families'.[6] He justified this adverse decision by arguing that by law mulattos were excluded from certain professions. In the course of the same year two further such cases were submitted from Cuba to the attorney general who consistently ruled against marriage. But in the latter two cases he met with the concerted opposition of the Crown's ministers who reasoned that 'although the marriages in question could cause grief to the individual families, they could not but be an additional benefit to the State, as all the laws that protect marriage are very convenient for the State, resulting as they do in an increase of the population which is the foremost and greatest policy objective'.[7] However, as the large number of illegitimates at the time shows, the population increased all the same.

Until 1805, then, the control over choice of spouse was exercised by the individual parents. The civil authorities had a say only in so far as sons or daughters challenged parental dissent.

In view of the persistent ambiguities of the interracial marriage policy in the Indies, the matter was submitted to the Council of the Indies which on 15 October 1805 issued the 'Royal decree on marriages between persons of known nobility with members of the castes of negroes and mulattos'.[8] This decree followed a somewhat earlier one (of 27 May 1805) passed in response to an inquiry from the Viceroy of Buenos Aires ruling that 'in cases where persons of age and known nobility *or* known purity of blood attempt to marry with members of the castes, recourse should be taken to the Viceroys, Presidents and Audiencias so that they grant or deny their permission'.[9] The October decree established, however, that those persons of known nobility *and* known purity of blood who, having attained their majority, intended to marry a member of the said castes [negroes, mulattos and others] must resort to the Viceroys, Presidents and Audiencias of the Dominions who will grant or deny the corresponding licence, without which marriage of persons of known nobility *and* purity of blood with negroes, mulattos and the other castes may not be contracted, even if both are of age.

Shortly afterwards, on 9 July 1806, the Audiencia of Puerto Principe in Cuba issued an edict reiterating the October 1805 decree.[10] Lastly, on 18 December 1810, the Viceroy of Mexico issued an edict concerning the implementation of the royal decree of October 1805 emphatically stating that this decree must be understood to apply to 'the persons of known nobility *or* known purity of blood'.[11]

The discrepancy between the May 1805 decree and the 1810 interpretation on the one hand and the October 1805 decree on the other is significant. If the October 1805 royal decree were taken literally, only nobles were formally required to obtain official authorization if they wanted to marry a coloured person. According to the May 1805 decree and to the Viceroy of Mexico's version, however, all whites regardless of their social status needed permission. None of the cases that gave rise to the 1805 decrees concerned nobles. All three white men whose intended marriages to coloured women motivated the inquiry by the Audiencia of Puerto Principe of 1805 were plebeians. Also, in a ruling by the Civil Governor of Cuba dated 28 March 1810, that is prior to the Mexican edict, in a case concerning a white soldier who wanted to marry a free negress, the Governor of Santiago de Cuba is instructed 'that on account of such inequality he be very much on the look out that such marriages be prevented'.[12] It is most likely that these decrees were aimed at all whites. But it would be largely fruitless to discover the true intentions behind the laws. Their very ambiguity already indicates the uncertainty with regard to interracial marriage at the time. More profitable is an analysis of the changing implementation of the decrees throughout the nineteenth century in Cuba.

For intraracial marriages, that is those where either both partners were white or both were coloured, the 1803 decree on marriage continued in effect. With the 1805 decree interracial marriages became, in contrast, the direct province of the civil authorities. The decision-making body being another, the interests determining these decisions were bound to be different as well. In fact the rulings on interracial marriages were often prompted pre-eminently by considerations of the stability of society rather than by family interests as such

*Interracial marriage*

PARENTAL OPPOSITION TO INTERMARRIAGE

A classification of the cases of interracial marriage licences collected at the Cuban National Archive[13] shows that roughly one quarter resulted from *parental dissent* to a mixed marriage. In more than half of the cases it was the man or the girl themselves who directly applied for official licence, and in the remainder the priests who were to celebrate the marriage refused to do so until an official licence was produced. As time goes on it is increasingly the candidates themselves who apply directly for official licence. During the first three decades the view predominated that mixed marriages could only be prevented through parental dissent. Plebeians – I did not find a single case of a nobleman wanting to marry a coloured person – had no need to obtain official permission for a marriage across the colour line. From the 1830s onward, however, it became generally accepted that inequality in colour constituted a civil impediment to marriage for which dispensation must always be obtained.

Already prior to the 1805 decree opinion opposed interracial marriage. And also after the 1805 legislation many parents oppose such marriages spontaneously, ignorant of the law. In 1819 one widow says of her son that 'forgetting religious sentiments and the good education she has always given him and overcome by a disgraceful and blind passion he tries to marry a woman who on account of her *parda* class and her condition of ex-slave can only do so with those of her own class, according to the royal decrees'.[14] One brother opposing his sister's marriage to a *pardo* is even vaguer: he argues that such a marriage is 'morally impossible and opposed to our laws and good manners'.[15] In both these instances reference to the laws is ambiguous, yet that mixed marriages are forbidden is beyond any doubt.

By the 1840s, however, the existence of the 1805 decree becomes widely acknowledged. One relative based his disapproval of the marriage on the 'remarkable inequality between the spouses' and begged the civil authorities that in accordance with the royal decree of 15 October 1805 they should forbid a marriage 'that would be so damaging to society under the present circumstances'[16] – these circumstances being slavery. This case dates from 1847.

The hostility to mixed marriages in the colonies, even prior to 1805, demonstrates that the Metropolis laws on intermarriage, far from constituting an imposition, did no more than provide a legal framework for pre-existing racial attitudes. However, with growing antagonism as a consequence of the sugar boom, the popularity of the 1805 decree increased proportionately and its interpretation by the authorities grew more and more restrictive.

Which were the specific objections parents raised against mixed marriages?

## Purity of blood

When parents objected to a marriage they did so because they felt it was a menace to family integrity and status vis-à-vis other families of their group. It is without exception the white candidate's family that opposes the marriage.

Again and again the dissenting parents talk of the 'absolute inequality' of the couple, of their own 'known purity of blood' and of the 'remarkable and transcendental stain' on their reputation, of the 'degradation of the offspring' and the 'disgrace and discontent' the marriage will bring to the family.

Particularly in the first half of the century parents frequently argue in terms of *limpieza de sangre*. The 1805 decree also talks of 'purity of blood' and it is thus possible that parents in their petitions merely repeated this phraseology. But the insistence on this point, and the specificity of the argument at times, indicate that this metaphysical notion of the blood as the vehicle of lineage equalities was still very much part of popular feeling, a legacy of the much older Spanish concern over purity of blood reinforced by the special socio-economic and ethnic conditions obtaining in the colonies.

One son objects to his father's remarriage to a 'light mulatto girl' because he 'belongs to a family of pure blood on all sides . . . [and] the marriage would be a stain on all the family which is composed of respectable citizens, farmers and *hacendados* useful to the public, being white'.[17] A mother says of her son that he is 'a white European and free of any bad race'.[18] Another father insists that 'he is free of any bad race, such as moors and mulattos'.[19] And one young man argues that 'his entire family has always been regarded, held and reputed as white, free of any bad race of negroes, mulattos, Jews or new converts'.[20] Domínguez Ortiz defines purity of blood as the 'absence of infidel ancestry'.[21] In the overseas possessions, although strictly speaking both Indians and Africans were of 'infidel' origin, in the end it was only those of African origin who were regarded as contaminated and thus to be avoided by those of 'pure blood'.

In the instances quoted above the accent is always on the white individual's own racial exclusiveness. More may be said on why the coloured partner is deemed to stain the family. Da. Nazaria Brito's uncle, for instance, argues that her marriage to a mulatto means 'the introduction into the same family of a subject through whose veins no white blood flows . . . [and] the eternal joining of a girl of the pure, white race . . . with an obscure man of an entirely opposite race to hers who will eternally bear the mark of slavery which he received from his parents'.[22] The dishonour deriving from such a marriage is often attributed to the slave background of the coloured individual. Thus, another father insists that 'he has had no other reason to oppose this marriage but that Casales is a notorious *pardo*, and grandson of slaves on both sides';[23] another objects because '[her] ancestors have all been slaves, her father . . . having become free not long ago at the death of his master'.[24] In the Cuban context 'impurity of blood' came to mean bad race, African origin and slave status. Slavery was regarded as a stain that contaminated a slave's descendants, regardless of their actual physical appearance.

The majority of these dissenting parents are concerned with the effect of a mixed marriage on their particular family's prestige vis-à-vis their peers. However, occasionally they seem to be aware of the more far-reaching social implications of intermarriage. As one says, 'the special circumstances of our society . . . which draw a dividing line between the white class and that of colour should not be trespassed against, and the civil laws prohibit such marriages'.[25] The son, the mother says, is driven by an irrational passion which makes him forget the unfortunate consequences of such a match. She herself, however, acts in the interest of family and State. Another parent points out warningly that 'This is a country where because of its exceptional circumstances it is necessary that the dividing line between the white and the African race be very clearly marked; for any tolerance that may be praiseworthy in some cases, will bring dishonour to the white families, upheaval and disorder to the country, if not extermination to its inhabitants.'[26] Nineteenth-century Cuba being a slave society, its social stability demands that the slaves and those who have their origin in slavery and, by extension, in Africa, be kept in their place and subordinated. In fact, in one instance a bride is rejected because her grandmother comes from Africa: as the dissenting parent says '[the young man] cannot be allowed to stain the splendour of his family by binding himself to a woman whose origin . . . is to be found on the coast of Africa'.[27]

Those within the white community are pure and those outside it are impure, and both purity and impurity are transmitted through the blood. Yet the relationship between the pure and the impure is not symmetrical.

The pure can all too easily become contaminated and impure, precisely by marriage to a member of the impure category. The impure, however, can in theory never shed their impurity entirely. As one parent asserts, 'a mulatto girl . . . never has nor will be able to leave the sphere of this class of humble people, on account of her colour in the society of that village, even if her complexion were white and her hair straight'.[28] Accordingly, there are a number of parents who object to the intended marriage not only in terms of the practical consequences for their own child but also of those for his/her offspring in a society divided along racial lines. D. Manuel Cordero is one of them. The bride's family is on both sides *pardo* whereas his is white. Therefore 'he cannot tolerate a marriage that will confound his grandchildren with the class of *pardos* to which [she] belongs'.[29] Another father is plain hypocritical:

as a good father who desires the happiness of my children, I would keep silent despite my son's poor luck, if he were to take as a wife a woman who does not dishonour his class, because although his suffering would pain me, on the other hand I would think that if only the rich were to marry, the poor people's fortune would be very hard for they would vegetate without procreating and without enjoying the respectable delights that an honorable and virtuous wife affords, but being a zealous parent, although unconcerned [*sic*] to preserve the purity with which his ancestors' blood has reached my son on both sides, I cannot permit that he marry someone who will be the infamy of my grandchildren . . . [for she] not only is of incomplete and defective but also stained ancestry, as the granddaughter of a mulatto woman.

Moreover, he (the son) 'would become aware in the course of time that his offspring will be disdained and will be unable to make a career due to the fact that this girl is a *parda*'.[30]

The Cuban kinship system was bilateral, that is to say children traced their descent through both parents and were related to the consanguines of both parents in the same way. When it came to the racial classification of an individual, however, the principle of hypo descent prevailed. It was always the racially inferior parent, regardless of sex, that determined the group membership of the offspring of a mixed union.

Offspring of mixed marriages were as a rule registered in the parish book for *pardos* and *morenos* (mulattos and negroes). But this system of classification was not accepted unquestioningly. There are repeated attempts to implement a patrilineal principle, as does the couple who argue that 'they understand that both the legitimate and illegitimate offspring follow the condition of the father and not that of the mother',[31] and the young man who contends that his bride, the daughter of a white man and a coloured woman, 'should be considered as white . . . because it is from the trunk that the leaves derive and receive their life'.[32] A third alternative form of classification of mulattos is suggested by the official who objects to interracial marriage on the ground, among others, that

since the husband cannot raise the woman to his rank, nor descend himself to hers, not only would they find themselves perplexed in the fulfilment of their respective social duties, but their offspring would pertain to one of those undefined and so common and awkward castes, who neither want to mix with the *pardos* whom they scorn nor are accepted by the white, by whom they themselves are disdained in turn.[33]

This description sums up well the predicament of classification of the offspring of mixed unions.

The constant endeavours on the part of the coloured population to advance socially by whitening themselves through marriage, or rather through informal affairs with lighter if not white people, conflicted with the downgrading principle as well. Thus one parent whose white status is questioned appeals to the authorities arguing that 'nature herself teaches that the one who has luckily and successfully begun to get out of the swamp should be protected and allowed to proceed until he is high and dry and clean'.[34] Yet, it is precisely against endeavours of this nature and the aspirations and presumptions implied in them that the decrees on interracial marriage were enacted.[35]

Around the 1840s the notion of purity of blood ceases to be an issue. Discrimination continues but is, roughly from then on, couched in other terms. Besides, the whole idea of purity of blood had been thoroughly brought into disrepute in Spain by the nineteenth century, the Inquisition was finally abolished in the 1830s and the last vestiges of tests of blood for offices disappeared in 1865.[36]

## Discord between the families

Official and popular practice was to identify the offspring with the lower-status parent, whereas the individual's aspiration was to be identified with the parent of higher status. As a consequence, in any marriage between 'unequal' partners a conflict of allegiances is bound to arise that produces family instability, a further reason adduced against such unions. D. Desiderio Sosa is well aware of this danger when he says that the marriage 'by necessity will bring discontent to the entire family'.[37] A priest advises against a mixed marriage because 'it would bring perpetual discord to the members of one and the same family, and to one of the families that were to be joined by it, through the shame caused by the idea of being degraded in quality in the eyes of their peers'.[38] And one official deems advisable an absolute prohibition of interracial marriages 'in view of the fact that the spirit of the institution of marriage is the solidarity or identification of spouses'.[39]

Occasionally the parents object to an interracial marriage also on the grounds that the woman is disreputable. One mother adduces this as her sole objection: '[she] has surrendered herself to a life of disorderly lewdness to the extreme of prostitution'.[40] And one brother feels he cannot agree to the match because she is a 'scandalous *parda*' who has lived in concubinage with his brother for seven years in the lifetime of her husband. He thinks this is reason enough to 'deny his consent for such an unequal monstruous marriage'.[41] One wonders whether the accent here is on 'scandalous' or on '*parda*'.

By and large these white parents pursued racial endogamy. A marriage across the race barrier was felt to degrade the white candidate's family for all time. This degradation could be conceived in metaphysical terms as taking the form of an indelible stain on the family's reputation among its peers, or as the contamination of its purity of blood. It could also be conceived and expressed in more practical terms as detrimental to the social status of the offspring of such a union and to family solidarity.

# CHAPTER 2

# INTERMARRIAGE AND POLITICS

## PRIVATE PURITY

It is surely the effect interracial marriage was felt to have on family prestige which led the authorities to insist on finding out whether the white candidate possessed any relatives in Cuba or in Spain who might object to the match before granting the licence. Some general guidelines which governed decisions on mixed marriages in roughly the first half of the nineteenth century are summed up by the official who demanded that 'reports be obtained on whether Maria Justa B. although *parda* is freeborn and her parents are the same, and on whether her conduct is respectable; with regard to the tailor José Flores, who is said to be from Cadiz, whether he has any relatives here who could be shamed and offended by a marriage with the said [girl]'.[1]

Thus, one aspect that is inquired into in the requisite reports on the candidates is the existence or non-existence of relatives on the part of the white party to the intended marriage 'who could be put to shame or offended by [it]'. Significant is an official's telling remark that 'the licence that M.'s father sent in granting her his consent to marry R. is sufficient proof of the equality of the two'.[2] She is said to be white whereas her suitor is reputed to be coloured. The official's reasoning is that marriage is only for likes, since the father agrees they must be equals. The law pays due attention to this interdependence of family honour and that of its members.[3] If one member of a family were to contract an unsuitable marriage this was sufficient to damage permanently the social prestige of the whole family. D. José Sánchez Griñán, a neighbour of Santiago de Cuba, feels keenly the harm done to his own reputation by his brother's marriage to a *parda* and consequently petitions the authorities that they issue an undertaking to the effect that 'no harm result [from this marriage] to the descendants of their common father, nor that it constitute an obstacle for them to be admitted to the honourable offices and prerogatives of their distinguished class'.[4] Moreover, several marriage licences are granted by the authorities because either 'he is entirely unknown or comes from a remote town' or 'he lacks any relatives in this town and there is nobody who could give any information on his background'.[5]

If then having a family and relatives is such an important factor with regard to the choice of spouse, clearly those who have no family, typically the foundlings, should meet the least official resistance to a mixed marriage. As a result of the discrimination they themselves were often subjected to on the part of the higher classes they were frequently forced to marry down. D. Manuel de Jesús was in such a situation: 'he is over forty years . . . has no known parents nor relatives whom he could tarnish; his bride is the legitimate daughter of a white man and a freeborn *parda*'.[6] The authorities have no objections to the marriage.

Furthermore, even if the white candidate has a family, but one which has fallen into disrepute for some reason or other, the marriage to an inferior person may take place. Since the family has already lost its honour it consequently lacks the quality that makes it liable to be offended by an unsuitable marriage. This is the situation of a white girl who wants to marry a *pardo*. Her mother is mentally ill, while her father lives in concubinage with another woman. Hence, the authorities rule that 'this marriage . . . is advisable so that [she] get away from a debauched parent who keeps in his own home the scandalous concubine'.[7] Similarly, a white family that already has a member married to a coloured person has a much weakened stand with regard to any subsequent mixed marriage. This is the case with Da. Maria de la Caridad Henríques, who objects to her sister's marriage to a *moreno* but is herself the widow of a *chino* (the offspring of a negro and a mulatto woman or vice-versa) and at present married to a mulatto. Her opposition is overruled and her sister is allowed to marry the *moreno*.[8] Cases such as this are also indicative of the persistent feeling of racial superiority cherished even by those who have, as it were, condescended to marry down.

In accordance with the general rule that the existence of relatives makes a marriage across the colour line more undesirable: D. Francisco A. Reymon Martin from the Canary Islands is denied the licence by the authorities although he adduces as an additional reason for his marriage his wish to legitimate two offspring he has had with the *parda*, for 'he has several relatives there who hold ecclesiastical careers, and one cousin at the Monastery of Sta. Clara who is a nun, and in this municipality another cousin who is held to be white and of pure blood'.[9] These relatives could well have opposed the marriage, and their dissent might have been accepted by the authorities. As it is, however, they did not object but it was the authorities themselves who decided against the applicant and in favour of family purity.

21

However, it is not the existence of relatives as such that leads the authorities to deny the licence. The social status of the applicant's relatives as indicated by their occupations plays a decisive role. Occupations bestowed high status as long as they were kept exclusive. In effect, coloured people were excluded from ecclesiastical offices as well as from the liberal professions. Authorities opposed these marriages also in order to protect the occupational prerogatives of whites.

The authorities then often deny their approval to a mixed marriage in the interest of family honour, occasionally even against the specific wishes of the family concerned. On one occasion a parish priest wished to go ahead with the celebration of the marriage and resented the official's interference. The latter then resorted to the higher authorities, requesting that something be done that this priest 'stop infuriating the public authorities and contracting marriages of remarkable inequality, even if the bride's parents approve of it; these poor people of good birth let themselves be bribed in detriment of the royal decrees'.[10]

It is significant that 'reasons of conscience' rarely succeeded in prompting the authorities to overrule parental opposition. Family honour usually prevailed with the authorities over considerations of individual morality. The parent who asks that his son be allowed to live in concubinage with the *parda*, for he would never grant his consent to the marriage, has the authorities' approval;[11] and so do other parents.[12] Only once do the authorities ignore the parent's objections, and only upon the Archbishop's intervention, who pressed for marriage.[13]

The authorities paid tribute to the wishes and interests of the white families even to the detriment of morality, as long as they coincided with those of the State.

## MUTUAL COMPENSATION OF STATUS

As part of the formalities in connection with interracial marriage the local authorities and the parish priest were required to submit reports on the social and moral standing of the suitor and the bride. The purpose was to permit the assessment of the two candidates in terms of the correspondence of their respective social, economic and moral status in the light of their different ethnic points of reference.

The primary criterion of social classification was colour. Other subsidiary criteria could diminish or further increase this basic difference. This mechanism of partial compensation is aptly described in the following ruling by the authorities:

The constant trend by persons of different colour to achieve marriage has always conflicted with the genuine sentiment of the inhabitants of these Antilles and the many Spanish possessions; and it has been opposed peremptorily and legally since 1805 by the Royal Decree of 15 October of that year, further defined in regard to its prohibitive character, following the declaration by the former Viceroyalty of Mexico . . . D. Jorge Barrera, who requests Y.E.'s permission to marry a woman of different race, is, as he says, of the common estate, but his certificate of baptism shows that he is free of the mixture with castes . . . If Y.E. . . . believes that the case . . . deserves a ruling . . . Y.E. may reach a decision on the basis of the prior reports which this law advises and indicates. This Section understands that those reports . . . cannot refer to any other aspect but the *social condition of both*; and more particularly of the one pertaining to the white race. . . . If, as the applicant states, he is of humble status, being the simple labourer he is, granting the permit . . . would surely be of less transcendence and importance.[14]

A number of specific attributes could make up for shortcomings or offset advantages in terms of ethnic status. Of one *parda*'s parents it is said that their 'good qualities of honesty and Christianity have gained them the highest distinction on the part of the first families of this municipality, so that this family only lacks the colour as it is commonly said, for anybody I asked were full of praise for them, as much with regard to the good upbringing and education M. has received as to the probity of the master carpenter her father'; while her white suitor is qualified as 'an individual of no regard whatsoever, occupied in carrying coal'.[15] The case is incomplete and it is therefore not clear whether the authorities eventually agreed that the excellent qualities of the girl compensated for her inferior colour. In another case it is reported that 'the quality of the suitor is not much above that of the bride . . . although he is held to be white, his purity of blood has not been certified and on the other hand the occupations he has held have been low, and, if not of the servile kind, he has worked as a hireling . . . [and] her quality appears to be open to doubt'.[16] In this case, little is known about the girl other than that she is a *parda*. The young man's status as a white man, however, is clearly offset by his lowly occupation. Appropriately, they are granted the requested licence.[17]

Conversely, the authorities deny the licence to the young man whose father was a lieutenant constable, 'by which distinction he deserves the greatest esteem', whereas the bride was a '*parda* on all four sides'.[18]

As regards the relative status of the white man, the authorities' approval of the marriage depended in part on the fact that he was 'neither noble nor a man of circumstances',[19] circumstance being determined by the inter-related criteria of occupation and wealth. The spirit of official policy was that 'his status is sufficiently humble so that this marriage will not cause a bad effect on the public'.[20] With respect to the coloured woman the emphasis has so far been on her own and her family's good reputation as a quality capable of improving her social status.

Most interracial unions are colour-hypergamous. When a match is colour-hypogamous, however, it appears that particular care is taken that the white woman be of utterly miserable circumstances. Thus, it is said of a woman that 'she appears to be white, but of a very humble condition; her conduct has been extremely reprehensible by virtue of the illicit affair she has been having . . . with the *moreno* José Joaquín for the period of eight years causing public scandal and persecution by the police'.[21] They are granted the licence. What makes a white woman ineligible for marriage within her own ethnic group, makes her eligible for marriage across the race barrier. Conversely, great importance is attached to the honesty and respectability of the coloured woman who wants to marry a white man.

Attributes other than her sexual respectability could compensate for the coloured woman's disadvantageous ethnic status as well. In the same way as poverty and a humble occupation could offset a white man's status to a degree that made him eligible for marriage with a coloured woman, the possession of wealth on the part of the coloured woman's family could at times improve her status sufficiently. Accordingly, one young man, a discharged soldier and by occupation a shoemaker, wants to marry a freeborn *parda* who is the legitimate daughter of a captain of the *pardo* militia and, moreover, a wealthy man owning property worth over 10,000 pesos. The authorities rightly believe that the marriage 'cannot do any harm' but cautiously add, 'it is not known for certain whether the suitor is of pure blood; besides he has no distinction whatsoever'.[22] Again D. José Florencio Acosta 'is engaged in agricultural work, and the bride lives under the tutelage of her mother . . . the circumstances of the young man are those of the poor while she has a certain inheritance the value of which is not known because it is in the form of land and cattle':[23] they may marry.

This last case dates from 1843. In contrast with it are two cases dating from 1853 and 1854 respectively. In the one it is again a poor white discharged soldier who wants to marry a *parda* who is the legitimate daughter of *pardo* parents, the owners of four slaves and 40 hectares of land. She would need no official licence to marry one of her father's slaves, yet she needs it to marry this poor man, and does not succeed in getting it, for 'reasons of politics and morality are opposed to allowing marriages between persons of different race, unless very special circumstances or considerations obtain'.[24] In the other case, a white man 'of good conduct ... but who does not appear to have any occupation or wealth of any kind' wants to marry a *parda* who lives with her parents 'who possess a quite substantial fortune'. The district officer argues, however, that

although the bride will come to enjoy her parents' wealth at their death, this will not be equivalent to what the suitor could earn with his work considering his youth and robustness, nor to the degradation he would suffer with such a marriage by becoming a member of the coloured class to which his bride belongs, and if there are offspring, they themselves would belong.[25]

The central authorities disagree with this opinion. Occasionally wealth might compensate for other social disabilities, although there are also those who under no circumstances would admit that whiteness can be bought.

In practice the attribute of colour did not classify people clearly into whites and blacks. Such an unequivocal distinction might have been the ideal of many. Those who opposed interracial marriage whatever the socio-economic circumstances of the candidates pursued just such a policy of systematic segregation. But even the censuses and the parish registers distinguished between mulattos and negroes, and among the mulattos themselves variations in shade resulted in differentiations in status. Thus it is said in one case that 'the suitor has no known relatives who could be wronged by the intended marriage' and it is added that 'neither would his career suffer under it since his bride is of good repute ... although it is said that she is a mulatto girl [but] of light colour'.[26] Here it is her good reputation as well as the lightness of her skin that compensate for her basically inferior ethnic status.

Similarly, one official remarks that 'the *racial difference* is not so marked for although the suitor is white he does not belong among those in society who are of a higher rank',[27] as if implying that on account of his low occupational or economic status his whiteness were of a somewhat darker shade. The rule is that the higher the rank the whiter the colour, and vice-versa. And indeed, as a neighbour reports on one girl, 'in the class of the coloured she is held to be among the most respectable on account of her distance from the black colour and from slavery and on account of the good manners of her ancestors which is what bestows distinction in the classes of colour'. Moreover, 'her father was a *hacendado* and her brother has been decorated by H.M. .... for his services rendered to the country in the persecution of fugitive slaves'. These outstanding endowments in terms of social status and lightness of complexion appear to

have made her worthy in the eyes of the authorities of a match as outstanding as that with a white man who 'belongs to the class of distinction
both on account of his birth as well as of his social status for he has been
Lieutenant of the 2nd Battalion of the Infantry Regiment of Havana'.[28]
That a white lieutenant should apply for a licence to marry a coloured
woman and that he could be granted the licence was exceptional.

Perhaps more common is the reaction of another lieutenant and of his
brother, a captain, both of Baracoa, who had lived peacefully in concubinage, for eleven and thirteen years respectively, with two *chino*
sisters who had borne them 'considerable offspring'. On the occasion of
one of the Archbishop of Santiago de Cuba's pastoral visits they were
asked to formalize their unions, but their mother intervened, indignant.
At last one of them got married and the other, not wanting to marry,
had to part company with his concubine, under ecclesiastical pressure.
What is significant is that in their depositions neither of the two women
expressed any desire to marry: presumably this possibility had never
entered their minds, and surely neither had the two men thought of it
until the Archbishop's visit.[29]

There existed, then, not one but several complementary criteria of
social classification. The social status of an individual depended importantly on his descent but also on economic performance. Social prestige did
not derive from each individual factor independently but was determined
by the combination of all. Disadvantages in one scale of evaluation could
be offset by advantages in another. But this compensating process operated
only within certain limits, i.e. a wealthy *moreno* could hardly aspire to ever
marrying a white woman, nor would a nobleman ever consider marrying
a *parda*. A degree of consistency was needed among the status-conferring
factors.[30] In the Cuban context it was precisely the low-class whites and
the freeborn *pardos* that were the most likely to marry.[31]

The most frequent union was that between a white man and a free
*parda* woman. And at times the girl is not only a freeborn *parda* of *pardo*
parents, but already herself the offspring of a mixed couple, the father
generally being the white party.[32] The result of all this was a highly
complex gradation of status, and a considerable measure of fluidity in the
middle sector, to the dismay of many.

PUBLIC SAFETY

In the early part of the century it was mainly parents who initiated the
proceedings over interracial marriage. Later on it is increasingly the candi-

dates themselves who apply for a marriage licence. In the beginning they resort to the authorities almost against their will, as D. Agustín José Rodriguez, who after ten years of concubinage with the *parda* Ma. Dionisia and after having had three children by her, in 1813 decides 'to provide for the worldly and spiritual happiness of his offspring and his concubine' by marrying her. The ecclesiastical judge, however, refuses to celebrate the marriage and D. Agustín resorts to the authorities to protest in view of the 'Royal decree of 1805 . . . according to which only the nobles and those of known purity of blood require a licence by the Audiencias, Presidents, or Viceroys'.[33] By contrast, in 1878 D. José de Jesús Fariño asks humbly that 'he be granted the superior permission . . . on account of the inequality in class [she is *parda*] and . . . in view of the fact that these marriages cannot take place without the competent licence by the first authority'.[34]

The authorities' attitude towards interracial marriage undergoes a similar transformation. In principle, official marriage policy was determined by the 'absolute need to maintain the social equilibrium of [the country]'.[35] As the economic and political conditions of the country underwent change, opinion as to means for achieving this goal changed as well. Everybody seemed to be agreed that mixed marriages, whatever the social status of the white partner, should be subject to some sort of control. Only rarely did any official reject an application by a plebeian on the ground that legally no such permission was needed. Less unanimous, however, were the authorities in their rulings on the individual cases of interracial marriage.

Until the fifties family interests, the individual performance of the partners to an interracial marriage and the socio-economic compatibility chiefly determined the authorities' attitude towards interracial marriage. From 1851 onward a new dimension is added. Instructions are issued that the reports include not only information 'of the particular circumstances of the [candidates] . . . their morality' but also on the 'political drawbacks that may result from [such a marriage]'.[36] Furthermore, while formerly reports by the priest and one local official were deemed sufficient, from that date onward counsel on the convenience of the particular marriage was demanded from the parish priest, the chief of the local police, and two prominent citizens as well as from the Syndic of the municipal council.[37]

## The 'Africanization of Cuba' scare

Until 1854 the only law in force regarding interracial marriage was the

October 1805 decree, reiterated by the 1806 edict of the Audiencia of Puerto Principe. In 1854, however, it was rumoured that the then Captain General Marquis of Pezuela had issued a new decree interpreting the October 1805 decree in the most liberal fashion, namely that only those recognized as nobles by law must obtain official licence for marriage to a coloured person. All other whites were said to be granted absolute freedom to marry whomever they wanted.

There is some doubt whether Pezuela actually issued such a decree. An official in 1875 in the proceedings of a case of interracial marriage refers to this decree as being of 22 May 1854, but I could not find it in the *Gaceta*. What can be established beyond doubt is that Pezuela introduced several measures in favour of the coloured people and antagonistic to the slave traders' interests. He reintroduced the militias of *pardos* and of *morenos* which had been suppressed earlier for fear of a rebellion along the lines of the Haitian revolution – coloured people were then forbidden to carry arms. He also established the right of the authorities to search plantations for clandestinely introduced slaves, and he declared the total freedom of the *emancipados*.[38] Furthermore, Pezuela obtained reports from the Bishop of Havana and the Archbishop of Santiago de Cuba on their views on interracial marriage. These reports favoured marriage between the races. They were submitted to the Real Acuerdo which ruled, however, that 'circumstances did not require the least alteration in the existing legislation'.[39] Interracial marriage should continue to be forbidden to all whites as established by the restrictive interpretation of the October 1805 decree.

Miguel Estorch, a progressive planter and staunch defender of Pezuela, writes in his *Apuntes para la historia sobre la administración del Marqués de la Pezuela*:

The slave dealers not content with having vitiated a section of the public opinion by means of slander . . . they endeavoured to get the fair sex and the family heads into the complot as well. To that effect they alleged that the *negrophile* governor, desiring to please his *charges*, had passed a circular authorizing marriages between *blacks* and *white women*. In order that the dismal consequences of such a measure would not be doubted and in order that the alarm in the midst of the respectable families increase even further, they invented several tales which ran from mouth to mouth . . . crossing even the Atlantic they reached the Mediterranean. They said that the blacks publicly wooed the young ladies in the hope of obtaining their hand in marriage.[40]

Although a progressive, Estorch attempts to whitewash Pezuela not by justifying the alleged decree as the only appropriate measure, but by denying that it was ever enacted. He agreed that slavery was outdated and even counterproductive. At one time he himself had experimented

28

with free white immigrant labour, although with little success since the Catalans he imported soon left the plantation and settled in towns as artisans. In a sense he approved of Pezuela's efforts to curtail the slave trade and to put a stop to the activities of the slave dealers, who were gaining an increasing economic hold on the planters. Yet he definitely felt himself to be among those 'respectable families' who would under no circumstances countenance marriage with a coloured person.[41] Hence Estorch concludes his description of the event approvingly, pointing out that 'as events did not support the stories invented by the slave dealers' malevolence, as there was not a single case of those that were said to be feared . . . the alarm subsided and nobody paid any more attention to the matter'.[42]

An instruction issued by the Ministry of Overseas Affairs to the ecclesiastical authorities of Cuba on 14 July 1854 shows that the rumour had indeed reached Spain, although here the alteration of the marriage laws is not attributed to the civil authorities but to the Church.[43] And a letter addressed on 8 August 1854 by General Concha, Pezuela's successor as Civil Governor of Cuba, to the Ministry of Overseas Affairs before taking up his appointment on the island once more alludes to the rumour, this time exposing Captain General Pezuela himself as the author of the measure:

It has come to my notice that lately the Captain Governor of Cuba has declared that permission should be obtained prior to contracting marriage between white people and those of colour, only if the white person is a noble by law, for which formerly such a permission was required in all cases and under all circumstances. This alteration I am referring to is of great social and political import and it is extremely important that it be suspended while the Government of H.M. engage in reviewing the legislation in force on the Island and resolve the matter in due course.[44]

General Concha's request was granted forthwith, for a royal decree was issued two days later, on 10 August 1854, ruling that Pezuela's alleged decree be suspended while the government undertook a review of the legislation in force on the island on the matter.[45]

Upon his arrival in Cuba Captain General Concha showed a peculiar degree of tact. In November of that same year he wrote to the Minister of State: 'The presence of my predecessor in this capital, and the desire that the remaining agitation be subdued induced me to defer for some days the publication of the Royal decree of 10 August . . . but on 26 October last I did circulate it to those concerned and announced the fact in an unofficial way.'[46]

Against Estorch's simplistic interpretation of the affair as a plot by the slave dealers accepted unwittingly as true by the Crown, it may be argued that Pezuela had indeed envisaged a change along the lines of the alleged decree restricting official control over interracial marriage only to those cases where nobles were involved as one more possible measure within his overall anti-slavery policy, directed from the very beginning against those interests that in order to perpetuate slavery sought annexation to the Southern States, and emanating from the wider aim of keeping Cuba Spanish. Pezuela's anti-slavery and anti-slave traffic policy was a temporary strategy which could be expected to ingratiate Spain with Great Britain, on whom one could then count to intervene to avoid Cuba's annexation to the United States.[47] Once Cuba had been secured for Spain, and the annexationist plotters were out of the way, the new liberal government in Spain brought to power by the Vicalvarada insurrection sent out the more 'racist' Captain General Concha, who then proceeded to abrogate the liberalizing measures, thus ingratiating himself in his turn with the slave dealer interests and other conservative elements of the island. Captain General Concha came back to the habitual Spanish policy: segregation was reimposed. The merchants, most of them slave dealers as well, had won the day. Their views are clearly set out by one of them in these words:

it is an undeniable truth that the coloured population has been for many years and even today is the one that imposes on the white both *insulares* [Cuban born] and *peninsulares* [Spanish born] the necessity to remain in intimate alliance in order not to weaken . . . the power that the white race has over the black one. I, who have witnessed for fifty years what has been going on in Cuba, have reasons and evidence which show to what degree the black race (without herself being aware of it) has contributed to the peace Cuba has enjoyed.[48]

The threat that 'Cuba would be African or Spanish' was credible as long as slaves kept coming in, and as long as the two races were kept apart.

A brief note the *Gaceta de la Habana* carried on 28 October 1854 reveals the favourable reception the restrictive 1854 decree had had:

We understand that the Government of H.M. has taken a decision in the grave matter of marriages between white people and those of colour. . . . Measures such as [this] will always find an echo in the country and deserve its most complete approval . . . there exist in our customs ideas and differentiations which cannot and must not be defied either directly or indirectly. Vague and unfounded rumours such as those spread some months ago make this declaration of conservative tendency even more necessary and opportune, which without impinging on any existing rights amply satisfies universal opinion.[49]

And the Governor of the Oriental province of Cuba went so far as to issue an instruction to his local officials upon receipt of the decree demanding its most scrupulous fulfilment, for 'the damage done by this tendency of mixing the white class with that of colour under religious considerations which should never aim at unbalancing the political ones, will be severe'.[50]

## The period of total prohibition

Despite these general expressions of relief, licences for interracial marriages, when requested directly by the couple, were granted almost unreservedly up to 1864. (Of ninety-one applications filed until that year, only eight were denied.) In 1864, however, a period of virtual prohibition of interracial marriage set in. D. Juan de la Cruz Benigno de Blanco was denied licence although he explains that he has been living in concubinage with the woman for over three years until the local parish priest admonished him to get married or separate, because as the authorities argued 'the royal decree of 10 August 1854 . . . suspended the prerogatives granted to Viceroys of these dominions by the Royal Order of 15 October 1805 to grant or deny the corresponding permit to contract this kind of marriage, until . . . a final resolution be adopted'.[51] Hence the request must be denied. This is a highly distorted interpretation of the 1854 decree. What it did was merely to reinstate the 1805 decree as it stood. In no sense did it suspend the authorities' prerogative to rule in matters of interracial marriage. In another case of the same year the official response is more categorical still:

The Government of H.M. has decreed that no licences be granted by this government for marriages when one of the parties belongs to the coloured race and while no other resolution is taken. D. Agustín Pardo who requests permission to marry . . . a *parda* finds himself in this situation. The Section believes therefore that the said petition should be denied and the proceedings be returned to the Governor of the Oriental Province who should be informed that in future no such petitions should be dispatched.[52]

In 1865 the War of Secession had ended with the defeat of the Southern slave states. This could not be without effect on Cuba. A confidential circular letter sent round by the then Captain General of Cuba in December of 1866 states:

The recent civil war in the neighbouring North American republic has had as a result the emancipation of the slaves; and it is improbable that this event should not have had a part in the slackening of the links of obedience and respect which the coloured race should entertain for the white and on which the tranquillity of this territory largely depends . . . It must be feared that news and doctrines will be propagated in this Island . . . which could contribute to their indiscipline.

31

In order to prevent any such pernicious consequences the Captain General then instructed the local officials that 'they fulfill and see to the fulfilment without excuse nor pretext of any kind, but with due prudence in their implementation, of whichever regulations have been passed regarding the respect and obedience the coloured race owes the white'.[53] Among the responses to this circular is one by the Governor of Puerto Principe, assuring the Captain General that 'the discipline of the free as well as of the slaves is maintained, in which important matter all classes of society with rare exceptions are interested; the planters because they form part of his assets, and those who have none, because of the superiority and racial antagonism'.[54]

From 1864 up to the mid-seventies the authorities follow the Captain General's segregationist instructions to the letter. Not a single interracial marriage licence is granted; no applications are dispatched. In the fifties some local officials had already voiced their misgivings with regard to the political consequences of interracial marriage: 'in the present circumstances it would be doubly damaging to open the hand and grant these licences, for the truly dangerous class or at least that which must be watched over in this Island, is that of the mulattos, whether free or slaves',[55] pointed out one official in 1852. He was presumably alluding to the Conspiración de la Escalera of 1844, an uprising allegedly instigated by free mulattos to overthrow the government and free the slaves, and which had as a consequence a massacre among the coloured bourgeoisie.

One interpretation given of the events of 1844 is that the clandestine activities of a few people both coloured and white were taken as a pretext to put a damper on the aspirations for social and economic advancement of the coloured population.[56] Practically 'all classes of society' had a vested interest in maintaining the status quo.[57] As the Governor of Guantánamo insisted in 1860: 'The laws of the Kingdom prohibit marriage between persons of white race with those of colour or African origin as a measure of order and good discipline in a country where there are negro slaves.'[58] And the Syndic of the municipal council of Cienfuegos elaborated further on the same theme. He was opposed to a marriage of a white man with a black woman although the white suitor was apprenticed to his coloured bride's father, because such a marriage 'in our colonies where there is slavery implies the awakening in an inferior and degraded class of the idea of equality, and other ideas of detrimental consequence for the common or public good'.[59] The Political Governor of Havana, referring again to the 1854 decree, made the same point:

From the union of these people bad consequences may follow, since the whites who received with so much displeasure the measure said to have been adopted concerning the union of the two castes, are today calm in the belief that this measure has been suspended; this marriage would revive the discontent among the whites, it would swell the coloured people with pride of such a right, and would produce at each step disagreeable events of great import, on account of the propensity of this race to excel the white and of the ambitious pretensions they harbour.[60]

It is what Stanley Urban called the 'Africanization of Cuba scare' that deterred these whites from permitting interracial marriage.

## Race and the national question

Merchants, slave dealers, some of them sugar planters as well, and the colonial power agreed that slavery must be maintained. This could be achieved only by keeping all the coloured people down. Not least the Haitian example had shown what could happen to a slave society. And the American Civil War, which did away with the hopes to save Cuba's slave regime through annexation to the Southern States, further weakened the faith of those in favour of slavery in the stability of the system. Even liberal-minded Cubans were aware of the exigencies of the system. Thus in a report of 1863 it is argued that

Even though the progress of the enlightenment has brought about a great change in the ideas one had on matters of this nature, in a country organized socially as is ours, quite some time must pass before public opinion marches in accord with these ideas. In effect, as a result of this same organization the coloured class here has always been at a great distance from the white, and any measure towards getting them closer and mixing them not only has disadvantages of great import, but being opposed to our customs will be looked upon disapprovingly. This is the way I think on the case . . . despite the serious philosophical considerations which would result if the matter were to be discussed at another level.[61]

Opinion on the merits of slavery was far from homogeneous and this is reflected in the different stands taken on interracial marriage. As late as 1866, one of the Cuban delegates to the Junta de Información held in Madrid in that year remarked that 'white people cannot stand Cuban sunshine; the negroes warm themselves by the fire in August'.[62] More enlightened Cubans had already began to question the economic viability and political desirability of slavery in the 1830s. Arango y Parreño became in his old age the prominent head of this movement against the slave trade. His views provide a significant index to changing socio-economic and political conditions. If at one time he had advocated the abolition of coloured militias in the interest of internal security, already in the first decades of the century he was campaigning for the abolition of slavery itself.

Sugar producers in the early nineteenth century found slavery a convenient and profitable form of labour. Later on they were not yet against slavery, but they found that slaves – imported under difficult conditions – were becoming too costly. Therefore they looked for alternative sources of labour such as Chinese and Yucatecan indentured, or white immigrant labourers. But precisely because the labour force was scarce in Cuba, in relation to the possibilities for sugar expansion, and because the standard of living of the free population was so prosperous compared to that of Spain, the imported white labourers settled down as artisans in the towns or as peasants on their own account – they could not be hunted down as the slaves were when they took to the mountains or forests.

It is true that in a seasonal industry wage labourers need not be maintained the whole year round, as slaves must be. This is not, however, a decisive argument, according to Moreno Fraginals, because the slaves were forced to work very long hours during the sugar milling season. But once the new machines such as Derosne's vacuum boiler and the centrifugal machine became available, some spokesmen for the sugar producers argued that it would be necessary to introduce this machinery to compete with beet sugar. Since such machinery could not be entrusted to irresponsible slaves, it would be advisable to substitute wage labour for slaves.

Incentives were needed. Even in agriculture, now that soil exhaustion had begun to set in (in the western part of Cuba) it was felt that improvements of techniques of cultivation would require wage labourers, or better still, as Pozos Dulces and others argued, sharecroppers paid by results. Indeed, because of such economic considerations slavery had already lost ground before emancipation in 1880, not only because of restrictions on the trade, and the 1868–78 war. The pattern of sugar production was to become that of a greatly reduced number of much larger mills buying cane from *colonos*. The Creole planters were naturally keen on remaining mill-owners – the one condition was to do away with merchants, with slavery, and with Spanish domination, all of which went together.

One may of course remain not wholly convinced by Moreno Fraginals' argument that slavery was incompatible with technical improvements.[63] But the economic argument tied in very well with the political problems confronting the progressive Creole planters. In the course of the nineteenth century the merchants (some also part-time planters) gained in economic and political power at the expense of the Creole planters. These merchants were often slave dealers and most of them had close connections with Spain, whose economic ties with Cuba (taxes, protected markets capital imports) were of great importance. The merchants, in alliance with the Spanish authorities, were strong believers in the theory that Cuba would either be 'African' or Spanish. Hence the restrictions on inter-marriage between whites and free coloured people. Hence also the advo-cacy of intermarriage by spokesmen for the progressive planters like Arango y Parreño who already in 1816 suggested the integration of the races:

I am aware of the strength of the preoccupations and the difficulties and risks involved in wanting suddenly to destroy or attack [the separation of the races] . . . but I wish that at least . . . a plan be designed at once to whiten our negroes, to identify in America the descendants of Africa with those of Europe. At the same time I want the destruction of slavery to be envisaged with prudence . . . and to consider . . . erasing its very memory. Nature herself shows us the simplest and most certain path to this end. She shows us that black yields to white and that it disappears if one continues mixing both races; . . . let us protect these mixtures instead of preventing them and let us qualify their offspring to enjoy all civil rights to the full. In my opinion this measure is worth more than all others that could be taken for the present and future security of Cuba.[64]

While the planters were still almost unanimously in favour of slavery, Spanish domination (or, alternatively, annexation to the U.S.) was needed mainly to counteract British pressure against the slave traffic. When the progressive wing of planters appeared, one finds General O'Donnell, (Captain General in the 1840s and the one who unleashed the violent persecution of those who had been involved in the Escalera conspiracy, and later Spanish premier) arguing that a repression of the slave trade would not only ruin the Cuban economy but do away with 'the guarantee of conserving the integrity of the territory and its dependence on the Metropolis'.[65]

The reformist planters thought, on the one hand, that technical improve-ments in the sugar industry were incompatible with slavery; on the other hand, that they should have a greater political say, which implied a reduction of Spanish colonial exploitation. Then they developed, through writers such as Arango y Parreño, Saco and Pozos Dulces, a coherent ideology: white immigration, 'whitening' through intermarriage, mechanization of sugar mills and a subsequent increase in their scale of operations, and the use of white sharecroppers paid by results. All of this was generously adorned with arguments on the higher cost of slave labour, pious remarks about the need for a rural middle class, dire predictions about a black insurrection and impracticable suggestions about sending the blacks back to Africa.[66]

Thus upon hearing of a new introduction of Africans, Saco strongly opposed the project for

this new introduction of Africans far from being beneficial for us, would only aggravate the enormous problems which slavery has already posed us. [Slavery] is one of the main causes hindering the rapid progress of the white population, it has poured its mortal venom into the midst of families and into the heart of society, evicted from the fields many whites who would have been honourable farmers, deprived them of work thus submerging them in vagrancy and demoralization, and led to the reduction or absorption of many of the small farms by the large ones.[67]

Regarding the inordinate fear of those who saw the greatest danger emanating from the offspring of interracial unions, he argued that since the greatest menace for Cuba consisted in the African presence and the cleavage between the blacks and the whites, racial mixture, far from intensifying the tensions, would on the contrary contribute to diminishing them:

Sr. Queipo [a defender of slavery and member of the Junta de Información of 1866] regards the illegitimate unions between white settlers and coloured women as a great evil. I fully agree with him in this respect, considering matters from the moral point of view; but politically it seems to me he exaggerates their importance. These unions, he says ... foment the procreation of the *mestizo* classes who are to be feared a thousand times more than the negroes by virtue of their audacity and their pretensions to be equal to the white ... If the *mestizos* were born of unions between white women and black men, this would be regrettable, indeed, because reducing our population [meaning our white population] it would weaken it in every sense; but since the opposite occurs, far from considering it a menace I regard it as an advantage. The great evil of the Island of Cuba consists in the static nature of the black race, who always preserving its colour and primitive origin, keeps itself apart from the whites by insurmountable barriers; but if one got it moving, mixing it with the other race, and allowed it to continue this trend, this barrier would gradually be broken down. This is what has happened in Cuba since the conquest to our days; and had it not been for this constant passing from one class to the other, we would surely have fewer whites and more *mestizos* today. This is the stepping-stone by means of which the African race rises to mix with the white ... Cuban opinion in less enlightened centuries not having been opposed to this form of social change it is not to be expected that it should reject it today.[68]

Political reforms and autonomy presupposed abolition, and abolition in its turn presupposed racial integration. In the view of Saco, the colonial government promoted the introduction of negroes 'not so much as agricultural labour but as an instrument of domination'.[69] The political question was then closely related to the racial question. The presence in Cuba of the African element was at the core of all the deliberations, from whatever angle one looked at it.

36

The proceedings on interracial marriage reflect well the differing points of view on slavery. The reports of 1860 on the marriage by a white man of Cienfuegos to a coloured woman contain both the segregationist and the integrationist views. A neighbour informs us that the white suitor 'was apprenticed to the master mason, the freeborn *pardo* . . . who is a well-to-do neighbour, of irreproachable integrity, religious and very respectful to the whites . . . on account of the humble circumstances of the suitor the marriage will pass unnoticed by the public', a view much akin to that put forward in another report to the authorities assuring them that 'no bad moral effect will [this marriage] have on the spirit of the people of that area, for the white proletariat treats the coloured class on a completely equal footing'.[70]

In the Cienfuegos case, however, there are two additional reports, one by the Syndic and the other by the local chief of police, both raising serious objections to the marriage. As the latter argues, 'it may lead to presumptions on the part of the coloured class who on account of their extreme ignorance may derive from the said marriage the idea of equality between the classes; and in my view this mistaken idea will bear dismal consequences for the future and the established good order'. Another official unmasks this attitude for what it is – 'the [posture] of the ardent adherents of slavery and the proscription of the coloured race', and refutes it very much along Saco's and Arango y Parreño's lines:

Even admitting that the white race can never come to an understanding with the black race, it is in the public interest to reduce the latter in every possible manner; they blend in fact every day, for the antagonists themselves who belong to the white race so often satisfy their sexual whims and sometimes produce the terrible example of mulattos who are the slaves of their own fathers though they already bear in themselves a white part.[71]

He shares Arango y Parreño's and Saco's view of the positive effects of racial intermarriage. But he does not comment upon the significant difference that obtained between consensual and legally sanctioned interracial unions.

By the 1850s Arango y Parreño's views on slavery and the policy to be followed to achieve the transformation of the sugar industry had gained the support of many Creoles. The insistence with which interracial marriage is recommended as a path to create the prerequisite free labour force indicates this. In 1848 the Captain General was advised by an official to grant an interracial marriage licence 'in view of the need to augment the population'.[72] And in 1861 the government department dealing with interracial marriages contended in another case which had

37

been earlier opposed on racial as well as economic grounds that 'the prohibition established by law of marriages between persons of the white race with those of colour, refers to persons of distinction but not to the commoners and still less to those of humble condition, considering that if the poor classes were absolutely forbidden to contract marriage at all, enormous damage would be done to the development of the population'. It was then pointed out that the applicant had no means but his personal labour to support a family, which was again discarded for 'one cannot qualify a person who is able to work as absolutely wanting of means of subsistence, and still less so in a country where there is such a shortage of labour'. The licence was thereupon granted.[73]

Scarcity of labour for the expansion of the sugar industry thus induced some spokesmen of the reformist planters to rule against the restrictions of intermarriage. They might genuinely have thought that the prohibition of interracial marriage was slowing down the rate of procreation, but perhaps they were only scoring debating points in order to draw the authorities' attention to the critical situation on the labour market. Perhaps the member of the Cortes who in the debate of 1873 remarked of the abolitionists 'So much love as you profess for the blacks, we shall see what you will do when a black will demand a daughter of yours in marriage',[74] saw through these planters' arguments.

Merchants, slave dealers and the colonial powers opposed interracial marriage in order to preserve slavery, but tolerated concubinage and sporadic sexual contacts, which rather than being an expression of equality of the races was only one more facet of a social system based on the exploitation of the coloured people by the whites. Reformist white Creole planters tolerated interracial concubinage but preferred outright marriage to create a whitish proletariat.[75]

There were also those who opposed both, advocating total segregation. As an official argued in 1857,

It is not only now that the enlightened Government . . . adopts with indefatigable constancy healthy measures which have always aimed at favouring the white colonization of the Island as the most effective means to aid its progress and curtail the aspirations of the coloured classes; and it is quite certain that white immigration would be of no avail if instead of mixing here with their likes they were to foment the coloured races by contracting unions with them in detriment of public order.

And then follows an exposition of his reasons along functionalist lines:

In effect, as the civil rights enjoyed by the different castes of America are different due to an imperious necessity of our wise institutions, the most immediate result of the *marriage or mixture* of one with the other is the decline of the indispensable subordination and respect with which the coloured class must regard the white.[76]

Not only interracial marriage but free unions will undermine the coloured people's discipline and subordination.

From a purely 'racial' point of view this official was right in fearing just as much the results of concubinage as those of interracial marriage. Where he went wrong, however, was in supposing that the coloured people's subordination would be greater if they were denied any chance of advancement on principle. On the contrary, precisely the possibility and the existence of racial mixture provided a safety valve for the system by creating an intermediate group, the mulattos, whose allegiance to the blacks' cause was often minimal. It was the blacks that were frequently the most rebellious; whereas among those that pursued fugitive slaves, for instance, one could find many mulattos.

In 1868 the Ten Years War, that is, the first war of independence, broke out in Oriente province. Its leaders, for military reasons, to gain the support of the coloured population freed their slaves. Among the laws passed by the revolutionary governments was one introducing civil marriage. It granted absolute freedom of marriage to men over eighteen and women over fourteen years of age, the only impediment accepted being consanguineous kinship.[77] Surely, the struggle for independence unfolding in one half of the island and its racial overtones contributed to increasing further the apprehension in the western half, more so as Spanish propaganda characterized the war as a race war. This naturally had its effect on official policy with regard to interracial marriage. Until 1874 no licences were granted at all.

In that year, however, an official remarked of a case of intermarriage that the only impediment that existed between the two candidates was 'the insignificance of colour'.[78] The segregationists in Cuba no doubt felt reassured when the period of extreme liberal and republican rule in Spain (1868–73) came to an end. In 1874 we find once again General Concha in Cuba, this time relaxing the anti-negro policy. After the fall of the Republic and the monarchist Restoration, the new Spanish authorities were able to move slightly to the left in their colonial policy, and try to outbid the independist rebels in their appeals to the coloured population. This would have been too dangerous a game for the liberals and republicans to play, since it might have been thought of them that they would take it seriously to the point of sudden emancipation. Gradual emancipation and even token integration were by the mid-1870s thought to be unavoidable and not without political use against the Cuban independist movement. The Spanish revolution of 1868–73 only dared to enact the Ley Moret, *de vientre libre* (the law of the free womb), which henceforth freed the sons and daughters born to slaves. There is no evidence that the Republican governments of 1873 attempted to reverse the very restrictive policy on interracial marriage then applying, and there is evidence that this policy went on until 1874 when once again the legislation was more liberally interpreted.

In view of the continuing uncertainty in the interpretation of the interracial marriage legislation, the Archbishop of Cuba in 1879, after the Ten Years War had ended in defeat of the *mambi* revolutionary forces and Spain had reimposed its absolute hold on the whole island, made an attempt to obtain a definitive statement from the civil authorities as to the practice to be followed, emphasizing that 'the difference of colour does not constitute in Canon Law an impediment'. The Cuban authorities forwarded this petition to the Minister of Overseas Affairs who in turn requested reports from the ecclesiastical authorities of Cuba, an occasion which the Archbishop seized to make his stand quite clear, for

bearing in mind the new status of the inhabitants of this Island, the partial abolition of slavery, the civil rights granted the free, the need to legitimate illicit unions through the holy Sacrament of marriage and the difficulties to obtain previous licence, and other moral disadvantages of great import . . . [he] believed that absolute freedom should be granted to people of different colour to marry according to the ritual established by the Church.[79]

Despite the urgent nature of the Church's appeal it took the Ministry of Overseas Affairs until January of 1881 to enact a decree at last granting freedom of marriage between the races. A year earlier the Law of Abolition of Slavery in the Island of Cuba had been passed.[80]

In theory, from 1881 onward no legal obstacle existed for whites to marry coloured people. Yet with such a tradition of racial discrimination and segregation, opinion was unlikely to change radically from one day to the next. In 1882 a young white man wanted to marry a *parda* who was pregnant by him, but his father was opposed on grounds of inequality. One official quotes the 1881 decree and favours the marriage. The Consejo de Administracion, however, accepts the father's objections since

this parental dissent cannot be viewed as an excess of paternal authority, even if the son's request is based on the Royal Decree . . . because even if this decree grants absolute freedom of marriage between the races, one cannot forbid a parent to oppose a marriage his minor son wants to contract with a person of colour, even if she is in the state the *parda* is in.

But this verdict is overruled for 'the father's fears with regard to his son's marriage to a person of different race have been destroyed by the Royal Decree of 27 January 1881',[81] and the supplementary licence is granted. In theory the fears were indeed unfounded once the coloured people had been granted full civil rights. Practice was still a different matter.

From 1881 onward the coloured population filed innumerable petitions for full civil rights.[82] And by 1894, fearing a renewed bid for independence, the Spanish government also actively supported the implementation of desegregationist legislation. Yet, as the outcome of the second war of independence was to show, José Martí was probably right in saying that 'Spain has come too late'. The process of acquiring national identity, largely synonymous with racial integration, which was characterized by the emergence of such coloured leaders as Antonio Maceo, Flor Crombet, Juan Gualberto Gómez, Martin Morúa Delgado and Rafael Serra, could no longer be delayed. Despite a renewed upsurge of racial hysteria in 1894, which found its expression in fears identical to those of 1854 – it was rumoured that the blacks were on the point of taking the white women and marrying them – the moment was nearer when, in the words of Maceo uttered in 1870, *no hay negritos ni blanquitos, sino cubanos* (there are no little negroes or little whites, only Cubans).[83] Racial tensions, however, survived in Cuba, though they became less acute.[84] Even nowadays, expressions such as 'good hair' and 'bad hair', and 'to advance the family' – meaning whitening – are used.

CHAPTER 3

# INTERMARRIAGE AND CATHOLIC
# DOCTRINE

## THE CONFLICT BETWEEN CHURCH AND STATE

The prohibition of interracial marriage and its moral implications had to be of direct concern to the Church. Marriage sanctioned by the Church was the secularly and religiously approved and prescribed form of conjugal union for equals in Spain. Unions between unequals, however, also occurred, or were at least attempted. The alternative in these cases could have been concubinage, as it was in fact in those instances where the social distance between the partners exceeded the accepted boundaries. This alternative was, however, unacceptable to the Church.

As far as the Church was concerned, absolute freedom of marriage existed among Catholics. From the ecclesiastical point of view the State should adhere to the same principle. There had been for some time jurisdictional disputes between the ecclesiastical and secular authorities with regard to marriage. Typical was the conflict that arose when Pope Benedict XIV in 1741, although accepting as licit the secret marriage commonly called 'of conscience' instituted by the secular authorities as an alternative in cases of social inequality between the partners, attempted to legislate on its temporal aspects.[1] By proposing that the offspring of these second-class marriages be granted the same civil rights as those of equal marriages, and thus in secular eyes defeating their very aim, he was felt grossly to have exceeded ecclesiastical prerogatives, for 'regulating inheritance and seeing to contracts is a right held by the civil republic and the authority of the sovereigns and not by the ecclesiastical authorities who should only attend to matters of conscience and the spiritual well-being of souls'.[2]

Although this dispute was on the surface only one more manifestation of the antagonism between Church and State originating in the latter's insistent claim to control the temporal aspects of Church government, a more fundamental principle, namely the role of the individual vis-à-vis society, was at stake. While the secular powers held a hierarchical view of society where individual aspirations were subordinated to the demands of society, the Catholic Church's teachings defended the paramountcy of the individual's spiritual salvation, dependent obviously on his performance in this world. The Church was in a dilemma. On the one hand, owing to her egalitarian ideology, the Church could not conceive of different kinds of institutions for different kinds of people; and on the other neither could she tolerate concubinage which was often resorted to in cases where the partners were thought to be socially incompatible.

A Committee of Ministers set up in 1775 to advise the Spanish Crown on ways to avoid unequal marriages maintained that the general principle that religious marriage had all the effects of a civil contract, even if it was entered into between utterly unequal partners and against parental will, was unacceptable, for

> by entitling the offspring thereof to become heirs to their parents' wealth, rights and honours . . . it results in lawsuits and enmities as well as in the dishonour of the families and the decline of titles, dignities and the oldest entailments through the offspring of unworthy marriages

and, as a consequence,

> some individuals of distinguished birth, bearing in mind the harm they would do their families and the glorious memory of their ancestors or fearing the justified indignation of their relatives . . . do not dare to contract such unequal marriages and live in perpetual concubinage blinded by their passion, to the detriment of their souls and scandal of the faithful.[3]

Without paying heed to the Church's moral misgivings, the Committee suggested as a solution for cases of social incompatibility of partners the introduction of a type of conjugal union analogous to morganatic marriage.[4]

As the subsequent legislation on marriage shows, the Crown kept the upper hand in this dispute. Although liberal ideas made their appearance in Spain in the late eighteenth century – disentailment of estates, sale of Church and communal lands, abolition or at least curtailment of the Inquisition, began to be discussed – they did not contribute to a less restricted view on marriage. As has been seen, the Royal Pragmatic on marriage was passed in 1776 and made extensive to the colonies in 1778. The penalty imposed on those marrying against parental will was disinheritance. This legislation was surely aimed at a regalist curtailment of both ecclesiastical and individual liberties, which here happened to coincide.

Ever since the enactment of the royal decree on marriage the so-called 'marriages for reasons of conscience' had been a source of conflict be-

tween the civil and the ecclesiastical authorities.[5] Should the clergy
celebrate a marriage when the couple were willing to go ahead with it
despite parental dissent and bear the penalties? The Crown gave this
answer:

I have decided [that] . . . although they submit to the penalties established by the
royal decree of 1776, the ecclesiastical judges should not accept their applications for
marriage, which would result in considerable detriment of the families and the State,
and that furthermore the clergy who are in a position to authorize marriages should
be instructed not to celebrate them in such cases.[6]

This decision was later reinforced: 'neither the submission to the penalties
established by royal decree nor the fact of having offspring and of volun-
tary or violent defloration are sufficient reasons . . . for the priest to
proceed with the marriage'.[7] As long as honour understood as family
pre-eminence did not conflict with female virtue, in the sense that female
honour was still intact when the honour of the family and the order of
society demanded a prohibition of marriage, all was well. But when the
impaired honour of the women required a marriage which on the other
hand was thought to damage the honour pre-eminence of the family and
the order of society, then the situation became problematic.

In 1798, in a more tempered recommendation designed to solve the
numerous queries that had been received from the overseas possessions
regarding the interpretation of the law in cases where the couple insisted
on going ahead with their intended marriage despite parental opposition
because seduction had occurred or the affair had already produced offspring, the Council of the Indies expounded the view that 'the most
appropriate and convenient solution in such cases is to leave it to the
prudence and discretion of the priest to compare the damage, scandal and
detriment that could result from such marriages with the consequences
that would have to be feared were they prevented, and allow or prohibit
them according to his conscience'.[8] In principle unequal marriage was
permitted when the honour of the girl demanded it, but the authorities
hoped that even the clergy might put political expediency above the
commands of their consciences which required them to redeem those who
had sinned.

But there was obviously good reason to fear that the clergy might in
fact be carried away by their consciences. This elicited from the Council
of the Indies a lenient recommendation which ended, however, with a
severe admonition:

As vanity and conceit frequently enlarge the pretended inequalities and once the
marriage has taken place the natural love and spiritual well-being of the children

44

usually calms those preoccupations and bad feelings, it seems that this solution is the most prudent for achieving the sacred objectives of the royal decree, and although it should not be thought that the Archbishops and Bishops will disregard them or due to excessive fears or scruples will be inclined towards marriage, it seems very convenient to beg and command them that they proceed with due vigour and correctness, bearing in mind that not any cause is sufficient but that it has to be a grave and very urgent one for them to condescend to authorize the marriages.[9]

The obvious alternative offered by concubinage was not left unattended: 'but if the grounds of conscience are overruled and marriage is frustrated or impeded, it will be equally his [the clergyman's] task to take appropriate steps and precautions to cut short any illicit affairs that might exist'.[10]

Finally, in 1803 the whole matter was re-examined once more, and this time the authorities made their stand quite clear. Moral considerations as extenuating circumstances were dismissed. Severe penalties were introduced for clergymen who dared to disobey the law: 'those vicars who authorize marriage for which the contracting partners are not qualified . . . shall be exiled and all their income shall be confiscated, and the spouses themselves shall incur the same penalty, that is expatriation and confiscation of their property'.[11] Since women usually married in their teens and young men in their early twenties, freedom of marriage beyond the ages of twenty-three and twenty-five respectively did not constitute an effective threat to the social order. Besides, as shown above, in 1805 a further royal decree was passed according to which not only minors but also those who had attained their majority were required to obtain a special dispensation from the civil authorities for interracial marriages.

Two points emerge from the legislation:

First, two models of society existed side by side, the religious egalitarian view, presumably also shared by the liberal extremists, and the State's hierarchical conception. The Church placed individual morality above considerations of political convenience: all Catholics were equal, and thus free to marry, all the more so if 'reasons of conscience' existed. The State, by contrast, severely restricted individual choice in the interest of the continuity of the social order, regardless of moral considerations.

Second, social class endogamy was the officially decreed form of marriage. I am using class here in the broadest sense.

## 'SOCIAL EQUILIBRIUM' AND CATHOLIC MORALITY

The conflict between the demands of 'social equilibrium' and those of Catholic morality were perceived by many. After all, according to

Catholic doctrine concubinage was a mortal sin, chastity being a central element of its value system.

In a report submitted by the Civil Governor of Oriente province in 1855 on the advisability of granting a marriage licence to a mixed couple, this conflict is made explicit:

> From the purely religious point of view this marriage imperiously demands government co-operation; but there is little doubt that the dissemination of ideas of equality of the white class with the coloured race puts in jeopardy the tranquility of the Island, the largest proportion of whose population consists of the said race; it is no less true that by authorizing marriages between one and the other [race] the links of subordination of the coloured people to the white will tend to be subverted and weakened, and . . . the day would come when those encouraged by the example of unequal marriages which favour them, will aspire impetuously to achieve a rank which society denies them and as a consequence public order would be upset; it is therefore the Government's duty to prevent such a situation at all cost.

The licence should therefore be denied. As an afterthought the official adds: 'this decision would make allowances for any reason of conscience that might exist since the failure to contract the marriage would then be the result of a decision taken by others than those desiring to marry'.[12]

The authorities could not easily deny the legitimacy of Catholic morality. Accordingly, marriage licences are repeatedly refused making a special point of the absence of 'reasons of conscience'. Typical is the ruling of the official who contends that 'he feels it would be very convenient that the licence be withheld as has been done in other cases, when there are no reasons of conscience that demand marriage'. Moreover, 'on account of her good manners [she] can easily contract marriage with a person of her own race'.[13] Conversely, as another official argues, 'one should not impede the marriage . . . and much less so when, as has been confessed, there has been concubinage and offspring . . . [for] one must bear in mind the damage done to morality by illegitimate unions and the terrible suffering caused to the offspring by being bastards'.[14] In these cases it is the sin committed prior to the petition that determines the authorities' decision. The general attitude is that 'reasons of politics and morality are opposed to the granting of these licences for marriages between persons of different race in the absence of very special circumstances or considerations'.[15] ('Morality' here means, of course, public order and not Catholic morality.)

Obviously, the authorities did not always abide by this rule, namely that interracial marriage should in principle be prevented except in those cases where moral considerations made it mandatory. D. José Campo Romero's is a case in point. Here the consequences of a prohibition of marriage as well as the authorities' reaction in the face of 'special circumstances' become manifest. The suitor is white, has no family in Cuba and does agricultural work. The bride is a freeborn *parda* of well-to-do parents. He is employed with her father. The local official believes that the marriage is not advisable unless 'reasons of conscience intervene and public morals suffer', which so far does not seem to be the case. The licence is withheld. However, the young man does not give up hope and appeals, adducing the precedent of other marriages with whites in his bride's family, yet with little success. Three years after the initiation of the proceedings the Bishop takes up the case, reporting that by now the couple have had a child and are living together and declaring cautiously that he cannot consent to their continuing cohabitation if they cannot marry. Only at this point do the civil authorities accede to the request, yet rebuking the Bishop that 'not always will it be possible for this Government to allow marriages of this nature and it expects of the apostolic zeal of H.E. that he know how to reconcile on similar occasions the high interests of Church and State'.[16] Another official is even more categorical:

The section understands well the significance of reasons of morality invoked by the applicant; yet, it is not such as, first, to warrant disregarding a mandate by H.M. Government, and second, to cause a conflict in the time to come in this country which harbours such a variety of races and which considerations of greater weight advise not to confound.[17]

'Reasons of conscience' did not, then, constitute an absolute must with regard to interracial marriage. Indeed, in a number of cases the requested licence, though granted, is made dependent on the respective status of the candidates.[18]

The authorities are well aware of the precepts of Catholic morality; they acknowledge them yet do not feel bound by them. On the contrary, they manipulate these values in accordance with the circumstances and as a rule subordinate them to the interests of the State. There is no doubt about the supremacy of the secular power. As long as a particular marriage appears to sustain or at least not to menace the established social order in a direct way, morality is allowed to prevail. When, however, the social order is felt to be at stake, morality is relegated to a second place. The integrity and continuity of the social order, from whatever point it is viewed, always prevails over religio-moral considerations.

The secular authorities' appraisal of religious morality is well set forth in the following statement:

*Interracial marriage*

The Archbishop of Cuba and the Bishop of this Diocese have opposed the prohibition of marriage between whites and blacks on the grounds that by these marriages the customs and public morals would gain much because in this way it would be avoided that many cohabit in detriment of Christian religion . . . although recognizing the inconvenience of concubinage, the high interests of public good make it appear advisable to prohibit marriages between whites and blacks.

And then is added, with the obvious purpose of showing the Church its place: 'concubinage can best be prevented by the Church by means of preaching and the good conduct of its own ministers'.[19]

### FREEDOM OF CHOICE AGAINST HIERARCHY

The secular authorities view society hierarchically, individual interests being subordinated to those of the collectivity. The Catholic Church by preaching the paramountcy of the individual's spiritual salvation defended freedom of choice in marriage which in turn implied the ultimate equality of all men. But Catholic doctrine is one thing, and ecclesiastical practice another. A number of authors have made much of the significance of Catholic universalism in softening racial attitudes in the Latin American slave societies.[20] It is thus interesting to see how both the lower and the higher clergy approached the question of interracial marriage in nineteenth-century Cuba. In a number of cases (21 out of the total 199) the licence is requested because the parish priest refuses to celebrate the marriage without official permission. Thus one priest regarded the marriage licence as indispensable, for the suitor was a soldier and 'at the same time a difference in class existed owing to [her] belonging to that of *pardos*'.[21] This clergyman did not question the government's restrictive marriage policy.

Some of the clergy went even further than merely abiding by official policy. Thus, another priest objected to a mixed marriage because 'given this inequality, the marriage if contracted could produce perpetual discord between the members of one family, and, for one of the two families to be united by it, the shame resulting from the idea of being degraded in quality in the opinion of their peers'.[22] Still another priest is well aware of the need for control of intermarriage: 'although it is true that inequality of class is not in Canon Law an impediment which forbids marriage, it is so, however, in Civil Law, and so desired by society itself which wishes every individual to keep to his station'. The white suitor had argued that he wanted to marry the girl out of gratitude. The priest had something to say on this as well: 'If gratitude is the only motive compelling [him] to contract this unequal marriage, what has this to do with the offspring who will be degraded and will have to lament to-morrow the damage their father has done them? In my view they will justly say that although gratitude is most praiseworthy, the price must stand in proportion to the benefit obtained.'[23] This priest is just as discriminating as his secular counterpart. Colour difference is equivalent to social inequality and thus forbids marriage.

Such an attitude is admittedly rare and extreme. Yet, a number of priests, without explicitly rejecting interracial marriage, do not accept it without reservations. They apply rules of social compatibility identical to those used by the secular authorities, namely that 'there is inequality of race between him and his bride . . . but [she] is of those *pardas* who in this village and even elsewhere could pass for white'.[24] Therefore, they could marry. Allowance must be made, however, in these instances, for the possibility that these priests saw their only chance of achieving the marriage to lie in arguing the secular authorities' case.

In fact, not only the higher clergy but also the lower orders sometimes attempted to implement the dictates of doctrine and morality. It is precisely the clergy who point out repeatedly the 'subsequent illicit affairs that usually result from the majority of the cases where marriages are not contracted for no fault of the candidates themselves',[25] or that 'neither the sacred canons nor ecclesiastical discipline prohibit the cele-bration of marriage between persons of different colour, and if this one is contracted perhaps an illicit union might be prevented';[26] or that the official who objects to such a marriage 'condemns [the poor classes] to complete celibacy or to a life of public concubinage in detriment of religion and dishonour of society'.[27] And there are also those priests who took an active part in getting those already living in sin to legalize their unions in Church – and among these free unions racially different partners were probably numerous – by admonishing them either to marry or to separate, to the extent of taking it upon themselves to obtain the licence if they were willing to marry. Thus the Archbishop pleaded that 'since he belongs to the lowest class of society and taking into account more than anything else his desire to remedy the state of sin in which he normally lives, to the scandal of the faithful and detriment of good customs, I have decided to forward [his] petition'.[28] In another case, he drew the civil authorities' attention to the fact that 'even if difficulties may arise from the fact that the coloured people advance in social status and pretensions by marrying white people, those arising from the degradation of white people to the class of the coloured through concubinage are greater and more important'.[29] To say that the whites who entered into concubinage with a coloured partner descended to their inferior class was a rhetorical device rather than a fact. Concubinage was preferred in many quarters precisely because, as opposed to marriage, it implied no descent in status.

Neither those living in sin nor their families nor the authorities, however, would always be swayed by religious or moral considerations. One priest in his zeal went so far as to present an apocryphal petition on behalf of his parishioner to marry a free negro woman, which was only discovered when the supposed applicant declared that

he did not know how to read or write and consequently the signature which foots the petition was not his: that he did not authorize anybody to submit a petition in his name for he has never thought of marrying the negress Candelaria Enrique and although he is having an affair with her, this is not nor can it be sufficient ground to marry her in view of the immense class distance.[30]

The ecclesiastical ideal was clear, but either it was not enforced with much conviction by the clergy, or, more importantly, it met with open hostility both on the part of the public and of the secular authorities. When Claret y Clarà was Archbishop of Santiago de Cuba (from 1852 to 1856), on the occasion of an extraordinary pastoral visit to Oriente province over nine thousand marriages were celebrated of couples of all colours who up to then had lived in concubinage 'thus giving a name to over forty thousand spurious offspring', over one hundred thousand devotional books were distributed and many 'repulsive works' were collected – perhaps masonic tracts preaching some measure of liberty, equality and fraternity – and seventy thousand people received the holy communion. It was an important enterprise which gave rise to a formidable polemic, for the missionaries

compelled by the firm purpose of inducing those living in concubinage to marry exhorted the population to disclose those who they knew were living in this way: without further justification and regardless of their social status people were forced to appear before the mission, even with their slave women with whom they were imputed to be having affairs; when they protested alleging racial inequality they were told that before God everybody was equal.

One Father Andoain was the priest who most excelled in these activities,

who coming from the Carlist ranks keeps his violent manners which he displays in the pulpit in raging sermons . . . at the pulpit [he] used an obscene and very improper style and in his sermons he broke forth into curses with an image of the Saviour in his hands, which he made the audience repeat and which were directed against all those who lived in sin . . . and the worst of it is that both from the pulpit and in private he has propagated doctrines of equality between the white and the black classes, thus causing immense damage to the Island.[31]

Attacks such as these by neighbours and officials of various parts of Oriente province were directed not only against Father Andoain but equally against the Archbishop himself, 'who is carrying out the visit of his Diocesis in such an unusual fashion and in contradiction with the custom of his predecessors, that the writer in his quality of faithful and loyal Spaniard thinks it necessary to inform Y.E. so that scandal and consequent damage be averted'.[32]

The secular authorities' and the white inhabitants' rage was first unleashed by the Archbishop's excommunication of one D. Agustín Vilarredona, a shopkeeper and tenant farmer who despite repeated exhortations by the missionaries persistently refused to marry his concubine. The case was taken to the Audiencia of Puerto Principe who ruled that excommunication was an excessive penalty, for 'cases of concubinage can neither be reputed as grave nor as irremediable' and besides their cognizance belonged exclusively to the secular authorities. Although the Archbishop insisted on the correctness of his interpretation of the laws, once Vilarredona had given up his life in sin, he eventually revoked the excommunication. The secular authorities' examination of the case turns exclusively on its legalistic aspects. It is only from a letter by Claret y Clarà that one learns that in fact the bone of contention was not solely Villarredona's concubinage, but that his concubine was a coloured woman.[33]

None of those complaining of the missionaries' activities denied the frequency of concubinage in the area; it is a 'deeply rooted evil' with which they, however, were willing to put up. They were up in arms, instead, against

the example set by the missionaries [which] had not . . . had salutary effects because instead of using persuasion and sweetness these clergymen have directed their endeavour against the sensual passions exasperating the people with dreadful penalties and even with excommunications; the style of their sermons which is resented by the locals, and their exaggerated threats are not the means that prudence advises . . . [these are] marriages that public opinion opposes in a country in which the separation of castes constitutes an important condition of existence.[34]

Concubinage was the lesser evil.

Feelings were greatly aroused. The controversy between the Church and the civil authorities over marriage in general and interracial marriage in particular produced a series of contradictory rumours. The Lieutenant Governor of Manzanillo felt compelled to report that instigated by the enemies of the government and the missionaries there were people who believed that 'it was the Government's intention to keep the country in a state of backwardness and fanaticism in order to govern it despotically'.[35] Alluding to the excommunication the official continued: 'it seemed to some as a kind of revival of the Inquisition, with which one more danger is added to those that we experience already'. To interpret the missionaries' efforts as symptomatic of a revival of the Inquisition appears to indicate a singular confusion in the minds of those spreading the rumour. It had been precisely the Inquisition's basic occupation to watch over the Spaniard's racial purity, while the Archbishop Claret y Clarà defended his missionaries against their imputed disregard for the laws on interracial marriage, arguing that 'in view of the great numbers it is not possible to pay much attention to the colour', and Father Andoain maintained that 'before God everybody is equal'.[36]

With the exception of Archbishop Claret y Clarà and his missionaries and a somewhat later Bishop of Havana, the clergy was largely law-abiding and of little initiative. Moreover, according to penal law they ran some risk in celebrating marriage between persons who lacked the necessary official licence. But then it was not clear whether the legislation demanded of a person of lowly status a licence to marry a coloured person. Archbishop Claret y Clarà discussed at length the complex legal aspect. The gist of his argument is that 'the Royal Decree and the Edict which are the present legal regulations ... do not prohibit unequal marriages, except if they are celebrated without licence, and they do not apply to all inequalities but solely to those resulting between people of noble origin and those of colour'.[37]

Some officials had based their proscription of interracial marriage on the Reglamento de Pedáneos issued in 1843 by the then Captain General Valdés and which in article 44 instructed the local clergy to 'suspend [while the appropriate official decision is taken] those marriages which on account of inequality of caste, status or for other motives in which it may be assumed that the affable union to which the State and the spouses themselves should aspire, and which is of such great interest to the families, will be of short duration'.[38] Undoubtedly this regulation was one more effort to, if not prohibit, at least render difficult interracial marriages. Claret y Clarà takes this regulation to task as well:

when sufficient time of continuous contact, obstinacy in an illicit affair, offspring which bring interests and affections closer to each other intervene, as they generally do in each and every one of these cases, it is unlikely that if peace reigns between man and woman with the blessing of the devil, it will be very different with the blessing of God.[39]

For all his religious fervour Archbishop Claret y Clarà did not campaign against the source of racial segregation itself, although in the eyes of many his policy had the effect of challenging the slave order as such. He was more concerned with freedom from sin rather than with freedom from bondage. The concluding passages of his report to the civil authorities reveal him as a realist. The so frequently-voiced fear that intermarriage would lead to open rebellion of the coloured people he refuted on the grounds that 'since some [of the mulattos] are thought of as white, instead of cherishing the least sympathy for the coloured race, they are the ones who are most opposed to it and who object most strongly to being associated with it, because nobody wants to descend from one class to another inferior one'.[40]

The foregoing report by Archbishop Claret y Clarà was submitted to the Captain General. His views were shared by the then Bishop of Havana as well as, not surprisingly, by Captain General Pezuela himself, who in a letter to the Ministry of Overseas Affairs strongly defends the Archbishop's activities, stressing that

such exhortations on the part of the parish priests is an obligation so much part of the cure of souls that the priest who without awaiting an instruction by his prelate acts in any other way and does not use all his zeal to regain the woman who has forgotten her duty, bears a grave responsibility, greater than in any other place in this Island of Cuba where concubinage is almost the rule, where there are parishes of over twelve thousand souls which until recently had no more than twelve married couples, while the Archbishop with his missionary activity of two years succeeded in transforming over twenty thousand public concubinages into marriage, not to mention the many people who have abandoned their illicit affairs.

Revealingly, he attributes the hostility encountered by the Archbishop to two sources, on the one hand the Cuban clergy who rebelled against the Archbishop's measures to moralize its members, and on the other to the then still hypothetical promoters of Cuban independence 'who cannot look on unshaken while he renders useless one of the powerful instruments of rebellion, the people [presumably the coloured people], through his extraordinary abnegation'.[41]

This understanding between the civil and the ecclesiastical authorities in matters of marriage was as rare as it was shortlived. After at least one attempt on his life,[42] Archbishop Claret y Clarà left the island in 1856 to become confessor to Queen Isabel II.[43]

In 1867 the then Bishop of Havana, Fray Jacinto Maria Martínez de Peñacerrada, raised once more with the civil authorities the issue of interracial marriages and its moral implications. Referring to the 10 August 1854 decree, he argued that it was then thirteen years since a revision of the laws on interracial marriage and a new regulation had been promised without any visible result. His attention had been drawn to the question of interracial marriage on occasion of a pastoral visit of his diocese – the western part of the island – where he had seen 'with no little sorrow that everywhere concubinages, predominantly between white men and mulatto women, continued to be widespread, resulting in an excessive number of natural offspring who with rare exceptions are not recognized by their progenitors and have neither family nor society, for the former consists of no more than a mother'.[44] Not being able to reconcile this state of affairs with the dictates of his conscience he took steps to remedy the evil, yet encountered on his path 'a wall which he could not surmount and which consists of the impediment established by the Supreme Government by the Royal Decree [of 10 August 1854] which . . . suspended the former legislation'.[45]

From 1864 to 1874 no licences were granted at all to mixed couples. Fray Jacinto Maria had come up against this restrictive policy. As he points out, the 1854 decree 'is acquiring an absolutely prohibitive nature with grave damage to the law of God, to the morality of the people, to women, to the family, to the wretched natural offspring and even to the political regime of this country'.[46]

The Bishop's request was submitted to the Consejo de Administración of the island, a body composed (in addition to the principal Spanish authorities) of a number of prominent Creole and Spanish planters and merchants, and was once more rejected on 12 July 1867 on the grounds that 'it is perhaps no mistake to say that the aversion against such marriages has even deeper roots today, for the superior race fears and wants to prevent the loss and damage of its genealogy, its pre-eminence and its dignity. This is the way of thinking of the wealthiest, most influential and most prominent sector of the Island.' Besides, official concessions in this field would be 'against the almost fundamental order of the country, the dignity of its families and the acquiescence of the submissive serfs to their status'.[47]

It was surely no accident that Fray Jacinto Maria when returning in 1870 from a trip to Rome was not allowed to land in Havana on the orders of Captain General Valmaseda. According to his own version of the conflict, widely printed in the North American press by exiled Cuban reformists, he had been 'very intimate with Captain General Dulce . . . and a cry was raised that he and I were traitors and supporters of the [1868 independist] rebellion'. Allegedly Fray Jacinto Maria had sent priests among the rebellious forces to preach to them and this had drawn upon him the wrath of the conservative elements. The Bishop's view on interracial marriage surely contributed to the growing enmity of the pro-Spanish elements which finally led to his banishment from the island.[48]

The position of the Church was, then, highly ambiguous. Among the lower clergy attitudes towards interracial marriage ranged from total opposition to active support. The higher clergy, or at least Archbishop Claret y Clarà and Bishop Jacinto Maria vigorously campaigned for interracial marriage. Since interracial marriage meant equality of the races which in turn meant abolition of slavery, they were bound to meet staunch opposition from many quarters. Claret y Clarà's friendship with the Marquis of Pezuela and his overtures to the poor and coloured people earned him the wrath of white Creoles, of both the annexationist and the reformist persuasion.[49] Fifteen years later Bishop Jacinto Maria's integrationist proposals were to antagonize the pro-Spanish elements.

In principle, there was no way of reconciling the Church's egalitarian teachings with the socio-economic and political interests of all the secular powers. Either the clergy's moralizing and catechizing efforts were severely curtailed by the government, or, as in the case of the two prelates, the government harnessed their support for its own purposes.[50]

But general indifference or even antagonism was not restricted to the Church's endeavours with regard to marriage. Its influence steadily declined in all spheres of life. As the traveller Trollope noted in 1859, 'Roman catholic worship is at a lower ebb in Cuba than almost anywhere else'.[51] This is not surprising for the clergy's corruption was proverbial. Even the 'saintly' Archbishop Claret y Clarà had no other choice but to put up with a clergy of very dubious morality.[52] And when Robert Richard Madden interviewed Domingo del Monte in 1838 about the state of the Cuban clergy, he was informed that 'The clergy here follows blindly the moral and political causes that compel the rest of the population to defend slavery'. Upon asking whether it was usual for priests to own farms worked by slaves, he was told that in fact most of them had farms and treated their slaves very much as did all the rest of the population.[53]

The loss of ground on the part of the Church is also reflected in the remarkable decrease in the number of clergy on the island. While in 1778 there were 1,063 practising clergy in Cuba, which made for a ratio of one priest for every 168 persons,[54] by 1846 their numbers had fallen to 432 giving a ratio of one priest per 2,080 inhabitants, increasing only slightly to 540 in 1862 when the ratio had fallen to one priest per 2,495 inhabitants.[55] Efforts to bring in missionaries to provide religious education for the slaves were categorically rejected in 1847, for 'it would be very difficult to reconcile the Catechism with the respect which is owed to property and the necessity of avoiding meetings of numerous slaves which could endanger the security of the towns'.[56] Moreover, most of the clergy lived in the towns. Thus in 1862 slightly under half of the priests in the island appear to have resided in Havana.[57] And most of them were *peninsulares* which certainly did not make for their integration into the local community.

# CHAPTER 4

# THE WHITE MAN'S VIEW

## THE SEX RATIO AND FREQUENCY OF INTERMARRIAGE

Sentiment in nineteenth-century Cuba was in good part hostile to interracial marriage. Nevertheless, throughout the century some 250 whites were keen enough to marry across the colour bar to apply for government licence to do so.[1] A factor relevant to the probability of interracial unions is the sex composition of the population. Table 2 gives the population figures by colour, status and sex from 1817 to 1862. It is possible to give age specific figures for three years, and to break them down by shade of the free coloured for two years (Tables 2a, 2b and 2c).

Throughout the century, there were 114 adult white men (1827), or 127 (1846), or 150 (1862) for every 100 adult white women. In the free coloured population, however, women outnumbered men. These two sectors, namely the white and the free coloured, generally furnished the partners to interracial unions. A considerable percentage of white males, unless they decided to remain celibate, had to resort to the coloured community for their women.

Some contemporaries also attribute the existence of interracial marriage to the white population's disparate sex ratio. As one official argues, 'bearing in mind that [he] . . . is of humble status . . . it would be difficult if not impossible for him to contract marriage with a white person'.[2] And Archbishop Claret y Clarà explained why poor whites have little chance of conquering a white woman:

Poor people like those living in the countryside, many of them from the Canary Islands and all of them although white of the humble class, do not find white women to marry because the latter's pride forbids them to engage in domestic chores. However poor these women may be, none of them or very few accept living without some black woman to wait on them; and perhaps there is no white woman who will ever adapt to the humble duties of the black women. Which unhappy *veguero* or *montuno* [peasants] can put up with such demands? And since on the other hand the coloured people do not shirk work, this is why the poor white prefer them.[3]

White women because of their relative scarcity were in a strong bargaining position. Moreover, the immigrants were mostly male. The

TABLE 2. *Population of Cuba by colour, status and sex, 1817–62*

| | Whites | | |
|---|---|---|---|
| Year: | Males | Females | Ratio |
| 1817 | 75,982 | 57,722 | 1.31 |
| 1827 | 89,526 | 75,532 | 1.18 |
| 1846 | 230,983 | 194,784 | 1.18 |
| 1862[a] | 432,624 | 324,986 | 1.33 |
| | Total coloured people | | |
| 1817 | 103,948 | 58,553 | 1.77 |
| 1827 | 146,623 | 96,856 | 1.51 |
| 1846 | 273,662 | 199,323 | 1.37 |
| 1862[a] | 431,573 | 262,915 | 1.60 |
| | Free coloureds | | |
| 1817 | 20,779 | 20,097 | 1.03 |
| 1827 | 21,235 | 24,235 | 0.85 |
| 1846 | 72,651 | 76,575 | 0.94 |
| 1862[a] | 111,268 | 114,670 | 0.97 |

[a] These figures do not include 34,771 Chinese men and 57 Chinese women, nor 712 Yucatecan men and 334 Yucatecan women.

Sources: *Cuadro estadístico de la siempre fiel Isla de Cuba, correspondiente al año de 1827* (Havana, 1829); *Cuadro estadístico de la siempre fiel Isla de Cuba, correspondiente al año de 1846* (Havana, 1847); *Noticias estadísticas de la Isla de Cuba en 1862* (Havana, 1864).

TABLE 2a. *Population of Cuba by colour, status and sex, 1827* (men over fifteen and women over twelve)

| | Males | Females | Ratio |
|---|---|---|---|
| Whites | 106,498 | 93,402 | 1.14 |
| Free mulattos | 16,101 | 18,974 | 0.84 |
| Free blacks | 15,502 | 17,667 | 0.87 |
| Slaves | 152,305 | 82,686 | 1.85 |

Source: *Cuadro estadístico de la siempre fiel Isla de Cuba, correspondiente al año de 1827* (Havana, 1829).

TABLE 2b. *Population of Cuba over sixteen by colour, status and sex, 1846*

|  | Males | Females | Ratio |
|---|---|---|---|
| Whites | 139,121 | 108,211 | 1.27 |
| Free mulattos | 20,915 | 24,577 | 0.85 |
| Free blacks | 22,562 | 23,998 | 0.94 |
| Slaves | 158,656 | 87,287 | 1.81 |

Source: *Cuadro estadístico de la siempre fiel Isla de Cuba, correspondiente al año de 1846* (Havana, 1847).

TABLE 2c. *Population of Cuba over sixteen by colour, status and sex, 1862*

|  | Males | Females | Ratio |
|---|---|---|---|
| Whites | 259,993 | 172,545 | 1.50 |
| Free coloureds | 42,876 | 58,529 | 0.73 |
| Slaves | 143,495 | 90,316 | 1.58 |

Source: *Noticias estadísticas de la Isla de Cuba en 1862* (Havana, 1864).

TABLE 3. *Percentage of illegitimate children of total baptisms by colour and status, 1846 and 1862*

| Year: | Whites | Free coloureds | Slaves | Total coloureds |
|---|---|---|---|---|
| 1846 | 19 | ... | ... | 75 |
| 1862 | 13 | 46 | 84 | 66 |

Sources: *Cuadro estadístico de la siempre fiel Isla de Cuba, correspondiente al año de 1846* (Havana, 1847); *Noticias estadísticas de la Isla de Cuba en 1862* (Havana, 1864).

white women available were thus the daughters either of local white families or of government officials who would hardly lower themselves and marry a poor white. As one young man remarks, 'the social status [he] has prevents him for approaching some other young woman of better presentation than the one he courts [she is coloured] for being engaged in agricultural work he lacks those refinements which could grant him entrance into society'.[4]

Demographic factors may explain why white men should choose coloured women for their companions. What they do not explain, however, is the form these unions took.

The figures on illegitimacy show that a substantial proportion of children were born out of wedlock (Table 3). But the censuses do not indicate whether the free coloured illegitimate children are the product of mixed or colour endogamous unions. Figures are also available on the frequency of marriage by ethnic group (Table 4).

TABLE 4. *Number of married women per 100 women over sixteen by colour and status, 1846 and 1862*

| Year: | Whites | Free coloureds | Slaves |
|-------|--------|----------------|--------|
| 1846  | 40     | 21             | 19     |
| 1862  | 51     | 36             | 10     |

Sources: *Cuadro estadístico de la siempre fiel Isla de Cuba, correspondiente al año de 1846* (Havana, 1847); *Noticias estadísticas de la Isla de Cuba en 1862* (Havana, 1864).

No census figures are available, however, on the frequency of *interracial* marriage or concubinage. Under these circumstances the only way to assess the actual incidence of interracial marriage is to count the marriage entries in the parish registers. Separate registers were kept for whites and for coloured people, mixed marriages being registered in the latter. I have gone through the nineteenth-century marriage registers of two parishes. One is the village of Sta. Maria del Rosario located about 30 miles outside of Havana. It was founded in the early eighteenth century by the Count of Casa Bayona and was one of the first places to have sugar mills[5] (Table 5). It is possible to make the population figures for Sta. Maria del Rosario age specific for all three years, and break them down by shade of the free coloureds for the two first years (Tables 5a, 5b, 5c).

The white man's view

TABLE 5. *Population of Sta. Maria del Rosario by colour, status and sex, 1827–62*

| Year: | Whites | | Free coloureds | | Slaves | |
|---|---|---|---|---|---|---|
| | Males | Females | Males | Females | Males | Females |
| 1827 | 1,286 | 1,068 | 96 | 100 | 802 | 380 |
| 1846 | 985 | 908 | 138 | 144 | 499 | 320 |
| 1862 | 2,571 | 2,425 | 419 | 409 | 1,240 | 933 |

Note: The 1827 and 1846 figures refer to the town of Sta. Maria del Rosario, those for 1862 to the whole jurisdiction.

Sources: *Cuadro estadístico de la siempre fiel Isla de Cuba, correspondiente al año de 1827* (Havana, 1829); *Cuadro estadístico de la siempre fiel Isla de Cuba, correspondiente al año de 1846* (Havana, 1847); *Noticias estadísticas de la Isla de Cuba en 1862* (Havana, 1864).

TABLE 5a. *Population of Sta. Maria del Rosario by colour, status and sex, 1827* (men over fifteen and women over twelve)

| | Males | Females |
|---|---|---|
| Whites | 756 | 679 |
| Free mulattos | 23 | 26 |
| Free blacks | 36 | 48 |
| Slaves | 612 | 286 |

Source: *Cuadro estadístico de la siempre fiel Isla de Cuba, correspondiente al año de 1827* (Havana, 1829).

TABLE 5b. *Population of Sta. Maria del Rosario over sixteen by colour, status and sex, 1846*

| | Males | Females |
|---|---|---|
| Whites | 552 | 516 |
| Free mulattos | 25 | 23 |
| Free blacks | 71 | 82 |
| Slaves | 399 | 225 |

Source: *Cuadro estadístico de la siempre fiel Isla de Cuba, correspondiente al año de 1846* (Havana, 1847).

61

TABLE 5C. *Population of Sta. Maria del Rosario over sixteen by colour, status and sex, 1862*

|  | Males | Females |
|---|---|---|
| Whites | 1,456 | 1,341 |
| Free coloureds | 218 | 331 |
| Slaves | 894 | 592 |

Source: *Noticias estadísticas de la Isla de Cuba en 1862*
(Havana, 1864).

The other parish is Regla, across the Bay of Havana and now administratively part of it. In 1812 it appeared in the census for the first time; it was then said to have a population of some 2,000. Its inhabitants were engaged mainly in fishery, coastal trade, work on the docks of Havana and smuggling[6] (Table 6).

TABLE 6. *Population of Regla by colour, status and sex, 1846*

| Whites | | Free coloureds | | Slaves | |
|---|---|---|---|---|---|
| Males | Females | Males | Females | Males | Females |
| 2,696 | 2,375 | 324 | 320 | 519 | 428 |

Source: *Cuadro estadístico de la siempre fiel Islas de Cuba, correspondiente al año 1846* (Havana, 1847). No age specific figures are available for Regla.

The marriage register for *pardos* and *morenos* of Sta. Maria del Rosario for the period 1805 to 1881 contains not a single marriage across the colour bar out of a total of 366 celebrated in that period. That of Regla covering the same period shows one marriage between a *parda* and a white man and one between a *parda* and a foundling (classified as white) out of a total of 260 marriages contracted. All marriages of coloured men were with coloured women and of all marriages contracted by coloured women 0.3 per cent were then with white men (i.e. 2 out of 626 marriages). Considering the 'racial' composition of the population, had marriages taken place at random the proportion of interracial marriages would of course have been much greater in both villages, as in Cuba as a whole.

Probabilities can be calculated from the preceding tables. The difference in the incidence of intraracial and interracial marriage is remarkable.

At least until further counting is done in other parishes, as one hopes it will be, it must be assumed that interracial marriage in nineteenth-century Cuba occurred *exceptionally* relative to the total number of marriages. The considerable number of *pardos* in the population testifies to the frequency of racial mixture. But these interracial unions tended to be consensual rather than legal, a fact stressed and lamented time and again by contemporaries. Archbishop Claret y Clarà in 1853, in order to refute the common argument that racial mixture would produce the coloured peoples' insubordination, pointed out that 'if that were an evil it no longer has any remedy, because the Island's population is mostly coloured, the result of the concubinages that have been so generalized for a long time; the concubines [the women] are all or most of them coloured and the white are very infrequent.'[7] As will be recalled, Fray Jacinto Maria, Bishop of Havana, in 1867 bitterly complained about the frequency of interracial concubinage in his diocese.[8] These prelates might have overdrawn the picture to get the civil authorities to take some action. Richard H. Dana, however, an American, gained very much the same impression when he visited Cuba in 1859:

Another of the difficulties the Church has to contend with [he reported] arises out of negro slavery. The Church recognizes the unity of all races, and allows marriage between them. The civil law of Cuba, under the interpretations in force here, prohibits marriage between whites and persons who have any tinge of black blood. In consequence of this rule concubinage prevails to a great extent between whites and mulattoes or quadroons, often with recognition of the children. If either party to this arrangement comes under the influence of the Church's discipline, the relationship must terminate. The Church would allow and advise marriage; but the law prohibits it and if there should be a separation, there may be no provisions for the children. This state of things creates no small obstacle to the influence of the Church on domestic relations.[9]

### PREFERENCE FOR CONCUBINAGE

Two thirds of the applications for an interracial marriage licence I recorded contain the official verdict. In two thirds of these the requested permit is granted. Although the formal requirement of official authorization in itself was surely an obstacle to interracial marriage, once this hurdle had been surmounted the authorities were not always disinclined to encourage the marriage. Thus it would not be accurate to attribute interracial concubinage solely to the official prohibition of marriage. As Solórzano had said, in the overseas possessions 'there are few Spaniards of honour who would marry an Indian or Negro woman'.[10] Parishioners in Cuba often reacted violently to their priest's exhortations to abandon their lives in sin. D. Melchor Mas, the parish priest of Sta. Filomena in Oriente province, encountered stout resistance from two white men to marrying their coloured concubines, for as one of them argued, 'he thought that between him and [her] a remarkable difference existed, he himself descending from the white race and [she] being *parda* as can well be seen'.[11]

How is it then that some whites took it upon themselves to swim against the tide, as it were, and marry a coloured woman at the price of social ostracism and degradation in the eyes of their peers?

Some of them gave in to the priest's moral exhortations. But there were also other legal and social pressures which might occasionally induce a couple to get married in the end. A single man or woman could be prosecuted for concubinage when the couple's conduct was thought to menace public morality.[12] The criminal statistics of nineteenth-century Cuba in most years contain some prosecutions for concubinage.[13] Again the couple either had to marry or separate, the latter solution being preferred by some.

The attitude of neighbours or friends had also some bearing on the couple's readiness to marry. As one white woman explains: 'the frequency of their communication and the fact that she has lived at his expense is public knowledge there, and in agreement with the advice of friends, and obeying religious sentiments . . . and in order better to serve God and avoid scandal' she now desires to marry.[14] Public opinion in most cases probably worked in the opposite direction. But this white woman had already disgraced herself by entering into concubinage with a coloured man, and thus it did not matter very much whether she married him as well. A white man could have abandoned his coloured mistress and married a woman of his own kind, but not so a white woman once she had lived with a coloured man. Few white men would want her after that.

## REASONS FOR INTERMARRIAGE

The majority of the applicants for a marriage licence, however, seem to have taken the decision to marry independently of direct external pressure. They present a series of reasons of a more or less personal nature,[15] revealing two rival concepts of society in general, and interracial marriage in particular. Many of the applicants are basically conformist. They accept that racial difference spells social inequality and is therefore in principle an impediment to marriage. But theirs, they argue, is an exceptional case. Particular circumstances warrant a marriage. The authorities could be won over by the degree to which social attributes offset racial attributes and the applicants appealed to this principle. The degree of conformity with the social norms of marriage comes across forcefully in the case of one young man. He argued that

> at first sight it might be surprising that a white should be ready to contract marriage with a *parda*, but if this white man lacks all esteem in society and is accustomed to associating with the *pardos*, there would be no objection . . . the applicant has the misfortune of being one of those men . . . cut off from society and in constant contact with the *pardos*.[16]

He is a foundling. The uncertainty surrounding his origin impaired his social status. He accepts the system that produces such injustices and only laments his personal misfortune which forces him to marry a coloured woman.

In other instances the 'excellent circumstances' or the 'good moral and religious conduct' as well as the 'good manners' of the coloured bride are remarked upon by the suitor as one of the attributes compensating for inferior birth.[17]

### Gratitude

Repeatedly the applicant explains his petition in terms of the gratitude he owes his coloured bride for her generous assistance in times of illness or other hardship, like the white man who upon his arrival on the island

> instantly fell seriously ill and reached the point of despair . . . in such a state he had no other refuge than the freeborn *parda*'s home where he was looked after with extreme care . . . She has a daughter . . . who was the one who took the greatest pains in his recovery and wanting to give a proof of his gratitude and not having anything better to offer he has decided to marry her.[18]

Whiteness is conceived of almost as a material asset exchangeable for services rendered. Occasionally the motive for marriage might be set forth in a more subtle manner but the underlying theme is the same: a poor, helpless and lonely young man, generally a stranger to the country, finds solace and care with a coloured woman and feels that he must pay her for her generosity in some way.[19] It was surely not easy for an indigent white man without connections to be assisted by his peers if he had nothing to offer in return. But, however poor, being white such a man still possessed an important advantage over coloured people. Moreover, once he had been taken into a coloured woman's home a more intimate relationship could well develop which, aided by his gratitude for her assistance, could on occasion be turned into marriage. As one man confesses: 'the close contact and his passion induced him to commit the weakness of offending the daughter . . . [he has therefore] decided to fulfil his promise of contracting marriage thus making amends to the mother, the daughter and public morality'.[20] In view of the generalized aspiration of 'whitening', a coloured woman was certainly easily persuaded to yield to a white man's advances.

A white man, alone and without relatives or friends, might also seek in a coloured woman a sympathetic person to look after him in emergencies and to defend his interests faithfully and unassumingly. Concubinage would probably not do, for what he sought was a less feeble bond which would withstand the strains of difficult times. Telling is the case of the old white man who had lived with a *parda* for some forty years. He had not married her earlier because of the legal impediment to interracial marriage. Now, however, 'he is prostrated in his bed, blind and without family or friends who could care for and assist him in the lamentable state he is in on account of his disease and his age, but for the Perez'.[21] And D. Francisco Rodriguez, a discharged soldier from Murcia, openly admits that he conceived of his marriage to a freeborn *parda* as a sort of health insurance: 'the great distance between his country and this, and being both without his family and without anybody to assist him if he should fall victim to an epidemic or any other disease, wandering about in this way he began an affair with the freeborn *parda*'.[22]

### Love and honour

But there were also those who were either contemptuous or oblivious of the social constraints on intermarriage. D. Hilario Cabrian Domingues decided to marry his *parda* bride 'out of his free and spontaneous will'.[23] Difference in colour is no obstacle to marriage and consequently no special justification is needed.

Love, by overriding social restraints, meant the assertion of individual freedom of choice over social conventions. Thus it constituted a potential threat to the social order whose preservation depended on the systematic curtailment of individual choice. Parents and relatives were well aware of the social hazards of romantic love. 'Driven or blinded by violent passion'[24] people tended to forget the harmful consequences of such unequal marriages. Love and passion are unpredictable and render people insensitive to their duties to family and society.

D. Juan Piñeiro, a discharged soldier from Corunna, argues that he wants to marry the girl because

they love each other with all the might resulting from a long time of communication, without the slightest reason that could weaken their determination to marry as demands the sacrosanct religion and educated society to which they have the fortune of belonging, so that in this way their amorous passion might develop links and grow roots which are respectable and indissoluble, avoiding thus the dismal consequences which they might otherwise suffer in detriment of their consciences.[25]

Marriage is desirable because it will turn their illegitimate passion into legitimate love. Yet applicants rarely rely exclusively on the persuasive power of love. Either they feel that love is not a forceful argument with the authorities, or they themselves are not convinced that it is a sufficient ground for marriage. Thus Piñeiro added that after all it was the father's status that determined that of the children. His bride being the daughter of a white man and a *parda*, they were equals and hence no obstacle to their marriage existed.

Another white man applied for a marriage licence because 'dominated by a natural love resulting from frequent communication . . . their hearts have become united in such a way that they have come to know each other carnally'. As if that was not enough, he claimed he had deflowered a 'punctilious, industrious and Christian young woman'; and, not least, he had no relatives who could object to the match. He deemed marriage indispensable to avoid scandal and to satisfy the girl.[26] By maintaining that this coloured bride's tarnished honour demanded marriage he accorded her a status equal to that of the women of his own group. It was obviously not true that there was a single standard of morality valid for all women regardless of their social status; but this is immaterial here. What matters is that by postulating the essential reputability of all women independent of colour he set himself clearly apart from those white men who had no objection to living in concubinage with a coloured woman, but would rather separate than marry her. Although, as I will show later, the great concern over female virtue had an eminently hierarchical meaning, it could also have the inverse effect of breaking the social barriers when it was used to achieve an unequal marriage.

Interesting in this regard is D. Luis Morejón's case. He insisted he had to marry his free *parda* bride for he 'is indebted to her in a way concerning his own conscience for nothing less than her honour is at stake which as an honest and religious man he must repair'. In other words, his own honour and conscience required of him to repair that of a coloured woman. At a later stage in the proceedings, however, he takes great pains to prove by means of documentary evidence that his bride is in actual fact white.[27]

Moreover, by alleging either sporadic sexual contact or prolonged cohabitation, as they frequently did, applicants could hope to exercise some moral pressure on the civil authorities. In effect, not infrequently the decision to marry follows a more or less extended period of concubinage which often had already produced offspring: 'I am not urged by the fire of lust but by the need to provide for my conscience because of the public concubinage', one white man asserts.[28] And Manuel Perez explains that 'his conscience does not allow him to continue any longer in this lamentable state of concubinage in which he has lived for seventeen years . . . in the interest of his peace of mind he wants to contract this marriage which he has not done before out of ignorance and misfortune'. It appears, however, that this sudden awakening of his conscience had been prompted by the local priest who 'with his pious exhortations and persuasive advice' had succeeded in convincing the applicant that he should take this crucial step.[29] What was at stake this time was not the coloured woman's honour or spiritual salvation but his own peace of mind stirred by the priest's recriminations.

## To give up a life of sin

Time and again white men speak of the need to 'serve God better', to 'put his soul in safety', 'to give up a life opposed to the precepts of morality and the rites of Our Holy Mother Church',[30] of the 'sacred duty . . . of an honest and Christian man',[31] and to 'achieve a state of divine grace'.[32] One young white man's application reveals a suspiciously bombastic style:

man being surrounded in the limited sphere of his intelligence by ignorance and error about a multitude of objects, which at times are bound to alter the eternal law of morality presenting itself rebellious to the idea of the good . . . however, these apparently invincible obstacles . . . come to nothing when the infinite mercy of the Lord wants to get his creatures out of the filthy bog of vice and shows them the only and true path of those fortunate in this life and the other.[33]

No doubt the parish priest had taken it upon himself to show him the path to a life of virtue.

These outbursts of religious fervour should not, however, be taken entirely at their face value. As seen earlier, the inhabitants of Oriente province were not at all impressed by the missionary zeal of Archbishop Claret y Clarà. As a whole the moral influence of the Church was limited.[34]

Either it required the active intervention of the priest to stir these men, or the protection of morality had to appear to the applicant as an argument of strategic value with the authorities. After all, the applications were submitted with the aim of marriage in mind.

In a few cases the white man wants to marry in *articulo mortis* or nearly so. One white man wanted 'to prepare himself for death in a Christian way'; besides, if he did not marry his concubine, they would have had to part company, admittedly an unsavoury prospect at his age.[35] It could be argued that none of these men would have thought of marriage were it not for the fear of dying in sin, which is quite another matter from living in sin. If, however, faced with death, people were likely to return to the fold of the Church this would indicate that religious values had a certain validity after all. But there is evidence that abuse was made of marriage in *articulo mortis* when the marriage could not be contracted otherwise. In 1867 some inhabitants of Havana filed one more complaint against Fray Jacinto Maria, their Bishop, for, among other things, having forbidden his priests under severe penalties to celebrate marriages under the pretext of *articulo mortis*. Yet, whereas the Captain General on most issues sided with the inhabitants against the Bishop, regarding marriages in *articulo mortis* he agreed with him:

In this respect I believe that the prelate has had more than enough reason to dictate the most severe regulations, because the scandalous abuses and frauds committed all over the Island by contracting or authorizing marriages under the pretext of *articulo mortis* without either of the candidates being in this sad situation, or having some impediment to contract a new union, are well known.[36]

No doubt difference in colour was among those impediments that could induce an individual to resort to a marriage in *articulo mortis*.

## To provide for his children

A coloured woman's honour could on occasion compel her white lover to marry her; and so could concern for his offspring by her. Thus one white man requested a marriage licence because he 'has had for the period of ten years a licentious friendship with the *parda* . . . and has had three sons in this union, with another one about to be born'; consequently, he wanted to 'provide for his temporal and spiritual well-being no less than that of his offspring and his concubine'.[37] Here the preoccupation for the illegitimate offspring and for their mother goes hand in hand. But on the whole the desire to provide for the offspring's future outweighs the concern for the woman who bore them: 'There is no more urgent ground [for marriage] than the offspring', argue two white men,[38] while another contends that 'he is a father and this duty alone more sacred than any other consideration compels him to contract the marriage'.[39] Still others justify their desire to legitimate their offspring in some such terms as that 'his conscience compelled him [to do so] in order to be able to justify himself before God and man',[40] or that 'upon his death they would remain in total abandonment and, worst of all, without name in the world, and would therefore be rejected by it, perhaps cursing those who had brought them into this world';[41] or that 'knowing the sufferings that might befall these two creatures in the future, the laws rejecting them for certain offices, their having been born out of wedlock'.[42] The illegitimate offspring's innocent misfortune added force to these appeals.

So much for the motivations of the applicants. It is difficult to know to what extent the reasons given are genuine. They certainly argued the official case, thus throwing light on the circumstances which made inter-racial marriage palatable to the authorities. As a rule these men were poor whites who, as Archbishop Claret y Clarà pointed out, had little chance of marrying a white woman. They could have entered into a consensual union with a coloured woman instead, but occasionally they wanted to marry. The majority seem to be prompted to take this step by very practical considerations, such as securing a faithful bedcompanion, or a free cook or a dedicated nurse. Only a few are inspired by such socially subversive feelings as love or the wish to repair the coloured woman's honour.

# CHAPTER 5

# COLOUR AS A SYMBOL OF SOCIAL STATUS

### REAL COLOUR AND LEGAL COLOUR

Ideally, and according to the marriage legislation, nineteenth-century Cuban society was divided into two large groups, those of European origin and those of African origin, physical appearance serving as the criterion of distinction. Yet the implementation of phenotype as the principle of social classification had by then become rather complex. A high degree of racial mixture had taken place which had significantly blurred the visible boundaries between the racial groups. This process of growing diffuseness of the racial attributes was in large measure the consequence of the coloured woman's sexual exploitation by the white man and derived additional momentum from the powerful aspirations of the coloured population to shed their apparently racially determined inferior social status by shedding their typical physical attributes.

A royal decree of 1788 reveals a keen awareness of the problems involved in the overseas possessions in segregating its population along racial lines, and points to its causes:

the difficulty of implementing [the] Royal Pragmatic on marriage in view of the various castes of people . . . and the fatal mixture of Europeans with the natives and negroes . . . results from the fact that those proceeding from these mixtures in order to conceal their defect, attempt to register their baptisms in the books for Spaniards and erase from them by reprehensible means the information on their ancestry, later justifying with ease and the aid of witnesses that *they are held to be white* . . . which causes affliction to those vassals who are *truly white* and who cannot avoid marriages taking place between their families and those who being mixed pretend the contrary.[1]

Undoubtedly, the difference between being 'held to be white' and being 'truly white' was not one of physical colour. In nineteenth-century Cuba physical appearance had become equally misleading with regard to a person's racial origin. Only too often was it difficult if not impossible to detect any actual physical difference between a person of Spanish and one of partial African origin. Pichardo in his *Diccionario provincial casi razonado de voces y frases cubanas*, first published in 1836, gives the following definition of the word *trigueño*:

The person of slightly darker colour or similar to that of wheat [*trigo*] in the same way as the person of lighter colour, milky with a pink hue is called *white* . . . In a racial context the word *white* is used even if the person is *trigueño*, in order to differentiate him from *negro* or *mulatto*; although there are some of the latter who are whiter than many of the white race.[2]

The proceedings on interracial marriage contain numerous allusions to the assessment and use of physical appearance as a criterion of social classification, and to its complexities. Thus, one neighbour in his report on a mixed couple points out the possible absence of physical differences between people of different racial origin: 'she is a *parda criolla* from Santiago de Cuba who can well pass as white outside this country and who is even of better colour than her suitor [who is of Spanish origin]'.[3] This is certainly not an isolated case.

The difficulties involved in social stratification along racial lines in an already racially mixed society emerge particularly clearly in the case of foundlings. By royal decree foundlings were of 'pure blood'.[4] The enforcement of this disposition in the overseas possessions 'on account of the great variety of castes' posed many problems,[5] for this prerogative rested, in the words of an official of 1786, solely on 'a fiction or privileged supposition'.[6] Consequently, the request by a foundling of the Orphanage of Havana to be granted the privilege of nobility was rejected because 'he is known to be a foundling and therefore *in reality* of uncertain origin'.[7] When confronted with requests of this nature by foundlings, the authorities in their endeavours to dispel these uncertainties and establish the 'reality' then took recourse to skin colour. In 1772 the Council of the Indies suggested that the ecclesiastical authorities of the overseas possessions be instructed 'not to dispense or ordain any foundlings whose *appearance* and well-known signs indicate their being mulattos or of other equally indecorous castes'.[8] And the royal consent to the Ministro Tesorero of San Luis Potosí's marriage to a foundling was made dependent on her 'colour indicating whether she was the daughter of whites'.[9]

Colour or physical appearance are conceived not as attributes conclusive in themselves but as mere outward 'signs' of a deeper condition. The symbolic quality of physical appearance in this context is perceived forcefully by the young white woman who rejected her suitor after having agreed to marry him because 'being reputed as coloured as it is said, she desists from her intention of marrying him, for if she had cherished this idea it was because he had assured her time and again that he was as white as she herself, concealing this circumstance . . . trying to deceive her under the pretext of being white'. He must have been of very light complexion to have been able to keep up the game until it was discovered that his certificate of baptism was registered in the book of *pardos*.[10] Consequently, his colour could not be the true reason for the girl's objections. It was his *legal colour* that counted in this case.

In another instance, the young man who wants to marry a *parda* insists that 'since his mother is white he has been baptized as white, but unfortunately . . . his mother took shelter with a coloured man and from this union resulted the applicant, whose *physical appearance, his kinky [apasado] hair and his brown colour* prove that he belongs to the coloured class'. The official dealing with the case, however, rejects the young man's demand on the grounds that

confused and blinded by the realization that the law separates him from the object of his love, he does not hesitate to present himself to Y.E. disdaining the rights and privileges he enjoys as a white man, to the extreme of not wanting to be such if in this way he can achieve his aim. The certificate of baptism [he] submitted is an irreproachable document; it certifies that he is white and as such he must be considered.[11]

Again, legal colour prevailed over physical appearance.

But this is not to say that physical appearance had no relevance at all. The inverse situation could well occur, physical appearance prevailing over legal colour. This is illustrated by one report which states that 'they say that they are from the interior; their origin is unknown here, but according to his appearance he seems to be a mulatto and is reputed by most here as such'.[12] Bacardí in his *Crónicas de Santiago de Cuba* tells of a man called Vidal whose whiteness had been questioned by another man. He took the case to the courts and won, upon which the following quatrain was in everybody's mouth for many days:[13]

> Señor Vidal, yo bien sé
> que es usted blanco en la Audiencia,
> pero en Dios y en mi conciencia,
> medio mulato es usté.

('Señor Vidal, I know well that in the courts you are white, but before God and my conscience you are half mulatto.')

Legal colour was then an alternative way of determining a person's racial status when his physical appearance was not an unambiguous guide. In addition to offering information on an individual's own status, the baptism registration indicated also the racial status of his parents.

Yet legal colour was no more a reliable guide to a person's true racial origin than was physical appearance. Although parish priests in the overseas possessions received repeated instructions[14] to make every effort to establish with accuracy the racial origin of the child before proceeding to its baptism and registration, this was in many cases an impossible task. As one parent commented, the 'registration of baptism of his children, some are in the book for whites and others in that for *pardos*, according to the judgement of the different priests who baptized them'.[15] Similarly, in a report on a couple to whose marriage a distant allegedly white relative is opposed, the practice of false registration due to the constant efforts by those of African origin to whiten themselves, is again described:

The certificates of baptism presented . . . have no value for lack of consistency . . . furthermore, in this country it is very common for anyone who in some way appears to be white to use the *Don* . . . being also usual that if one of the parents is white the baptism will be entered without further investigation into the book for whites . . . [however] I cannot but say that according to the opinion of distinguished persons they are in truth all mulattos, with the difference that some try to cover this up whereas the others don't but are respectable and industrious.[16]

Presumably many white parents endeavoured to bestow their own racial prerogatives on their mixed offspring by omitting their coloured mother's name in the registration. This particular technique of whitening was not infrequent: 'the suitor is neither white nor of distinction being the son of a known *parda* and a white man of low sphere; and although his baptism has been entered in one of the books for Spaniards this has been done by concealing the mother's name, a circumstance which indicates some trickery'.[17]

In nineteenth-century Cuba both factors, real and legal colour, were resorted to. If physical appearance was deemed to be an unsatisfactory or misleading guide, then recourse was taken to the registry of baptism which provided information on a person's genealogy and thus his ancestors' physical appearance. Both reference to a person's physical appearance and reference to that of his ancestors were techniques to determine his racial origin. The parent who asserts categorically that his son's bride 'will never be able to leave the sphere of these humble people on account of her colour in the society of this village, *even if her skin were white and her hair straight*'[18] shows that it is not physical appearance in itself that is the cause of discrimination, but what a person's own or his ancestor's colour stands for.

In the Cuban context colour stood for African descent, but in the view of some white parents and numerous officials it was also 'the mark of slavery which has descended from his parents'.[19] Physical appearance and family pedigree are both no more than means of recognizing the same thing, i.e. an individual's social origin.

The view that the white Cuban's prejudice is not a prejudice against people of a particular physical appearance as such seems to be supported as well by the use of the Spanish concept of purity of blood, which was the product of the earlier efforts of the Spanish Crown to achieve national unity through religious unity. Once a substantial amount of racial mixture had taken place purity of blood was surely a more rigorous criterion of classification than purely physical appearance. Even those who had become physically undifferentiated could still be said to be unacceptable on account of the impure quality of their blood. This may explain why the concept of purity of blood, which had become largely discredited in Spain by the end of the eighteenth century, should have experienced a revival in Cuba.

The adjustment and balance of the social order in nineteenth-century Cuba required discrimination for functional reasons. Interracial marriages were to be restricted, if not outright prohibited, because the 'equilibrium' of the society demanded it.[20] The antagonism was not directed against people of colour because of their colour as such, but because their colour indicated that they were, or had their origin in, slaves. It was the slaves and their descendants who needed to be segregated in the interest of the slave system. Initially, a direct relationship had existed between physical attributes and slavery. All slaves were of dark complexion, kinky hair, etc., all non-slaves were of white colour, straight hair, etc. At that time physical appearance was indeed an efficacious criterion for distinguishing non-slaves from slaves. The existence of two occupationally distinct groups preceded the use of physical appearance and especially skin colour by the dominant group as the criterion to legitimate the segregation and subordination of the dominated group.

In the analysis of nineteenth-century Cuba a direct link can thus be established between racism and slavery. But, for instance, the changing meaning of the concept of 'purity of blood' should make one wary of an interpretation of racism in simply economic terms. This concept, it is true, had always had a racial connotation, but of very diverse meaning. Whereas in Spain it was initially applied to distinguish Old Christians from New Christians, in the Spanish colonies it gradually acquired a new meaning. In this context 'purity of blood' is used to differentiate those of African/slave from those of European/free origin. Thus, I would suggest that race is often used as a symbol for other socially significant cleavages in society, such as the division of labour in nineteenth-century Cuba, and religion in fifteenth- to eighteenth-century Spain.

Such an interpretation of Cuban racism at once raises the question as to why the free coloured people were discriminated against as well. Two points can be made in this respect: on the one hand, the legislation on interracial marriage was enforced with significantly less rigour in the case of freeborn *pardos* because of their greater removal from 'black colour and slavery'.[21] This is clearly evidenced by the process of mutual status compensation. On the other, it is repeatedly argued that it is precisely the free mulattos who are the people 'that must be watched with greatest care', surely because by their conflicting attributes of dark colour but free status they put in doubt both the consistency and the continuity of the system.

### MARRIAGE BETWEEN CHINESE AND WHITES

The social classification of the Chinese is of some help in explaining the nature of racial discrimination in nineteenth-century Cuba. Beginning in the early 1850s and as a result of the growing labour shortage, over 100,000 Chinese indentured labourers from Canton were introduced into Cuba over a period of some twenty years.[22] This gave rise to acute classificatory embarrassment. Their skin colour was lighter than that of many Spaniards. Their legal colour posed a major problem to the authorities; for, as one official asserted, 'although they are considered as whites, public opinion and custom places them in a condition inferior to whites'.[23] And the Junta de Agricultura, Industria y Comercio of Matanzas in 1864, when reporting on ways of moralizing slaves and Chinese, attributed the high rate of murders of overseers committed by the latter to the fact that 'they [the overseers] have not yet persuaded themselves that the Chinese are free men, but regard them as of equal or worse status than the black slaves'.[24]

Moreover, a ruling by the Real Acuerdo in 1861 concerning a petition by a young Chinese to be allowed to marry a free *parda*, opposed by the local Syndic on the ground that there was 'such a variety of races that people the Island', favoured this particular marriage but with the proviso that 'it is not possible to establish any general rules for future cases of this nature, for in each one the special circumstances . . . must be taken into consideration'.[25] It is plainly the conflicting racial and occupational status that prevents a social classification of the Chinese along traditional lines. 'These men are placed between the races', remarked an official from Cárdenas.[26]

In the case quoted above it could be argued that the girl's free status could make her eligible also for marriage to a white. In another instance, however, a Chinese wants to marry a *parda* slave woman and in fact succeeds in obtaining the official licence the parish priest – classifying him as white – deemed necessary. The petition was filed on behalf of the Chinese man by a white neighbour, who pointed out again that 'in reality in public opinion the said Chinese are not at the same level as those that are properly white'.[27] Yet, in still another instance where a Chinese wants to marry a white woman no objections are raised by the authorities, for 'according to the certificate of baptism he encloses he belongs to the class of whites'.[28]

So far it would appear that the Chinese could marry freely people of any colour, from a *parda* slave to a white woman. Up to this point their legal colour seems to be highly ambiguous. Consequently, and in view of the numerous queries regarding the classification of the Chinese for the purposes of baptism and marriage, the Consejo de Administración in 1864 took up the matter for discussion. Refering to the Ordenanza de Colonos of 1853 and to the Reglamento de Colonos of 1854, the Council decided that the Chinese were to be considered as whites. Further to substantiate their ruling the Council contended that 'the Indians to whom the Chinese are usually assimilated have been declared equal to the whites by the Royal Decree of 12 March 1697, which declares Indian *caciques* and *principales nobles* like the *hijosdalgo* of Castille, and the other Indians equal to those of pure blood of the general estate in Spain'. Hence, the Chinese like the Indians were legally white.

One would consequently expect that the Chinese would require an official licence to marry coloured women, in accordance with the restrictive interpretation of the 1805 decree in fashion at that time and with the 1854 decree. Evidently the Consejo de Administración was aware of the legal implications of declaring the Chinese white and to cope with this point it established, contrary to the usual practice, that the Chinese were exempt from the literal requirements of the 1805 decree, arguing shrewdly that it was not likely that there would be nobles among those Chinese coming to Cuba as indentured labourers. As regarded the registration of baptism, as long as none of the parents were coloured, the children were to be registered in the book for whites.[29]

By not requiring the Chinese to obtain a marriage licence even if they wanted to marry a coloured woman, the authorities betrayed their innermost doubts about the true racial status of the Chinese. In the final analysis, the Consejo de Administración's ruling that the Chinese were exempted from the formal requirement of a marriage licence whatever the colour of their spouse meant that they had either no legal colour, or they had them all. In this light, the Lieutenant Governor of Colon is correct when he remarks on a marriage between a Chinese and a white girl that

the Chinese race is assimilated to the black race as regards the effects of the Royal Decree of 15 October 1805, and the ideas that existed when this decree was enacted have not changed on the whole, for although this new race had not been introduced into the Island then, and although it is thought to be purer than the African race, it is nonetheless looked upon with a certain aversion by the whites. The great majority of the whites reject this kind of marriage and it appears only just to respect their views, and, if you like their anxieties, the fruit of the social organization of the country.[30]

If the racial status of a person with respect to the coloured people was determined by whether he required a marriage licence or not, by not needing a licence the Chinese automatically became part of the coloured in-marrying group. Presumably the authorities were well aware of the dangers inherent in ambiguous classification of the Chinese, for the rule that they be registered as whites was justified on the grounds that 'they should not feel degraded from their rightful status as whites'.[31] The inefficiency of slave labour in a time of rapid mechanization of the sugar industry was by then a much debated question. The choice of contract labour in preference to slave labour had surely been influenced by this consideration, apart from the latter's increasing shortage. It might have been thought a matter of economic sense to prevent a degradation of the Chinese to the level of the slaves and thus undermine their expected efficiency.

In those cases recorded where Chinese attempted to marry coloured women the central authorities raised no objections, with the exception of the official quoted earlier (p. 76) whose opposition on functional grounds was, however, overruled in favour of the priest's view that 'it is preferable that they live united by the sacred bond of marriage than scandalously in concubinage and in the usual mortal sin', and the progressive Creole planters' argument that 'the disadvantage would not be great because if the great need of the country is to attract settlers, this aim can be achieved in no way better than by authorizing legitimate marriages'.[32] In theory, the Chinese indentured labourers had two choices upon termination of their contract – either to leave the country at their own expense or to renew the contract. Even though they perhaps cherished a desire to return to their own country, under their conditions of work they rarely acquired the means to do so. Thus it did not require the bond of marriage to prevent them from leaving Cuba. Presumably it was felt to be preferable to create a proletariat by mixing the Chinese and the blacks than by mixing blacks and whites.

That despite their legally white status the Chinese were far from being classed by public opinion in this category emerges also from two cases in which the respective families of two free *pardas* were opposed to their marrying Chinese 'without more basis than the minute difference in colour'[33] which should have favoured the Chinese if the criterion had been whiteness. And one mother could say that 'she'd rather see her [free *parda* daughter] living with a negro or dead than married to a Chinese'.[34] This attitude had clearly nothing to do with a preference for a whiter skin colour but emphasized rather occupational differences. As a consequence of their 'being rejected by the white women but also by those of colour', the Chinese were said to succumb to other 'unspeakable vices',[35] and are to this day.

## MARRIAGE BETWEEN AMERICAN INDIANS AND WHITES

Cuba had lost most of its native population in the first century after the conquest. By the nineteenth century only a few Indians were left in isolated areas of Oriente province.[36] But attempts were made to introduce Yucatecan Indians to resolve the acute labour shortage. Thus, a few cases of marriage of Indians occurred in the nineteenth century. At least as regards marriage, the legal status of American Indians was far from clear in Cuba.[37] While in one instance a *moreno* slave who intended to marry a Yucatecan Indian woman – whose social status had to be very low having come to Cuba as indentured labour – is denied the licence because the Indian woman 'had been baptized as white';[38] in another case a *pardo* who wanted to marry the daughter of a white man and an Indian woman is granted official permission despite her father's dissent, for 'both are *pardos*'.[39]

In skin colour, though not in phenotype, the Indians presumably were often not much distinguishable from the Spaniards. Their occupational status, however, was generally lower than that of the whites. As Konetzke concluded in his article on the early practice of Indian slavery in the Spanish overseas possessions

the introduction of slavery reinforced the differentiation between the dominating class of Europeans and the indigenous population. Slaves constituted a disqualified and defamed social group and it is for this reason that one shunned their intimate contact. Slavery creates a greater obstacle to the integration of a community than racial difference. It rigorously divides society into the free and the slaves.[40]

Significant in this connection is the seemingly generalized practice in Oriente province of Cuba to register the baptisms, marriages and deaths of Indians in the books for *pardos* and *morenos* rather than in those for whites.[41]

## COLOUR AS A SYMBOL OF THE DIVISION OF LABOUR

By the nineteenth century it had become well established that African origin implied slavery. The Cuban economy run with slave labour perpetuated colour prejudice as a conventional device to justify slavery. The criterion chosen to classify the population hierarchically was physical appearance and particularly skin colour, this initially being the most consistent and also the most salient difference between the two groups. As long as these two groups kept entirely to themselves, skin colour as a principle of social classification would have been unambiguous and hence highly successful. Yet with progressive miscegenation and the appearance of a free coloured group, colour as a distinguishing mark of a person's occupational status became increasingly equivocal and unreliable. Typical in the ambiguous nature of their status were the free negroes and the slave and free mulattos. As M. Douglas writes, 'whenever the lines are precarious we find pollution ideas come to their support'.[42] In effect, in the Cuban case once the racial attributes became blurred recourse was taken to the more abstract notion of 'purity of blood' that had already been applied in Spain throughout three centuries, or to its equivalent, legal colour.[43]

If the status of the mulattos was often a source of incoherence, more so was that of the American Indian and the Chinese. The mulatto was the product of the mixture of the two groups themselves, and by instituting the principle of hypodescent the problem involved in his classification was, at least in theory, solved. The Indians and the Chinese, however, were extraneous elements for which the system made no provisions. A special third category could have been created to take up Indians and Chinese. Yet such an additional category would have reduced the clarity and workability of the system in terms of the interaction between the different categories, apart from the integrating rather than segregating effect of an intermediary category.

In the case of the American Indians official policy revealed a degree of incoherence, which, however, never reached the point of an admitted incapacity of the system to accommodate a category of people, as was the case when the Chinese were declared wanting of any legal colour. The

Indians were always considered as legally white. Their skin colour, however, was probably closer to *pardo* and their social status as regarded income ranged from medium to desperate in the case of the Yucatecan indentured labourers.

The Chinese and the Indians (especially the Yucatecan labourers) were then in varying degrees a classificatory embarrassment. For while they were physically rather white – in comparison to Spaniards – occupationally they were as if of African origin.

The defenders of slavery would have wanted to enforce a neat dividing line between the racial-cum-occupational groups. Only coloured people should be slaves, and only free people white. But the system contained its own seeds of destruction. Miscegenation was the consequence of a demographic disequilibrium but also one more manifestation of the dominant sector's exploitative practices coupled with the coloured woman's pursuit of the white ideal. The product was the mulattos, who, though the partial descendants of slaves, approximated physically to their white fathers. They increasingly posed an administrative and social problem. On the other hand, about half of the artisans were free coloureds, as a result of the scarcity of white labour to exercise these functions. The mulattos, the free coloured artisans, the Yucatecan Indians, the Chinese indentured labourers are all instances where the system of classification breaks down.

CHAPTER 6

# INTRARACIAL MARRIAGE

MARRIAGE BETWEEN WHITES

The issue of slavery deeply divided opinion within the white community. For political and economic reasons some sectors favoured interracial marriage, but many abolitionists would probably have thought twice about marrying their daughters to a coloured person. Even the common man prided himself on his purity of blood, his sole mark of distinction. One should not think, however, that race obliterated any other criteria of status definition among whites themselves. Differential socio-economic status within their own ranks played a role with regard to marriage, and gave grounds for parental opposition. Opposition to marriage among whites was often motivated by such criteria as birth, wealth, occupation and religion. There was clearly nothing very specific to Cuba in all this as compared, for instance, with Spain and other European countries at the time, where possibly the opportunities for individual advancement were more limited than in Cuba. More characteristic of Cuba, however, was the preoccupation over race which reinforced the concern over ascription.

The stated aim of the 1776 Royal Pragmatic on marriage was to prevent any marriages that gravely offended the family's honour and threatened the State. No instructions were issued, however, neither with the Pragmatic nor in later legislation, on the terms on which an intraracial marriage could be deemed unequal and therefore objectionable. Canon law established a number of specific impediments to marriage such as consanguineous, affinal and ritual kinship. Social impediments were left to custom, and became explicit only when parents, making use of their legal rights, opposed a marriage by their minor children before the civil authorities.

*Reasons for parental dissent*

White parents could be opposed to a marriage for various reasons. The fundamental attitude is illustrated by the parent who complained that 'a young man . . . who does not belong to [my] class has robbed me of my

82

daughter'.¹ But what are the criteria that defined 'class' in nineteenth-century Cuba?²

The concern was often in some way or other with the extraction, the lineage of the rejected candidate. As one parent remarked categorically: 'There cannot be marriage for there is no equality of lineage.'³ One spoke of himself and his family as 'persons of honesty and some birth',⁴ another argued that the bride's family 'is by origin incompatible with that of the suitor'.⁵ Frequently there was no specific proof that the unwanted suitor or bride was actually of inferior 'birth'. However, his or her status was such that their extraction was open to doubt. Either the family was simply little known, or he or she was illegitimate or a foundling. One mother had no other objection to giving her approval but that she 'was ignorant of the girl's conduct and that of her family'.⁶ Another parent was against the marriage because the young man was illegitimate, which fact made him unsuitable for 'intercourse and communication with the people'.⁷

The only registries that existed in nineteenth-century Cuba were the Church registries kept by the parish priests, one for whites and one for *pardos* and *morenos*. The baptism certificate was regarded as evidence of a person's racial status. But many frauds occurred in registration, a fact which certainly must have intensified unease in cases of marriage where the family origin of the candidates could not be established beyond doubt. To shed their doubts, parents not infrequently insisted on seeing the baptism certificate first before granting their approval to the intended marriage.⁸ The origin of illegitimate children was particularly ambiguous and therefore suspect.

Until the end of the century illegitimate children were second-rate citizens to whom all offices of 'distinction' as well as crafts and trades were closed.⁹ Their legal rehabilitation by Charles III had little effect on public opinion. They continued to be considered 'infamous', 'stained', and 'defective by the nature of [their] birth'.¹⁰ Illegitimacy was thought to confer an 'indecent and shameful' mark.¹¹ Few were the more enlightened who shared the official's view that 'In the times we live in illegitimacy is not a mark of infamy but should rather be seen as a misfortune worthy of compassion and not as a stain.'¹²

In the overseas possessions the implications of illegitimacy were particularly serious. Solórzano, in his *Politica Indiana*, made precisely this point when he said of illegitimates:

the most common case is of those born of adulterous or other illicit and punishable unions, because there are few Spaniards of honour who marry Indian or negro women; this defect of birth makes them infamous, at least *infamia facti*, according to the weighty and common opinion of serious authors; they carry the stain of different colours and other vices.[13]

It was without doubt basically the possible 'stain of different colours' that elicited parental rejection of illegitimates.

Another mother contended that 'she does not like her son's choice because the girl was brought up by the Casa de Beneficencia',[14] that is the orphanage, which meant that she was a foundling. Although by law foundlings enjoyed all the prerogatives of legitimate offspring and were officially registered as 'seemingly white' in Cuba,[15] in practice, as one official remarked, 'they are treated with the greatest disdain and considered as bastards, spurious, incestuous and adulterous'.[16] When it came to making the royal legitimation extensive to the overseas possessions, it was thought to be highly problematic 'on account of the multitude of castes that abound . . . and the constant phenomenon of parents abandoning their children at the door of some private person when they are the result of a punishable and wicked union or of obscure quality and contaminated origin'.[17] Again it is their doubtful extraction that made them undesirable.

A person could be rejected as unsuitable for marriage also on very specific grounds, one of them being a difference in the professional background of the two families. As one parent said:

It is public knowledge that his family from its most remote ancestors has served His Majesty in distinguished offices, some of them in the Navy and others in the Ministry of Marine, without there having been any persons in the descent of its lineage that have practised crafts or trades, as does at present [the bride's] father – he is a watch-maker and silversmith – and this mere fact convinces one of the great difference that exists between his social status and that of the bride.[18]

The bride's father, however, got his own back by refusing his consent as well, on the grounds that the young man did not work. Striking is the case of D. Felix Quiñones and Da. Josefa Bacallao. He was the son of a butcher. The girl's father stated emphatically: 'this circumstance alone is proof of the considerable distance that exists between the bride's birth and that of the suitor', for 'by introducing confusion and inequality into the families of pure and distinguished origin the respect and consideration which has always been the basis of a good relation and internal harmony are menaced, and at the same time the place due to honourable families in society is endangered'.[19]

There existed in Spain legislation ruling on the offices and trades fit for the different estates. The artisan classes were rigidly divided into those associated in guilds constituting as it were the aristocracy of the working classes, and those who practised the so-called *oficios mecánicos* (mechanical trades) occupying the lowest social rank. In the course of time the *oficios mecánicos* came to be regarded as of little or no prestige. Only in 1783 were the discriminatory laws abrogated in Spain, which attached a variety of disabilities to these mechanical trades,[20] surely a triumph of the ideas of the Enlightenment. This liberalization, however, was not simultaneously made applicable to the overseas possessions, despite repeated appeals by the local authorities who complained of the 'general preoccupation of the genteel families who choose to live in idleness and misery rather than take up any of those occupations which are generally reputed as infamous'.[21] In 1807 a change of the legislation in this respect was rejected on the grounds that

on the Peninsula, where there are only nobles and commoners, this ruling produced sinister consequences. . . . This would be all the more so the case in America with the multitude of *pardos, zambos,* mulattos, *zambaigos, mestizos, cuarterones, octavones.* All these are vitiated at their very roots and are corrupt . . . and since it is these who practice the crafts of ironsmith, shoemaker, and all other mechanical trades, if the said decree were to be made applicable to those countries, disorder and consequences detrimental to the State would result, for it would be thought that it dispensed the vice they bear in their very origin.[22]

Although by the mid-nineteenth century in Cuba the crafts and trades were practised in almost equal proportion by free coloured people and by whites,[23] and it could happen that a white man was apprenticed to a coloured master, it is quite possible that the presence of coloured people in the crafts and trades reinforced their inferiority in the eyes of the upper classes. As one young man remarked, 'in this country to be a tailor diminishes the white man who takes up such an occupation'.[24]

There is the highly controversial view that attributes to traditional Spanish culture the idea that 'manual tasks, skilled trades, industry and commerce were so much base and dishonourable drudgery'.[25] The haughty attitude towards mechanical trades displayed by the parents quoted above would seem to support this view. On the other hand, however, time and again the prestige of hard work is underlined. Time and again young men are approvingly described as being 'of good conduct and leading an industrious life'.[26] To be 'a hardworking man, who earns his living with his personal labour',[27] or 'an industrious artisan who earns enough in his job as a cigar-maker',[28] was a source of praise. Moreno Fraginals describes the ideology of the new Cuban entrepreneurial class which had nothing but contempt for the purchasers of titles and nobility. They defended the pride of being an active man as the only genuine value in the new economic life.[29] And Arango y Parreño, the prominent spokesman of this new bourgeoisie, maintained at the turn of the century that 'honours should only be bestowed in accordance with a person's abilities and virtues and not on account of his birth'.[30]

Also, differences in wealth of the families involved could give rise to parental dissent. As one official reported: 'the two families are among the most magnificent of this town, that of the bride is quite rich and the other, although not so much so, is only slightly less wealthy'.[31] Hence they could marry. In another report, it is remarked that 'the position his family occupies is that of poor people living as they do on a cattle farm on lease and that of Da. Rosa Casanova is good, for her father owns in this municipality a coffee plantation with fifty negroes working on it', and 'the education of Casanova is somewhat more finished in consequence of her advantageous position than that of Burrundarena'.[32] And another suitor is rejected because 'his education differs greatly from that of his bride's family. She has a good education, while he does not even know how to sign his name.'[33] He lacked the refinements that wealth bestows on the rich.

A further criterion was religion. In principle, 'Jews, heretics, and other unbelievers' were forbidden by the Spanish Crown to establish themselves in its colonies,[34] but this was surely no obstacle for those who wanted to do so.[35] And indeed, one parent whose son wanted to marry a French woman from Santo Domingo demanded of her 'evidence of Christianity', and objected because her father had 'never gone to confession, to mass, nor had he attended any public religious act'.[36]

The individual traits of the marrying couple played a role as well in defining their eligibility. Typically of a newly settled territory in a period of formidable economic expansion, individual enterprise could to some extent overcome social distinction based on ascription. Thus parents often objected to the suitor precisely because he was thought to lack enterprise, because he was poor, lacked a profession, and thus the means to meet the cost of married life. But occasionally these objections contained a status element. The candidate was rejected not only because of his alleged lack of enterprise but also because this implied that he would be unable to achieve the life-style that was expected of him. As one official commented: 'even if lack of means is not a legal impediment to marriage, this must be fully taken into account when the families are of some standing, and the means of subsistence are not in proportion to the class to which they belong'.[37] Nevertheless, here the suitor's ineligibility was determined by his personal performance rather than his family background. It was up to him to improve his economic standing and thus be able to marry up.[38]

Finally, moral conduct was significant as well. Young men were required to be 'of good conduct'. One suitor was rejected for not doing anything but 'attending dances, playing billiards and going cock-fighting and molesting young girls'.[39] In the bride's case, her reputation was equally if not more important. She was expected to be modest and respectable. Any doubt about her sexual integrity made her ineligible in the eyes of any decent family. One parent alluded, among other reasons, to the previous dishonour of the girl at the hands of a sergeant as a ground for opposition, an imputation which was vigorously refuted by the young man, for

it is not true . . . that Da. Rosalia found herself before I met her in the lamentable and corrupted state alluded to . . . nobody but I can affirm this with the certainty and conviction that is born of experience . . . I swear by God and man that I have seduced Da. Rosalia and that she had not been touched by anybody else, and I make this oath because I found in her undoubted and very marked signs of an immaculate and evident virginity.[40]

## Marriage among kin

The preservation of the whites' socio-economic pre-eminence depended importantly on class endogamous marriage. But wealth and racial purity could be maintained intact even more successfully through marriage among kin. According to canon law, in Spain and its overseas possessions consanguineous kinship in direct line up to the fourth degree including collaterals, affinity to the fourth degree and ritual kinship constituted impediments to marriage. Nevertheless, all consanguineous or affinal prohibitions to marriage could upon request be overcome by papal dispensation[41] with the exception of consanguinity in direct line, i.e. between parents and children, and in the first degree in the collateral line, i.e. between siblings. As the Bishop of Havana noted in 1858: '[this is] a country in which the short number of its white population makes marriage with kin very common, particularly within the well-to-do classes'.[42]

Despite earlier misgivings on the part of the Church[43] and presumably in order to ease the process of dispensation for marriages among kin in the colonies, the overseas prelates were repeatedly given special powers to grant these dispensations themselves.[44] In the case of Cuba it is not quite clear whether and for how long the local prelates held these powers.[45] At any rate, the Archive of the Ministry of Overseas Affairs in Madrid holds

235 papal dispensations granted to Cubans between 1800 and 1870. And the Bishop of Havana in 1858 addressed a vehement letter to the Minister of State and Overseas Affairs greatly concerned over the consequences of his lacking these powers: 'any brother-in-law who cannot obtain a dispensation from the undersigned to marry his sister-in-law, the same as any uncle with his niece . . . disappear to any of the ports of the American Union . . . and within two weeks they return' dispensed and married.[46] The Catholic bishops of the United States held these powers; the reasons, the Bishop of Havana assumed, were that the simplification of the legal requirements with regard to marriage between kin would prevent the defection of the faithful and the strengthening of the Protestants there.[47] While the Bishop of Havana neither on that occasion nor later succeeded in obtaining special powers, the Archbishop of Santiago de Cuba was granted these *facultades sólitas e insólitas* in 1860.[48]

The significance and extent of marriage between kin in nineteenth-century Cuba is difficult to assess. In the absence of a systematic reconstruction of marriage patterns in a given area in a given period of time, which could only be done on the basis of the parish marriage registers, it is impossible to know whether the incidence of family endogamy of any form exceeded random frequency.[49] In a homogeneous egalitarian society where romantic love would be the only motive for choice of partner, the probability also exists that a few people fall in love with their nieces, sisters-in-law or cousins. But on the basis of the dispensations granted and a tentative analysis of some genealogies taken from the Conde de Jaruco's monumental *Historia de las familias cubanas*[50] it is possible to specify the kind of kin that were most likely to marry when family endogamy took place, and to propose some interpretation of the sociological implications of these marriages.

The papal dispensations concerned mainly marriages with ego's deceased wife's sister and with his brother's or sister's daughter.[51] These two patterns have different structural implications. The marriage with the deceased wife's sister reproduces an affinal link. It has the effect of renewing an alliance between two distinct families and hence looks outward. The marriage with the brother's daughter/sister's daughter, on the contrary, reinforces the solidarity of the consanguineous group.

The applicants for papal dispensation give a number of reasons in support of their requests. A man generally desired to marry his deceased wife's sister because he was concerned 'to see to her situation', and/or felt he must 'provide for the care and education of the children'.[52] In the former case the sister-in-law was usually past her prime, 'over twenty-four years of age', as they say.[53] If women had not managed to secure a husband by their mid-twenties, and since social and legal norms ruled out an independent existence, they had to rely either on their parents or on siblings to provide for their future, or enter a convent. Under these circumstances a marriage to a widowed brother-in-law who had already proved his worth was surely a welcome alternative for all parties concerned.

Not infrequently it is pointed out that she suffered from what in canon law was called *ob angustiam loci*, meaning that in her town there were no men of her station except her own kinsmen.[54] A son-in-law might himself feel a certain obligation towards his family of procreation in terms of protecting its women, 'freeing them from the risks and dangers of the world'.[55] Besides, any misdemeanour on their part would reflect, if not on his, certainly on his children's reputation, and this he would surely want to avoid.

On other occasions there might not be a shortage of suitable men but the woman herself lacked an essential prerequisite for marriage. Often she is said to be 'poor', she 'lived in poverty' or 'had no wealth nor hope of a dowry of any sort, with whose inducement [she] could hope to make another marriage'.[56] The lack of a dowry could severely handicap the chances of a young woman on the marriage market.[57] A widowed brother-in-law who might have already received a dowry in his first marriage with the sister and in addition felt some responsibility for his sister-in-law might be more willing to do without one the second time.

The existence of children by his previous marriage constituted a strong incentive for a man to seek remarriage. The children's unmarried aunt, having probably already assumed part of the mother's functions, would seem an appropriate candidate. As one applicant says, 'the children I have from my former marriage will find in her a person who will take their mother's place'.[58] Besides, by marrying her any possible embarrassment is avoided. Thus one applicant, whose wife's single and orphaned sister had already lived with them before her sister's death, argues that

he has been left without children and in the age of sickness and afflictions; now his helplessness and critical situation has become extreme for his sister-in-law . . . who has lived with them for many years, today wants to leave him to save appearances and her reputation. This lady has no wealth and hardly any means to subsist and this step would thus require a great sacrifice on her part and would undoubtedly be her doom and perhaps even her death.[59]

Living under the same roof, the contact between brother-in-law and sister-in-law at times was more than fraternal, one more ground for seeking marriage, 'to remedy the scandal caused by their excessive inti-macy',[60] the result 'of a crazy passion due to which they came to know each other carnally and to procreate'.[61]

Although the marriage with the deceased wife's sister from the man's point of view only duplicates an existing affinal link, it has a positive hierarchical value. The widower, instead of establishing a relationship with a new family, solidifies his and his children's structural position as determined by his first marriage, and in addition guarantees the sister-in-law a marriage within her own group.[62]

Marriage with the brother's daughter/sister's daughter was second in frequency, but only seldom are reasons given for this choice,[63] possibly because this form of family endogamy was so common that it had become generally accepted and required no extenuating circumstances to be dispensed.[64]

Archbishop Claret y Clarà in 1852 in his *Auto de dispensas matrimoniales* talks disapprovingly of 'those kinsmen who marry among themselves out of calculation and family interests' and 'who do not know how to love except within the circle of their kinsfolk, disdaining strangers whom they regard with contempt and scorn'.[65] Due to the substantial outlay involved in obtaining a papal dispensation – 500 to 600 pesos at least[66] – or in travelling to the United States, only well-to-do families could contract such marriages, precisely those families whose 'family interests' would make such a marriage seem most desirable. It is surely to these families that Claret y Clarà alludes. Thus Da. Carolina Maribona, a young girl of fourteen years, upon her father's death had inherited a sum of over 100,000 pesos. Her suitor, a young man of twenty-one, a law student who earned little money and having many brothers had little to expect in the way of inheritance, was rejected by the girl's mother who wanted to marry the girl to her own brother. The mother herself had no right to the girl's inheritance, but if she succeeded in marrying the daughter to her brother the money would revert to her family.[67] Inheritance as well as filiation were reckoned bilaterally in Cuba. Both sons and daughters were heirs to their parents, and these in turn to their children, should they die without offspring.[68] In the absence then of any legal device to prevent the dispersal of property, recourse was taken to family endogamy.

Only rarely does a man want to marry his mother's or father's sister, presumably for reasons of relative age. Besides, canon law was more hostile to this kind of union than to uncle–niece-marriages because it was thought to be incompatible with the obedience which the husband as nephew owed his aunt who was at the same time his wife.[69]

Archbishop Claret y Clarà in 1852 sorrowfully remarked on the 'multitude of those living in the sad state of concubinage not few of whom are kin . . . cognates, affines and even ritual kin in various degrees'.[70] Lacking legal sanction these unions between kin could not have the purpose of keeping family property intact. The Bishop of Havana attributed the frequency of marriage between kin to the ethnic multiplicity of the country. Also, in the rural areas of Oriente province, which Archbishop Claret y Clarà visited, the coloured population was substantial. A white person, unless he was willing to take a coloured spouse or concubine and have mixed offspring, had often no other choice than to take a relative. If both parents were white, regardless of whether they married or lived in concubinage, the offspring would be white. Given that social pre-eminence depended on both socio-economic as well as racial exclusiveness, it may be argued that the upper strata of Cuban society were compelled by economic as well as racial interests to practice intra-kin marriage while the lower strata, having their whiteness as their sole mark of distinction, could well perpetuate this through concubinage.

An analysis of three genealogies selected from the Conde de Jaruco's *Historia de las familias cubanas* does not take us much further in the assessment of the social significance of intra-kin marriage in nineteenth-century Cuba.[71] But one point is worth noting. Cousin marriage is absent in the papal dispensations, whereas the genealogies (see Figs 2 and 3, pp. 143–7 below) indicate that this form of intra-kin marriage did occur. If intra-kin marriage, particularly among consanguines, is interpreted as a strategy followed to preserve socio-economic status, the total absence of cousin marriage would have been odd. Given that brothers and sisters are prohibited from marrying, marriage between uncle and niece is the next best alternative, from the point of view of family solidarity. Bearing generation difference in mind, however, cousin marriage would seem to be a good alternative.

## MARRIAGE BETWEEN COLOURED PEOPLE

### *The coloured person in law: some honour worth preserving*

The Royal Pragmatic on marriage of 1776 embraced 'all from the highest classes of the State without exception to the commonest of the people . . . because of the importance of choosing an appropriate partner in marriage'.[72] When in 1778 it was made extensive to the colonies, however, the

Pragmatic lost its all-inclusive character: 'mulattos, negroes, *coyotes* and other people of similar castes or races, publicly held and reputed as such' were excluded from the requirements of parental consent for marriage 'save those who serve as officers in the militias or who differ from the rest by virtue of their reputation, good conduct and services rendered'.[73] With the stated exceptions coloured people were regarded as a separate community to which the laws of the Crown did not apply, a despicable and worthless mass. Only those who proved positively useful and loyal to the State were conceded some 'reputation', that is 'honour' worth protecting. Otherwise their condition might have reflected on those reputable citizens with whom they were bound to interact.

In 1803, however, the law was again revised and a decree on marriage by *hijos de familia* was passed explicitly applicable to 'any class of the State they might belong to';[74] this modification was reiterated by royal decree of 15 October 1805 and also by the edict of the Audiencia of Puerto Principe of 1806 stipulating that 'negroes, mulattos and other castes who are under the said ages . . . are required to demand and obtain parental consent in the same way as all the others'.[75] This reform indicates two things: at least for the effects of marriage, coloured people were elevated to the status of full citizen; and by introducing parental consent as a formal requirement also for marriages among coloured people, a measure of social mobility and consequent internal stratification of the coloured community was acknowledged.

There is ample evidence that the generalized discrimination by whites, rather than having an equalizing effect on the coloured people, produced marked cleavages within their ranks. The whites were well aware of the positive value of the cultural hegemony they exercised over the coloured community. The maxim was 'divide and rule'. By a *composición* and against the payment of a fee a *pardo* could obtain from the King a dispensation of his colour, thus becoming eligible for offices hitherto closed to him.[76] But care should be taken that such a privilege be bestowed only upon '[those] *morenos* and *pardos* who by means of authentic documents . . . can prove their free and legitimate descent through four generations.'[77] Surely not many qualified in these terms. For, as a ruling of 1806 by the Council of the Indies read, in principle 'it is useful and necessary to keep [the members of the contaminated castes] in their place and in a class excluded from the public offices and honours, distinctions and prerogatives of the whites and of the legitimate mestizos'.[78] In short, there was room for individual mobility of the coloured, but the authorities were careful to preserve the exceptional character of this advancement.

*Reasons for parental dissent: inequality in colour and 'condición'*

The mobility aspirations of the various strata often came into conflict over marriage. The differences in the social structure of the coloured community are reflected in the reasons for parental dissent to marriage. Generally, parental dissent was prompted by differences in 'colour' and in *condición* (legal status). The basic attitude of all these parents was that 'all men should endeavour to advance instead of regress',[79] advance both in relation to one's colour by 'whitening' oneself and in terms of one's distance from slavery. The lighter the skin and the further removed from slavery, the greater the chances of ascending the social ladder. Typical was the attitude of the mother of a mulatto, who objected to her son's intended marriage to a *morena*, the daughter of an African negress, because he should rather aim at improving his lineage'.[80] But differences more subtle than that were perceived as an obstacle to marriage. Thus José Benites y Benos, the son of a white man and a *parda*, arouses his father's wrath when José attempts to marry a *parda* on both sides. Although 'it is true', as he argues, 'that the Reina descends from *pardos* . . . they are of such light shade that they look white, as she herself; she has reached a degree that permits one to say that her blood has been purified through the mixture of her ancestors with the white', the father opposes the marriage because of the 'conspicuous inequality' between the two.[81] It was not her complexion but her 'blood' that despite successive purification was still conspicuously 'darker' than that of her suitor.

Better still than preserving past gains, one should 'advance one's family'. The mother who disregards all rules of politeness and says bluntly that 'she does not want her daughter to marry a *negro*' although the daughter herself is a *morena* has no qualms to confess her ambitions.[82]

Table 7 gives the respective 'colour' of the candidates involved in the disputes and the dissenting party. In all cases of dissent but two, the candidates to the projected marriage are of different shade. And it is always the lighter person's family who objects to the match.

Often free parents were opposed to a marriage because the bride/suitor was a slave: 'how could he give his consent', argues one father, 'when the suitor, being a slave, lacks the means to maintain her'.[83] A son objects to his father's remarriage because the woman is 'a morena . . . slave and therefore of inferior quality';[84] his father is a free *moreno*. Specifying the source of his anxieties the son adds, 'this marriage in addition to being repugnant to the mind in a man of his age is only the result of the *morena*'s mistress's suggestions . . . our maternal inheritance is at stake'. The slave's

TABLE 7. *'Colour' of candidates and dissenting party*

| Suitor | Bride | Dissenting party |
|---|---|---|
| pardo | morena | his father |
| moreno | china | her mother |
| moreno | parda | her father |
| claims to be white | parda | his relatives |
| pardo, white on one side | parda on both sides | his father |
| moreno | morena | her mother |
| pardo, on both sides | parda, white on one side | her father |
| claims to be white | parda | his mother |
| moreno | parda | her mother |
| moreno | parda | her mother |
| pardo | claims to be white | her father |
| pardo | ? | his mother |
| pardo | morena | his mother |
| pardo, white on one side | parda, white on one side | her father |
| moreno | parda, white on one side | her mother |
| pardo | ? | his mother |

mistress presumably intended to sell her to her future husband and the son did not doubt that his father would want to buy his spouse's freedom. By law a slave did not automatically become free by marrying a free person, but those free persons who married a slave surely hoped to set their captive spouses free.

The practical difficulties involved in a marriage between a free person and a slave were only too real, and the difference in legal status between them was fundamental, but that, for instance, between an ex-slave and a freeborn person would seem insignificant. Still, it was thought to be important in terms of marriage. As one mulatto argued: 'he cannot approve of such a marriage, for, although he is by birth mulatto . . . his parents and grandparents and those of his wife had all been free from captivity; it causes him therefore great pain to see a daughter married to a *chino* [offspring of a negro and a mulatto woman or vice-versa] who has only recently been a slave'.[85] And of one girl it was said 'that she is regarded as one of the most respectable women of her class owing to her removal from the black colour and from slavery . . . [Besides] her brother has been decorated by His Majesty with the Grand Cross for services rendered to the country in the persecution of fugitive slaves.'[86]

The greater the removal from slavery, then, the more social worth a person had.

TABLE 8. *'Condición' (and colour) of candidates and dissenting party*

| Suitor | Bride | Dissenting party |
|---|---|---|
| free pardo, claims to be white | parda, ex-slave | his father |
| moreno slave, criollo | free parda | her mother |
| free pardo | parda slave | ? |
| moreno ex-slave, de nación | free morena, criolla | her mother |
| free chino | freeborn parda | his father |
| moreno ex-slave | free morena | her mother |
| free moreno | morena slave | his son |
| moreno slave | free morena | her mother |
| free pardo | slave | his mother |
| free pardo | morena slave | his mother |
| free moreno | morena slave | his mother |

Table 8 sums up the respective candidates' *condición* (and colour) as well as indicating the dissenting party. With the exception of one case (in which, nevertheless, such an inequality is alleged) there is always a real difference in legal status between the candidates who, however, in most cases are equal in 'colour'. The opposing party throughout is the family of that candidate who is thought to be further removed from slavery.

Finally, in some individual cases factors other than difference in 'colour' and legal status make a marriage undesirable in the eyes of some parent. Occasionally objection is taken to the suitor's economic standing, his moral reputation, and, as among whites, the bride must be of proved virtue. Thus one candidate is said to be a 'drunkard',[87] another one a 'loose, thievish and disslute *moreno*'.[88] And one worried father describes well the perils of marrying a fallen woman:

I do not approve of this marriage planned by my son to his own detriment and that of society at large in whose interest it is to promote good marriages . . . my son's bride once eloped with a *pardo* . . . this scandalous event makes for an unhappy marriage because of the dreadful hold her lover is likely to have over the heart of the woman who will not be able to be faithful to my son who has come to know her only when she had already lost her reputation.[89]

If she had shown signs of moral weakness before marriage, how was she to be trusted thereafter?

Relative social status among coloured people was, then, pre-eminently dependent on 'colour' and legal status. Individual performance could enhance an individual's status but advancement on this scale was decisively checked by ascription. 'Between negroes and mulattos', says one *pardo*, 'the only inequality there is is that between the free and the slaves.'[90] In the final analysis it was an individual's status with regard to slavery that mattered. Skin colour was a means to assess this status. *Pardos* occupied a higher place on the social ladder, not only because of their phenotypical approximation to the whites but because they were likely to be further removed from slavery. In effect, population figures show that at least until 1846 there was always a predominance of mulattos among free coloured and a marked excess of negroes among slaves.[91]

Among coloured people a very general aspiration was to become as light and to get as far away from slavery as possible. Instead of developing a consciousness of their own worth they made their own the white discriminating ideology imposed on them from above. The same disdain with which they were regarded by most whites they often applied to their peers. It is true there were occasional outbursts of rebellion, such as the famous conspiracy of the *escalera*. And the whites made much of the menace to the social order constituted by the coloured population. It is significant that those who participated in this conspiracy were the most educated and socially advanced of the coloured people, who were bound to feel most strongly the injustice of the system. And at the other extreme, it was the slaves who proved the most rebellious, killing overseers, escaping, or as a last resort committing suicide. The middle sector of the coloured community, however, those who had managed to make some status gains but had not yet come up against the upper limits of mobility, probably constituted the most status-conscious and conformist group. They not only accepted passively the constraints imposed by the social order but lent it their active consent. An attitude such as that of the mulatto woman Angela Campos was certainly rare among them. When her daughter's suitor, a white man, approached her with the request to allow him to live with the daughter, she rejected him 'for her daughter was a virgin [and] she [wished] that she marry one of her own class'.[92]

Admittedly, the number of cases of parental dissent to marriage among coloured people that were taken to the authorities was small compared to the size and the number of marriages of the coloured population. It could therefore be argued that few parents really cared whether their children's marriages were colour-status endogamous or not. But Table 9, summing up the marriage entries for coloured people in the parish registers of Sta. Maria del Rosario and of Regla, substantiates the view that coloured people, when they married at all, did so with their own shade and *condición*.

The multiple rifts within the coloured community can also be apprec-

TABLE 9. Frequency of endogamy of colour and of condition in marriages of coloured people in the parishes of Sta. Maria del Rosario and of Regla, 1805–81

| Parish: | Number of marriages of coloured people | | | | | | Total number of marriages of coloured people |
|---|---|---|---|---|---|---|---|
| | of same shade | of different shade | shade known | of same condition | of different condition | condition known | |
| Sta. Maria del Rosario | 277 | 13 | 290 | 328 | 38 | 366 | 366 |
| Regla | 214 | 30 | 244 | 227 | 31 | 258 | 260 |

Note: The registers distinguish two colours only – pardo and moreno – and two types of condition – slaves and free.

iated when one records the numerous colour-status categories that occur in the marriage proceedings. Coloured people distinguished at least nine different types of free coloureds:

pardo, white on one side, freeborn
pardo, white on one side, ex-slave
pardo on both sides, freeborn
pardo on both sides, ex-slave
chino, freeborn
chino, ex-slave
moreno criollo, freeborn
moreno criollo ex-slave
moreno de nación, ex-slave

and three categories of slaves:

pardo slave
moreno criollo slave
moreno de nación slave.

This is surely symptomatic of a marked absence of common identity.

### A coloured petty bourgeoisie?

It is interesting to take a look at the occupations of the young men involved in these marriage disputes.[93] Well represented are the military and the crafts and trades. Agricultural occupations are practically absent. The professions are predominantly urban, not suprisingly if one bears in mind that the majority of the free coloured lived and worked in the towns. It is largely from these occupations that what Deschamps calls a 'coloured petty bourgeoisie' was recruited.[94] It is this sector which – due to economic expansion – had managed to carve out a relatively comfortable place for itself, which they were keen, if not to improve, at least to consolidate.

The members of the coloured militias occupied the apex of the coloured people's social hierarchy. The special prerogatives of the militia not only granted them social prestige but also allowed them to live in comfortable circumstances. The militias were organized on a coloured basis; there were those of *pardos* and those of *morenos*, a distinction which was again reflected in the marriage pattern. Thus, the captain of Morenos Manuel Salazar, married Tranquilina Barba y Peñalver, the legitimate daughter of Gabriel Doroteo Barba, captain of the Battalion of Morenos Leales of Havana between 1835 and 1836, who had been decorated with the Royal Effigy of Her Majesty for his services in Pensacola, Florida, and who was the owner of two houses and several slaves. His wife was Maria Isabel Aróstegui, a free *morena criolla* who had brought a dowry of 6,000 pesos to the marriage.[95] And José Lorenzo Póveda, *alférez beneficiado* of the Battalion of Morenos Leales of Havana, by profession a shoemaker, married Dolores López, a free *morena* and sister to the lieutenant of the Battalion of Morenos, Joaquin López. Póveda was one of the 739 *pardos* and *morenos* who had to leave the island in 1844 as a consequence of the violent repression unleashed by O'Donnell.[96]

Occasionally coloured people themselves possessed slaves and were often accused, perhaps not quite objectively, of being the harshest masters. The captain of the Battalion of Morenos, Ciriaco Acosta, in his testament lists apart from several houses and landed property six slaves. He had married Maria de la Regla Santa Cruz who had herself brought a house to the marriage.[97]

The artisans also in a way constituted a privileged group. Francisco Uribe, the fashionable tailor, owned two houses and twelve slaves when he died in 1844. The masons José de la O. Lanet, José Maria Aróstegui and Faustino Ladin had made a position for themselves. The musician Tomas Vuelta y Flores, who was also a sergeant of the Battalion of Morenos of Havana, left at his death in 1851 sixteen houses, and several slaves valued all in all at about 45,000 pesos.[98]

As the coloured poet Juan Francisco Manzano was to write: 'I remember many blacks and mulattos, some of them possessing a considerable fortune, who in their way of life, their dress, their behaviour and their manners of speech imitated those white gentlemen who were still left in Cuba; there was no lack among them of people fond of reading serious books and even of making verses.'[99]

It is understandable that this sector of the coloured community which had achieved eminence despite official and social prejudice should be bent on controlling the marriages of their children.

# PART 2. HONOUR AND CLASS

'If the maiden seduced under promise of marriage is inferior in status, so that she would cause greater dishonour to his lineage if he married her than the one that would fall on her by remaining seduced (as when for instance a Duke, Count, Marquis or Gentleman of known nobility were to seduce a mulatto girl, a *china*, a *coyota* or the daughter of a hangman, a butcher, a tanner) he must [not] marry her because the injury to himself and his entire lineage would be greater than that incurred by the maiden by remaining unredeemed, and at any rate one must choose the lesser evil ... for the latter is an offence of an individual and does no harm to the Republic, while the former is an offence of such gravity that it will denigrate an entire family, dishonour a person of pre-eminence, defame and stain an entire noble lineage and destroy a thing which gives splendoura nd honour to the Republic. But if the seduced maiden is of only slightly inferior status, of not very marked inequality, so that her inferiority does not cause marked dishonour to the family, then, if the seducer does not wish to endow her, or she justly rejects compensation in the form of endowment, he must be compelled to marry her; because in this case her injury would prevail over the offence inflicted upon the seducer's family for they would not suffer grave damage through the marriage whereas she would were she not to marry.'

Biblioteca Nacional, Madrid, Manuscritos de America, *Dictamen de Dr. Tembra acerca de la consulta que se hizo sobre si el Cura o cualquier juez eclesiástico puede o debe impedir los matrimonios entre consortes desiguales, celebrados ya esponsales o con juramento de cumplirlos, sin consentimiento paterno*, Mexico, 1752, Leg. 18,701[14].

# CHAPTER 7

# ELOPEMENT AND SEDUCTION

Social class endogamy was the officially and socially preferred form of marriage both among whites and among coloured people in nineteenth-century Cuba. Most marriages conformed to this pattern. When a young couple, however, decided to disregard established norms on choice of spouse they could do two things to get away with it. They could either appeal to the authorities for a supplementary marriage licence overruling parental dissent, or, more drastically, they could elope. Once the families and society had been presented with this *fait accompli* parents would presumably find it much harder to uphold their initial objections. Such practice was not uncommon in colonial America nor in nineteenth-century Cuba.

Already in 1780 we find the Audiencia de Chile complaining about 'the excesses that have been noted there, and that are subject to punishment, of those who remove daughters from the authority of their fathers and take them to the open fields and to a deserted place and keep them there for a few days in an attempt to marry them under the pretence that the parents are against it'.[1] And Cuban popular literature contains repeated allusions to elopement. In *El Perro Huevero*, a contemporary satire, Mónica, the daughter of Matías, elopes with Mamerto *el indiano* and later promises to marry him. When the play was staged in Havana shortly after the onset of the Ten Years War the Voluntarios caused a riot: for it was generally assumed that Matías, a cock-fighter and gambler, was no other than the Spanish government, that Mónica was the island of Cuba who endeavoured to free herself from the colonial yoke, and Mamerto represented the rebels.[2]

There existed, however, two slightly different forms of elopement. The Council of the Indies in 1780 had spoken of 'elopement for reasons of marriage';[3] this is the type of elopement brought to the courts.[4] It was resorted to as a means to overcome parental dissent and aimed at immediate marriage. Parents would initially attempt a settlement outside the courts; if they were unsuccessful they would take the case before the authorities.[5] But the elopement was also a way of commencing concubinage, common among the lower strata. The young man would take the girl away and they would set up house together on the understanding that once his financial circumstances improved they would marry. In this case parents, who had presumably done the same in their time, after an initial show of outrage would acquiesce in the end. As one girl explained:

Andrés García had been courting her for about a year; at the beginning her parents were quite pleased . . . [but then] they became opposed . . arguing that he was a poor man . . . she wants to marry him but with the proviso that he do so at his convenience since he had told her of his circumstances and if she had run away with him it had been out of her free will.[6]

Elopement with a view to premarital concubinage was fairly frequent; at least Francisco Figueras suggests this:

although only a minority of these cases went to the courts, the elopement with dishonest intentions became the most frequent offence. Above all in the countryside . . . the elopement became the most common and expedient way of constituting a family; although it must be said . . . that the majority of those who established this type of union, once they had offspring and had acquired some wealth did not wait any longer to honour and strengthen their union by means of the more stable bond of the sacrament.[7]

An important reason leading these couples to opt for concubinage rather than marriage is said to be their precarious financial situation. It might seem paradoxical that poverty should be conceived as an obstacle to marriage but not to concubinage. After all, the costs of married life were surely not any higher than those of a life in concubinage. Moreover, marriage fees were not all that heavy. The clergy fixed them very much at their own discretion but the so-called *pobres de solemnidad* were able to obtain exemption.[8] Given their frequency, free unions presumably received some social recognition. On the other hand, marriage was very much a symbol of status, resorted to by those who possessed such status in order to protect it. For marriage to have such a social meaning it would demand a measure of public display and ritual which in turn demanded a substantial expenditure. It was almost certainly the outlay involved in the marriage celebrations which prevented these couples from entering a legal union from the start, coupled with the fact that they had no property or status to protect in this way.

As Figueras says, only a few of these cases were brought to the courts. This is understandable. The young man was thought to act in good faith and the girl's parents trusted him to marry her if and when he could. There was thus no reason for parental or official intervention.

I shall discuss here only the well-documented instances of elopement with a view to immediate marriage.

### ELOPEMENT WITH A VIEW TO MARRIAGE

It is difficult to assess the exact incidence of elopement with a view to marriage in nineteenth-century Cuba. There is plenty of evidence, however, indicating the degree of its institutionalization. The moment the whereabouts of a girl are unknown elopement is suspected. Immediately parents jump to the conclusion that she must have run away with a lover. Typical is the following case. The mother reported the disappearance of the girl to the local police, and when asked why she thought the daughter had eloped she replied: 'she had no other reason, though she thought this was very well founded, but that the said Herrera had demanded her daughter in marriage which she granted considering him an honourable man and of the same class as her daughter'. Later it turns out that the girl had left on account of constant quarrels with her half-brother.[9] Or elopement is alleged by parents as a subterfuge to exert pressure on a young man to marry the daughter. One uncle goes so far as to forge a letter in order to rid himself of his niece; as the attorney comments:

Da. Manuela Guelvenzu had been living at the home of her uncle D. Andrés Bustamante for some time . . . and since he is poor she had to take charge of most of the affairs of the household . . . she was probably rather a burden to her said uncle, who to alleviate somewhat his precarious situation had the idea of accusing Menéndez of elopement with the said girl, making use of the fact that she had run away from his home because of the ill-treatment she received at the hands of his wife, and for this purpose made up the letter . . . so that Menéndez would find himself in the difficult situation of having to choose between a marriage or the penalties established by law . . . in which case he [the uncle] would always be the winner for if [the young man] married the girl his expenses would be reduced and if he did not [Menéndez] would have to give her an endowment and with this they could live more comfortably at least for some time, but he did not take into account that the truth invariably triumphs.[10]

Neither was the elopement a novelty to the authorities. One parent is outraged at the equanimity of the local police chief who upon being informed of the elopement advises the father to calm down, for the fugitives would marry in the end; he could be certain that his daughter would reappear not later than the following morning.[11]

The widespread familiarity with elopement in nineteenth-century Cuba must not be taken, however, as an indication that this was the normal way to get married among the upper strata, in the same way that to run off to

Gretna Green, though a strategy well known in England for minors to get married, was not a generalized practice. In Cuba the norm was class endogamous marriage. The aspiration to exogamous marriage as manifested in this type of elopement must be treated as a deviation from this norm. After all, had class exogamous marriage been the general rule, parents would have had no reason to oppose it, nor would youngsters have had any need to elope.

It is in relation to the lack of freedom of marriage on the one hand, and religious morality, which demanded virginity of unmarried and chastity of married women, on the other, that elopement must be studied.

### ELOPEMENT BY WHITES

The initial stage of courting was carried on more or less in secret. Once the parents became aware, however, that their daughter had a suitor, they started making inquiries into his background and tried to ascertain whether his intentions were honest.[12] One father describes this ritual well:

As soon as my daughter had passed puberty, she was courted by D. Ramón Cabastani, known as Tarragona, and from the moment I became aware of their courtship I tried to find out from Cabastani himself what his intentions were. I got a respectable reply, and when he said that he would marry her very soon I granted him entry into my home.[13]

The assurance by the suitor that his intentions were honest was not the only prerequisite for the establishment of the second and formal stage of courting. More important was the view the parents held of the candidate's social acceptability. The preoccupation to ensure that the chosen spouse conformed to their expectations, however, was not peculiar to the girl's parents. The young man's were equally solicitous to secure an appropriate match. When the evaluation of the candidate turned out negative, then a campaign set in to cut short the courtship.

It was at this point, when parents objected to the match and placed obstacles in the path of the young couple, that the latter resorted to elopement. The aim of this drastic step was to reverse the attitude of the dissenting parents towards the intended marriage, to create a situation which would compel the parents actively to promote the marriage. Usually the young couple disappeared for a few days, and the girl was deflowered. Then the young man gave himself up, or they were found by the police. The essential point was that the girl had lost her honour. In view of a daughter's shame, few parents would persist in their aversion to her suitor. The rationale behind this manoeuvre was that, whereas initially the family's honour was thought to be damaged by a marriage with an unsuitable candidate, in the face of the daughter's shame it was precisely the family's honour that now demanded the marriage.[14]

## Reasons for eloping

Fairly typical was Da. Inés Ros' explanation: 'at about seven in the evening, when talking to her fiancé at the door of her home, she begged him to take her with him for she saw no other way of getting married in view of her parents' opposition'.[15] But the opposition did not need to be as explicit as that. The mere inkling that the parents might be against the marriage sufficed another girl, who ran away 'fearful of a denial by her father with regard to their plans, and profiting from the opportunity of his absence'.[16] Elopement as a means to overcome parental dissent to marriage was so much part of the whole complex of marriage that it also provided an excellent means for betrayal by men who alleged that their parents could only be persuaded to agree to the marriage if confronted with an elopement. Typically, however, elopement occurred with intent to marry. In thirty-six out of the fifty-six cases of elopement due to parental opposition, the explicit purpose was said by the young man to be marriage, and in only two was it seduction.

Ill-treatment ranked second among the reasons for elopement. An analysis of the proceedings reveals, however, that ill-treatment was only one particular form of parental opposition to a marriage. One girl

was so much harassed by her mother, for she victimized her all day trying to get her to put an end to her affair with the said Miguel, but since she had given him her word a long time ago she always resisted and insists on it, which was the reason that induced her to tell the said Miguel to take her away from where she was staying to the house of her uncle while the preparations for the marriage were made.[17]

And it was said of another parent that 'not liking the marriage he had ill-treated her'.[18] Presumably the fear of ill-treatment and punishment often succeeded in discouraging marriage, but it could clearly also have the opposite effect and drive a girl even more quickly into the arms of her man.

The reasons for parental dissent to marriage among whites have already been discussed. For the most part it was their concern over social exclusiveness and family purity that compelled parents to object to a marriage. Youngsters thus eloped mainly to overcome social inequality as an obstacle to marriage. But how effective was this device?

## The efficacy of elopement: the triumph of virginity

For elopement to be conceived as an institutionalized instrument to achieve marriage in the face of parental dissent, it was necessary that it should succeed regularly in overcoming their opposition. And, in fact, it often achieved this end. As one parent said, 'in view of the elopement, he is no longer opposed to it, but rather on the contrary the marriage should take place the sooner the better, so that public virtue does not remain unredeemed'.[19] If parents were intransigent, recourse could still be had to the civil authorities who had powers to grant supplementary marriage licences overruling parental dissent. An official reacted in the expected way when remarking:

Now a very significant circumstance has been introduced. Da. Paula Calero has run away with her lover and has been deflowered by him. The first circumstance stains her honour, the second fills her with ignominy. Public morals, domestic decency [would profit by] the example of another marriage, instead of by a young girl whose chastity has been violated and who perhaps, or not even perhaps, will not find an honest man who will want to take her in marriage. When a woman has gone astray, there are many who want her, not for anything good but to repeat the harm done.[20]

Elopement was successful as a means to overcome parental dissent because it inflicted a very concrete loss on the family, which could only be made up, at least partially, through marriage. There is considerable evidence that offended parents regarded it in this way. A suitable marriage could only be achieved if the girl was a virgin. Otherwise, she became a perpetual liability for the family and a stain on its reputation. As one parent lamented, '[he] snatched from her . . . the most valuable jewel nature has given her and which she will never be able to recover . . . resulting [in] the scandal of the family'.[21] What the practical consequences were of the loss of a woman's virginity for her family is explained lucidly by another mother: 'This grave offence by the said Ojeda has plunged a respectable family into profound consternation; although poor it enjoys the best reputation in all the neighbourhood and on it are based all its hopes and well-being, because it is this that offers the best chance to place and marry the daughters I have.'[22]

A parent's dissent was prompted by considerations regarding honour-precedence, that is regarding the social worth of the family, but once the elopement had occurred the foremost concern was to safeguard the girl's reputation despite the decrease in social prestige of the family this might entail.[23] Incidentally, the elopement may be just as effective in overcoming parental dissent to a son's marriage, although a man's prestige did not suffer by it in any way. One explanation would be that parents, by contributing to protect the honour-virtue of other people's daughters, symbolized their claim that their own daughters be accorded the same treatment. In addition, the legal sanctions on elopement – marriage, or alternatively endowment and banishment – must have contributed to its efficacy.[24]

It was the loss of sexual virtue of a daughter and the resulting loss in social worth of the family that made the elopement successful in achieving marriage in the face of parental opposition, for a family's honour was intimately related to that of its women. Legally, criminal action could only be taken for elopement when actual defloration of the girl had occurred. Indeed, it seems to have been an essential part of its ritual, and was often achieved under difficult conditions. One girl tells us:

It was about seven in the evening when she went from her home to the corner of the Calzada del Monte where a carriage was waiting for them with a pair of horses and after getting into it they drove towards the Cerro . . . and while the carriage proceeded at a very slow pace, upon his tender entreaties and offer of marriage, she gave way allowing him to enjoy her virginity, without having alighted or gone into any house.[25]

Two hours later the suitor gave himself up to the police.

### SEDUCTION: THE AFFIRMATION OF VIRILITY

So far I have only discussed elopement and shown that it was one possible way of overcoming social inequalities as obstacles to marriage in a hierarchial society that aimed at preserving its social order through class endogamy. I have also shown that the device through which the purity of the group was achieved was virginity, that is female purity. By controlling the access to female sexuality, control was exercised over the acquisition of undesirable members by the group.

Typically, elopement aimed at marriage. The young man dishonoured his bride precisely to be enabled to honour her later. In these cases, male conduct appeared to be in perfect agreement with the demands of virginity. I have, however, also found evidence of seduction, which is access to the sexuality of a woman achieved through deceit or under false pretences. The following case of a father who resorts to the authorities to obtain redress is typical:

It is as a peaceful and honest head of family that I resort to you . . . having a numerous family which I maintain with my personal labour, under great hardships and privations. It was my bad fortune that at the end of my life I should suffer the cruel fate of seeing a seducer corrupt one of my unhappy daughters, who has stained my honour even more by carrying in her womb the fruit of the criminal conduct of a man who knew how to triumph with flattery over her innocence and candour . . . The astute man who, aware of her innocent heart, knew how to cast a net not only to enjoy her virginity but to impress on her the ineffaceable sign of his crime, namely the pregnancy of some months which has been the reason why I discovered the sly conduct of that man who, under the promise of marriage, offended the obligations established by society and all rules laid down by law and morals. My family had become aware of the affair between my daughter and Balio, and although they never imagined that he would commit such an outrage, they took appropriate steps to break it up to avoid any event they might regret later, but as he had undoubtedly made his plans he knew how to make use of the moments when I rested from my hard toil to carry out his crime, the punishment of which I demand in the interest of a wretched daughter whose honour has been basely violated . . . Many nights Balio secretly entered my own home to satisfy his lewd desires in the bed of the victim of his seductions, which were undoubtedly all the more successful as this young girl, brought up among peasants in the simple ways of rural life, could not offer all the resistance required by the . . . bold conduct of Balio. And the worst is that after this attack that brought tears to the eyes of the whole family, he refused any settlement that would repair the damage done; as I did not want any lawsuit or that the painful condition of my daughter should become more public, I approached this man to demand of him some solution that would prevent this event from becoming known; but with inexplicable stubbornness . . . he has refused everything.[26]

Whereas elopement was a designedly overt affair, for the loss in social prestige that results from the community's knowledge of it was precisely the source of pressure that led to parental approval of the marriage, seduction was typically secret. It occurred generally in the girl's home and was, in most cases, detected when the girl became pregnant. As in elopement, a promise of marriage preceded the event.

In seduction, the normal course of events was that the young man started courting the girl. He tried to win her confidence and that of her parents by promising marriage and behaving in a generally respectable manner. Once he had consolidated his position in relation to the family, he got down to persuading the girl to accede to his desires. And when his intentions were crowned with success he beat his retreat as best he could under a variety of pretences. As one bride told the court: 'It is exactly two months since he stopped seeing her and her mother . . . as a consequence of having noticed that she was pregnant, and having pressed him repeatedly to fulfil his promise of marriage he abandoned her for she does not know what reason, although she suspects it was to evade his responsibility'.[27]

To get away and live in hiding was doubtless not all that easy. Therefore, more often men resorted to less drastic but also less effective ways of turning their backs on their responsibility. By far the most common strategy consisted in discrediting the girl's reputation. By doing so, the fundamental requisite for marriage which was the girl's respectability was done away with. The situation was inverted. Since she was not respectable, he did not have to marry her. Only the seduction of a virgin constituted an offence. Thus one girl's conduct was questioned, for one 'who repeatedly leaves the parental home in the middle of the night to go to amuse herself in a hen house with a man, is no candid virgin liable to be seduced with a promise of marriage'.[28] Another girl was claimed to be disreputable for 'she used to attend dances at a tavern in this neighbourhood, not disdaining to thrust herself into the arms of negroes and mulattos to dance with them'.[29] Both men were, nevertheless, found guilty.

In both elopement and seduction, the woman on the whole was expected to play a passive role.[30] She acquiesced, confident in the good faith of her suitor. She was necessarily largely passive for she was the pawn that was played in the competition for honour. It was in relation to her that the attitudes of the other parties were adjusted. These parties were the couple's parents, predominantly the girl's parents, and the suitor. They were active, regulating their behaviour according to their aims. In the typical elopement, the parental attitude with regard to marriage was basically negative. That of the young man was positive. The parents believed that the intended marriage would curtail their prestige, whereas the young man – if we bear in mind that opposition was generally prompted by considerations of social inequality – was likely to increase his. In seduction, the position was reversed. The young man's attitude was negative towards marriage, whereas the parents', both before and after the event, was positive.

Seduction thus appears as the opposite of the typical elopement. In elopement the young man was intent on guarding the girl's honour; in seduction the girl was a prey to the male's sexual aggressiveness and desire to assert his virility. While a father's honour might suffer by the corruption of a daughter in the same way as a brother's honour suffered by a sister's disgrace, a man's honour was also enhanced by the seduction of a virgin. When a woman told her lover 'to take her away if he is a man',[31] she was precisely challenging his virility.

These two attitudes, namely the high evaluation of female virtue on the one hand, as exhibited in elopement, and male aggressiveness on the other, as shown in seduction, seem to conflict. Nevertheless, they do exist side by side, and necessarily so for, in order that virginity as such be conceived an essential possession of women, the probability of its destruction must exist. This probability of destruction is made credible by the occurrence of seduction. The guardian of a betrayed girl described lucidly the two alternative types of male conduct when the seducer had succeeded in triumphing over her virtue: he 'boasts about it and relishes his artful behaviour and her unhappy condition', while she had thought him a 'sincere and honest man'.[32] These different and apparently conflicting concepts of male conduct are the expression of the structually necessary dual role of the man: as the defender of the family's, and more specifically the sister's, honour (one brother is said to be the 'keeper of the sister's honour'),[33] and also as the aggressor against the honour of all other women. Moreover, a general principle basic to any form of competition becomes apparent here. The destruction of other families' honour directly enhances that of one's own. Thus, seduction is complementary to the typical elopement in the same way as the assertion of virility is complementary to the high evaluation of virginity.[34]

### ELOPEMENT BY COLOURED PEOPLE

Elopement with a view to marriage occurred also within the coloured community. As among whites, it is considered as a possible way of overcoming parental dissent to marriage: 'the free *moreno* Ignasio Galban ... gave himself up to me', reported a police officer, 'declaring that he had carried off the *parda* Maria Ana Flores with a view to contracting the marriage they had agreed upon; her father's opposition prevents them from putting into effect their plans and for this reason they have taken [this] decision'.[35] As has been seen, parental opposition among coloured people was generally prompted by differences in 'colour' and legal status.

As among whites, female honour was evaluated highly by the coloured people. Coloured parents likewise spoke of the 'honour' their daughter had 'lost' at the hands of a man, which demands to be 'repaired', or 'saved'. And, conversely, a daughter's respectability and modesty were emphasized. Thus, as proof of the good conduct of her daughter, one *parda* insisted that 'when she went out into the street she always went accompanied as a respectable young woman should'.[36] And a grandmother said of her granddaughter whom she had brought up that 'she had kept her virginity ... for ... she had taken great care with her so that she might become a virtuous woman'.[37] Suitors faced with parental dissent exploited this evaluation to put pressure on the families to overcome opposition, and successfully so at times. As one parent commented, 'being aware now that his daughter is pregnant, he cannot but rush to give his consent so that they might marry as soon as possible and her honour be covered in this way'.³⁸

However, considerations of social prestige might outweigh those of honour-virtue, as in the case of a mulatto girl who wanted to marry the son of a slave woman: 'under no circumstances would he grant her his approval . . . because the young man is unequal; as regards the elopement he is ready to take charge of his daughter in the state she is in, and demands that the criminal suffer the appropriate penalty',³⁹ fulminated one parent.

### INTERRACIAL ELOPEMENT: PRE-EMINENCE SAVED BUT HONOUR LOST

Parents might, then, persist in their opposition regardless of their daughter's dishonour. This was particularly the case when the couple were of different 'race'. The elopement failed to induce the dissenting parents to change their views about the marriage. They preferred to put up with a dishonoured daughter rather than allow their 'lineage' to become impure. One white parent summed up the whole line of argument very well:

[The suitor has had] the inconceivable audacity to seduce, carry off and perhaps even rape a respectable white girl . . . and has thus been guilty before the law of an extremely grave offence, an offence of a kind that demands that it be brought before the courts of the Island of Cuba at all costs. This is a country where, because of its exceptional circumstances [i.e. slavery], it is necessary that the dividing line between the white and the African races be very marked, for any tolerance that might be praiseworthy in some cases will bring dishonour to the white families, upheaval and disorder to the country, if not extermination to its inhabitants; [he] will never approve of a marriage of their daughter to a mulatto, for this would be covering one stain with another much greater and indelible one; on the contrary, they rather swallow their pain and shame in silence than authorize it publicly.⁴⁰

At this point considerations of social prestige conflicted with the concern over honour-virtue. So far honour-pre-eminence was sustained by honour-virtue. Now repairing the sexual honour of a woman implies the destruction of social pre-eminence.

As long as the social distance between the families and candidates remained within the accepted boundaries, virginity sustained honour-precedence, which in turn sustained the social order. But beyond these boundaries this relationship became inverted. Important in this respect is a remark by the Council of the Indies, made in 1783, that 'any stain in one or other of the ancestors contaminates the whole generation'.⁴¹ In principle, family honour and the honour of its individual members were intimately related and interdependent. But here, greater honour-precedence had to be bought at the price of the daughter's honour-virtue.

The authorities generally shared the parents' intransigent view. Thus a mother explained that

the free *pardo* Manuel Morejón succeeded in seducing Da. Lorenzo Pacheco, her daughter, by extracting her from her maternal home and keeping her with him for three months, after which he demanded her consent for the marriage. Since she [the mother] did not know the status of the seducer and desiring that he repair her daughter's honour, she agreed to the marriage ... When at this point she was informed of Morejón's inferior quality she could not but openly resist the said marriage and therefore expressed her opposition to the parish priest.

The authorities approved of her attitude, for 'it is and should be very painful for any white family to see its offspring married to people of humble colour' and besides 'it is advisable to teach the *pardos* to refrain from undertakings which exceed their rights and to warn the unwary young women not to comply with what not only offends them but also their families'.[42]

One may view elopement in terms of a challenge. Faced with this challenge to his social prestige, a parent had three possible courses of action, depending on the respective honour of the parties to the challenge. If the challenger was, broadly speaking, his equal in honour, marriage was the adequate solution. If he was inferior in honour, the appropriate action was the criminal's conviction. But if he was his superior in honour, the parent must put up with the shame. This last possibility emerged in cases of seduction. Accordingly, one negro father humbly remarked: 'It is not my intention to bring any action for seduction against D. Antonio Cordovés [a white man] as established by the laws; not because I might offend public morals by using an action that is not reserved to a certain class of people; but because I believe that this would not be in the interests of my daughter.'[43] It is unlikely that he considered his daughter dishonourable. He was, rather, aware of the improbability of obtaining satisfaction in the form of marriage. In fact, the young man denied all the charges although they were amply proved. The girl's father was only realistic in his appraisal of the position, and demanded a form of redress that was more likely to be forthcoming. In this sense, honour defines the boundaries of the in-marrying group.

There is then a fundamental contradiction. While social inequality demanded a high evaluation of virginity, this, under the risk of elopement, implied freedom of choice in marriage which in turn was only admissible under conditions of social equality. It is for this reason that there were necessarily boundaries to the efficacy of elopement. For honour-virtue to be effective as a device to safeguard the social hierarchy, elopement had to succeed at times; but, if it were always allowed to triumph regardless of the social distance obtaining between the partners, the upholding of virginity would ultimately bring about the very situation it was originally intended to prevent, namely total social equality.

### THE HONOUR OF THE COLOURED WOMAN
#### *A double standard of justice and morality*

As has been pointed out, virginity also enjoyed high esteem among coloured people. In sharp contrast with this image of the respectable coloured woman are such statements as 'Talavera is a free *parda* . . . One attributes to her the frailty that is common among women of her kind',[44] or 'although a *parda* she lived respectably',[45] and such proverbs as *no hay tamarindo dulce ni mulata señorita* (there is no sweet tamarind fruit, nor a virgin mulatto girl). These disparaging assessments were made by white men. It may therefore be argued that they were merely the expression of the biased attitude of the white male in his relationship with the coloured woman. It was often the coloured woman who satisfied the sexual needs of the young white man. In a report of 1863 on the advisability of introducing a register for prostitutes in order to fight venereal disease, it was argued that because of the existence of a number of women who only sporadically offered their sexual services, such a register would be ineffective:

the young men who are not yet of age or still live under the tutelage of others and those who keep some respect for public opinion yield only occasionally to an opportunity or temptation without going out to look for it, and try to hide their weakness and prefer to resort to less known and more discreet women.

Such opportunities were probably not all that scarce for

this class [the slaves] engages in domestic service and very many other of the vilest occupations [and] is in frequent and at times very close contact with the higher classes; its women enjoy as such the greatest freedom and as a result of their condition neither observe scrupulous principles of morality nor regard their favours very highly . . . If we go on from the slave population, both African and *mestizo*, to the free coloureds, we will find another numerous and equally uncontrollable group of prostitutes . . . who are no better as regards their moral qualities.[46]

Cirilo Villaverde in his novel *Cecilia Valdés*, a critical account of society in nineteenth-century Havana, gives an excellent description of the predicament of the coloured woman. Cecilia Valdés, a *parda*, is courted by a young white man of good family. She is the product of an affair the young man's father had with a coloured woman which he has succeeded in keeping secret, and the young people therefore do no know that they are half-brother and half-sister. She is of very light complexion. The young man promises her marriage, succeeds in gaining her favours but in the end marries a girl in his own class. Cecilia Valdés is not only an instance of a coloured woman victimized by the white man but also a casualty of the social system. She had a suitor, *pardo* like herself, but had always rejected him in preference for someone better. She prided herself on her white features, and, misjudging the social system, believed that she could escape. She admits this quite openly: 'of course I like the whites better than the *pardos* . . . I would blush with shame if I married and had a throw-back for a son.' Her *parda* friend Nemesia is much more realistic in her assessment of their chances vis-à-vis white men. She tells Cecilia to bear in mind *señá* Clara, a friend of theirs who keeps telling them that 'each one should keep to his own kind'. When Cecilia pretends not to understand she elaborates the point further:

Doesn't *señá* Clara have more experience than we? Of course. She is older and has seen more of the world than you and I. Well, if she so often repeats this proverb, she must have good reason for it. Here, between us, nobody told me this but I know that *señá* Clara always preferred the whites to the *pardos*, but all the same she married *señó* Uribe. She got more burns and has had more disillusions than hair on her head and this is why she now consoles herself by telling girls like you and me 'each one with his own kind'.[47]

As a remedy, the report on ways and means to curtail the effects of prostitution suggested education and work opportunities for coloured women. Bachiller y Morales in 1864 more correctly attributed the moral corruption of the coloured woman to the double standard of morality prevailing. He argued that the seductions by whites of coloured women and their consequent demoralization would diminish drastically 'if the seducers were subjected to the general laws which demand that this type of offence be repaired through marriage. If the castes were always granted this right and not only in exceptional cases, the hope of marriage would be a means of avoiding the lewdness of coloured women.'[48] Normally, a coloured woman had little chance of redress in her relationship with a white man. Even if the man in question was willing to honour his obliga-tion, it was often the case that his family, sharing the general evaluation of the coloured woman's honour, would be opposed, not to mention the obstacle posed by the requirement of official licence for interracial marriages.[49] In a society such as this, it was, however, more likely that white men from the very beginning felt free of any responsibility. Although there is no evidence that the laws on elopement and seduction were not applicable to free coloureds, in practice, as Bachiller y Morales indicates, it was difficult for a coloured person to enforce these laws against a white.[50]

Doubtless, such frustrated marriages were bound to have a demoralizing effect on coloured women. Marriage remained the ideal also among the coloured people: 'she had the greatest confidence in her son Jacinto who is married in the Church and has a family which bestows honour and morality on him', said a coloured mother.[51] Another parent rejected a proposal by a white man to live in concubinage with his *parda* daughter and demanded that they 'marry in Church'.[52] Concubinage, however, was frequent and so was the so-called matrifocal family: 'everywhere adultery and concubinage persist, largely between white men and mulatto women, producing an excessive number of natural offspring, which, with the exception of a few who are recognized by their progenitors, it can be said have neither family nor society, for this consists of no more than a mother'.[53] The marriage rate of the coloured population was noticeably lower than that of whites. Among the whites marriage appears as the norm, among the coloureds concubinage is as frequent as marriage.[54]

Significantly, those who wanted to draw attention to the dangers of interracial marriage often talked only of coloured men wanting to marry white women, although in reality the reverse was more common. Parental opposition to such hypogamous unions was fierce. This is explained by the fact that women were regarded as the true perpetuators of the lineage. This notion of women as the link between the generations emerges also from the legislation regarding the so-called 'crimes against honesty' and specifically adultery. It dealt extremely rigorously with infringing women but very leniently with men: 'a sensible and just differentiation [in a hierarchical society] because apart from the consequences of any infidelity between spouses in weakening social bonds, in attacking good manners, in introducing war and discord into the home, *the woman can bring bastards to the marriage*'.[55] This inequality was perfectly logical. Consequently hypergamy was more tolerated. Yet, even if opinion was on the whole more lenient towards hypergamy, parental opposition could be just as intransigent. D. José Antonio Ramírez's father is a case in point. The young man had eloped with his bride, upon which both families agreed that they should marry

provided they were equal in class; but as it now turns out from the certificate of baptism of the young girl . . . that her mother is a free *parda*, the young Ramírez's

father withdraws his consent and opposes the marriage claiming that if his son had
been visiting the young girl's home and had run away with her, it was only because
he thought her white, because for such they had been passing themselves off in this
neighbourhood.[56]

As a corollary of the central role played by female honour, man's
sexual conduct was of less social consequence. Hence hypergenation,
that is procreation between upper-class men and lower-class women,
could be tolerated and did not constitute a menace to group integrity.
These hypergamous affairs, however, by necessity had to remain extra-
legal, for their honour-precedence forbade upper-class men to formalize
these unions in marriage. As one white man asserted, when exhorted by
the local parish priest to marry his negro girl: 'he has never thought of
marriage, and although he does have an affair with her, this affair has
neither been nor can it be sufficient reason to marry her on account of the
immense class distance, nor is it necessary for neither does the *morena*
[negress] herself intend nor want to get married'.[57] This trend was reinforced on the other hand by the desire on the part of the coloured
women to advance socially through whitening according to the maxim
'rather mistress of a white than wife of a negro'. If one adds to this the
more immediate impact of slavery on the status-consciousness of the
coloured woman – prostitution was one of the ways to obtain the means
to buy their freedom, and concubinage with the master to improve their
living conditions – the truth behind such sayings as 'there is no sweet
tamarind fruit nor a virgin mulatto girl' becomes clear.[58]

As to coloured men, the lack of honour of their women severely
undermined their role as their guardians, and had as a consequence their
own laxity in matters of sexual conduct. Revealing of the coloured man's
sexual frustration is the remark attributed to a mulatto that 'he wished
the revolution [1868] would come to this village so that he could enjoy
many white girls'.[59] Even if the young mulatto was falsely accused of
this expression of rebellion, at least those whites who put it into his
mouth were well aware of his likely frustration. There was thus a clear
gradation of honour-virtue which ran parallel to that of social status.

At this point the general lines of the argument may be restated. It has been
shown that elopement was an institutionalized means to overcome
parental dissent to marriage. The reasons that induced parents to oppose
a given marriage were as a rule the product of their desire to preserve
family honour in terms of social status. Family honour and individual
honour were intimately related. Dishonourable conduct on the part of

one of its members directly affected the prestige of all the relatives. From this it is concluded that nineteenth-century Cuba was a rigidly stratified social order in which ascription and only secondarily personal achievement defined an individual's place in society.

This preoccupation with heredity was lent additional force by an acute anxiety over racial purity that had characterized Spanish culture over the previous centuries and that in Cuba gained new vigour on account of slavery.[60] It was this emphasis on family origin coupled with the continual efforts made to preserve family status through social class endogamy that was designed ideally to grant the system the necessary permanence.

The high evaluation of female honour, positively sanctioned by Catholic morality, effectively provided a suitable mechanism to control marriage. Family integrity was preserved through the protection of the moral integrity of its women. Consequently, and presumably in part for biological reasons, it was through women that family attributes were transmitted from generation to generation. Men, in their role as the guardians of the family's women, fulfilled only the supporting function of seeing to the socially satisfactory transfer of these attributes.

At the level of ideology, the emphasis on social class endogamy as the prescribed form of marriage must be seen as the manifestation of a hierarchical view of society, whereas elopement, by rejecting the established social criteria of choice of spouse, constituted a timid assertion of individual freedom and equality and thus became a direct challenge to the system. It was because of this fundamental contradiction that limits had to be set to the efficacy of elopement. Thus honour, conceived as a device to guarantee group integrity, delimited its boundaries.

CHAPTER 8

# CONCLUSION:
# SOME ANALYTICAL COMPARISONS

This acute preoccupation with individual and family honour is by no
means restricted to nineteenth-century Cuba. These are values which
seem to have played a central role not only in Spain but also in other
European countries before the nineteenth century. Contemporary literature gives evidence of this. Unfortunately, few attempts have so far been
made at a systematic sociological study of these concepts. It is only
recently that a few anthropologists working in the Mediterranean area
have endeavoured to reach an understanding of the concepts of honour
and shame in terms of the social order in which they prevailed.[1] Before
attempting to draw some parallels between nineteenth-century Cuba and
these Mediterranean societies, and suggesting a more general explanation,
a short review of these studies is necessary.

### HONOUR IN THE MEDITERRANEAN

I shall concern myself mainly with Campbell's, Pitt-Rivers' and Lisón's
studies, and in them specifically with the female aspect of honour.[2] While
being well aware of distinctions between these communities and nineteenth-century Cuba, there are nevertheless certain parallels which seem
to make such an analytical comparison worthwhile.

   J. K. Campbell, in his study of the Sarakatsani, a Greek shepherd community, aims at explaining the resolution of the conflict between their
conceptualization and implementation of honour on the one hand, and
their religious ideals on the other. Sarakatsani hold two systems of values:
one social, which prescribes as a paramount duty of all men the defence
of family prestige vis-à-vis all other families, the result being a permanent
competition for honour; and one religious, which espouses the brother-
hood of all men before God. The community consists of a group of
families. Essential to the family's honour is the conduct and reputation of
its women. Sanctions on deviant behaviour by women are rigorous:
the penalty for sexual immodesty is said to be death.[3]

Lisón, in his study of a Spanish town, portrays a slightly less restricted picture. Women are expected to behave with modesty. Although sexual aggressiveness is said to be an important source of male prestige, its satisfaction will never be achieved at the cost of a virgin. And if a woman should forget her duty, she is liable to face expulsion from the village. Yet marriage may in part repair the damage done.[4]

Pitt-Rivers, in his study of honour in Andalusia, draws a similar picture as regards village and middle-class honour. The ideal of female purity is attained in the village through the vigilance of men whose honour-precedence depends importantly on the sexual virtue of the women of their families. The sanction for dishonourable conduct is the loss of shame and consequently of social worth. A distinction seems to be made, however, between outright shameless women, that is prostitutes, and women who have had the misfortune to be seduced and abandoned. The loss of family honour through the loss of a daughter's virginity may be remedied through marriage. Yet the idea that Pitt-Rivers conveys is that on the whole, as regards female honour, practice coincides with the ideal at the village level. And this is so because it is a face-to-face community. Public opinion reigns supreme. Social status is achieved through virtuous conduct, it is not ascribed. The possession of shame defines the limits of the community. In contrast, the women of the aristocracy are said to enjoy a high degree of sexual freedom. For one thing, they are outside the boundaries of the village, and its sanctions have no effect on them. But also, their honour is 'impregnable' in the sense that it is social status obtained by birth and not an honour achieved by personal conduct and therefore requiring defence by men.[5]

Female virtue is thus the ideal in all three communities, and on it family honour depends. What varies from one to the other is the rigour of the sanctions applied on deviant behaviour. Among the Sarakatsani the penalty for dishonour is death. In Belmonte de los Caballeros it is expulsion from the village. In the Andalusian village it appears on the one hand that marriage with the seducer is an acceptable solution, and on the other that unmarried mothers may be received back into their families. I shall come back to this point.

As to the explanations offered by these authors, Peristiany, the editor of a collection of essays on honour and shame in the Mediterranean,[6] tentatively suggests that these values 'are the constant preoccupation of individuals in small-scale, exclusive societies where face-to-face personal as opposed to anonymous, relations are of paramount importance',[7] a view which, as has been seen, is also shared by Pitt-Rivers who argues that 'the smaller the community the more effectively' do sanctions operate. Therefore 'honour has gone to the village'.[8] However, although nineteenth-century Cuba certainly cannot be characterized as a small-scale, exclusive society, it can surely be safely asserted that there also public opinion was the arbiter of personal conduct. I believe that the question to be asked is not so much how personal conduct is sanctioned, but why. I suggest that an answer to this question may be found in the nature of the social order in which these values obtain.

As has been shown, nineteenth-century Cuba was a hierarchical society in which family origin was an important status determinant. A correlation between social class and honour obtained. It was precisely the women of the lowest stratum, that is the coloured women, who had least honour. Among the Sarakatsani a 'hierarchy of prestige' exists 'based upon a fairly precise knowledge of the genealogy, wealth, moral character and conduct of each family'.[9] The poor are not granted recognition of their merits, for, as Campbell states, 'all Sarakatsani are born with honour into families of honour ... with the exception of those persons in certain families at the lowest level of the prestige hierarchy'.[10] Moreover, the conflict felt to exist by the Sarakatsani between the religious and the secular norms, as in Cuba, seems to result precisely from the pursuit of a hierarchical ideal standing in direct opposition to religious doctrine which is basically egalitarian.

Equally, Pitt-Rivers in his brief discussion of elopement in his Andalusian village and the defied parent's unwillingness to agree to the desired marriage on account of the daughter's suitor's social incompatibility,[11] offers evidence of a differential evaluation of honour within the village itself depending on an individual's place in the social hierarchy. And Lisón talks explicitly of 'endogamy of social position'.[12] On the basis of these indications I would maintain that, as with nineteenth-century Cuba, we are dealing here with hierarchical rather than with homogeneous societies, and that family origin plays a major role in determining a person's status within society.

What matters in these communities is at least to maintain one's position within the gradation of social positions. And this is basically achieved through isogamic marriage, which in its turn is ensured through exercising a strict control over female sexuality. In this light, religious doctrine, which especially in Greece and in the Aragonese village prescribes female sexual virtue, rather than being the origin of its high esteem fulfils a complementary function in the sense of reinforcing a value which is essential for the survival of the social order. That religion in this connection is not a primary fact is also shown in the Andalusian case. Though the Andalusians are notoriously poor Catholics, female honour there plays as important a part as in the other communities.

I would then suggest that the distinctive characteristic of these communities is not their size or the lack of anonymity of interpersonal relations. What appears to be important is the manner of status determination directly linked to the nature of the social structure.[13] As has been seen, Pitt-Rivers also alludes to this as part of his explanation when he refers to the upper-class women, though in the reverse sense. In Cuba, and so it seems also in the other societies, ascription and only secondarily personal performance seems to define an individual's place within the status hierarchy of the community. Family prestige and that of its members are intimately related and personal conduct is the source of great concern to the entire family. If personal achievement alone were the determinant of status, each family member could be allowed freedom to forge his own place in society, and his conduct would be irrelevant to the prestige of his relatives. This is also implicit in Rivière's analysis of The Children of Sanchez.[14] In the more mobile context of Mexico City individual performance comes partially to replace ascription as a status determinant, and consequently female honour as an index of family prestige decreases in significance. Furthermore, the hereditary principle as the primary status determinant implies permanence, which is the prerequisite for a hierarchical social order. I suggest then that the value attached to virginity is inversely proportional to the degree of social mobility and thus of individual freedom obtaining in a social order. That is to say, in an unstratified egalitarian society no restraints should be applied to its women's sexual freedom.

To restate clearly the steps of my argument: Nineteenth-century Cuba was a hierarchical society. The explanation for the system of stratification obtaining must be sought in its economic base characterized by a highly unequal distribution of the means of production. This unequal distribution of resources was preserved by an emphasis on heredity, with regard both to property as well as to status, coupled with a class endogamous marriage pattern. As Nur Yalman pointed out, 'where affiliation is through one parent only, status differences can be kept up by unilineal pedigrees without recourse to endogamy rules'.[15] In Cuba, however, filiation was bilateral. Thus the control over the choice of spouse was fundamental for the maintenance of the system. The control over the choice of marriage partners can be carried out in different ways, for instance through child marriage, a rigid segregation of the youngsters before marriage, etc.[16] In

Cuba it was achieved through strict control over female sexuality. This is not to say that a hierarchical social system always presupposes an emphasis on female purity, but rather that where there is such an emphasis this is generally related to the existence of status groups.

To come back to the varying rigour of the sanctions applied on deviations by women from established conduct in these different contexts. The relative importance of ascription or achievement as status determinants is a question of degree. I would suggest that the varying severity of the penalties on deviant behaviour by women is directly related to the relevance of family origin as a source of status. Moreover, the greater the stability and the higher the level of consensus in the society, the less likely are infractions of the norm. Under such circumstances, drastic penalties such as death would affect only a very few and thus be viable, apart from contributing by their very rigour to preserving the stability of the system. This might be the case of the Sarakatsani. Nineteenth-century Cuba, however, was marked by the lack of consensus, as manifested in the elopement, and by a degree of social fluidity. Had such deviations from the norm of female purity been punished by death, the society would clearly have become unviable.

A further point can be derived from this structural similarity between the ethnically homogeneous Mediterranean peasant communities and multiracial nineteenth-century Cuba, namely that ultimately race relations are class relations.[17] As an old Spanish epigram has it:

> Tienen los que pobres son
> la ventura del cabrito.
> O morir cuando chiquito,
> o llegar a ser cabrón.

('The poor have the same fortune as the kid; to die in infancy or to grow up to be he-goats.' *Cabrón* has the double meaning of he-goat and cuckold.)[18]

## MATRIFOCALITY IN THE CARIBBEAN

As has been shown, as a consequence of the correlation between social status and honour, lower-class women lack honour, and their unions with upper-class men will generally be relegated to the realm of illegality. At this point it seems appropriate to recall the Bishop of Havana's appraisal of the coloured woman's predicament in nineteenth-century Cuba: 'everywhere adultery and concubinage persist, largely between white men and mulatto women, producing an excessive number of natural offspring, which, with the exception of a few who are recognized by their progenitors, it can be said have neither family nor society, for this consists of no more than a mother'.[19] A further consequence of the gradation of honour is the instability of the lower-class woman's family.

Much has been written on the so-called 'matrifocal' family in the multi-racial societies of the Southern States of America and the Caribbean. This is not the place to discuss at length the various interpretations given for this phenomenon. Suffice it to review briefly the most recent studies on family organization in the Caribbean as a background against which to explain my own view.

A basic assumption underlies all these studies, namely the idea of the social, economic and cultural homogeneity of the Caribbean area deriving from its common past as slave societies and its African heritage. Some authors have regarded this particular type of family organization as a modified form of African cultural survival,[20] others as the product of the disruptive effect on the slave family of the conditions obtaining on the plantations run with slave labour.[21] The approach of these early students was basically historical. Still others, taking a structural-functional view, have interpreted matrifocality as the consequence of the relations of production characteristic of post-slavery plantation systems. The first systematic studies of family organization, in particular communities in the Caribbean, are those carried out by R. T. Smith in British Guiana and by E. Clarke in Jamaica.[22] Both of them attribute the prevalence of matrifocality, that is female-headed households, to the current social and economic conditions which make for economic insecurity and consequently low social status of the males which in turn undermines their socially expected roles as husbands and fathers. As Clarke asserts:

The important point for an understanding of the contemporary situation is that conditions which make it impossible for men to perform the roles of father and husband as these roles are defined in the society to which they belong, persist in present-day Jamaica and it is in conditions as we find them today that we shall most profitably look for the explanation of the 'unstable' features of family life to which such prominence is being given.[23]

On the basis of intensive field studies of three rural communities she then discovers a correlation between economic stability and frequency of legal marriage.

R. T. Smith's study is in a sense more ambitious, for whereas Clarke seeks her explanation in the socio-economic factors intrinsic to the communities studied, Smith maintains that the working of the three Guianese communities he investigated can only be understood fully if they are treated as part of total Guianese society. He concludes that 'the matrifocal system of domestic relations and household groupings . . . can be regarded as the obverse of the marginal nature of the husband–father role'.[24] This marginality of the male is determined by the nature of the Guianese social order which R. T. Smith defines as being a colour/class system. At both ends of the social hierarchy status is basically ascriptive and consequently static, determined essentially by racial criteria. Low racial-cum-social status implies an equally low occupational status. As a result of this social and economic immobility, the husband–father's role as the economic head of the family and his status-determining function is annulled. Consequently he is only head of the family as long as the wife is absolutely dependent on him for her subsistence, that is while the children are small, but becomes gradually marginalized throughout the developmental cycle of the family, his basic functions then being taken over by the wife–mother.

Edith Clarke and R. T. Smith thus arrive at basically the same conclusions: (*a*) it is the specific socio-economic role assigned to the male in these communities that determines the type of family organization obtaining in them; and (*b*) the role assigned to these men is in turn determined by the socio-economic nature of their society.

M. G. Smith, in an introduction to the second edition to Clarke's study, severely criticizes R. T. Smith on several counts.[25] I shall not take up this controversy in all its details, but there are a few points which are pertinent here. In contrast to R. T. Smith, M. G. Smith maintains that a social phenomenon must be analysed with primary reference to its internal constitution before attempting a study of its articulation with the wider social system.[26] Accordingly, his study of West Indian family structure[27] is above all an attempt at defining the problem, establishing a typology of family forms and discovering the internal mechanisms governing them.

It is on the point of definition of the family that the two authors diverge fundamentally. R. T. Smith bases his definition on co-residence of the couple. Thus he equates household unit with family unit, and his discussion of matrifocality turns essentially around the progressive switch of authority from the husband–father to the wife–mother throughout the developmental cycle of the family, rather than around those units which lack a male from the start, and its causes. The 'matrifocal' family is defined in terms of the distribution of authority rather than of the actual physical absence of a husband–father. And, most important, the matrifocal family is not conceived as an alternative choice to a 'patrifocal' family, but as a form which evolves from the latter in a developmental process which most families undergo. Men start out with the best of intentions to constitute a stable family, but owing to socio-economic factors are later hindered from fulfilling this aim.

M. G. Smith, by contrast, defines the matrifocal family as a unit often resulting precisely from the absence of intent to establish a stable family. He regards the various forms of family organization as possible alternatives determined by the type of mating resorted to. The mating system is the central formative principle of the family structure. Marriage and concubinage are two different choices producing two formally distinct types of family organization. Although concubinage may evolve into marriage, the two mating forms may also constitute alternative arrangements. It is significant here that R. T. Smith denies any normative distinction between marriage and concubinage. Taking co-residence as an essential feature of the family, he has no place in his developmental cycle for what M. G. Smith terms extra-residential mating and its consequences in terms of family organization.

The type of material underlying the present study is insufficient to establish a comprehensive typology of family forms in nineteenth-century Cuba. Nevertheless, some suggestions are possible relating to the questions debated by the two Smiths. As the Bishop of Havana pointed out, 'matrifocality' in Cuba was often precisely the result of the particular type of mating characteristic of interracial unions, which in its turn was the consequence of the coloured woman's marginality within the gradation of honour of the global society. These unions could be relatively stable and even occasionally end in marriage. However, they could just as well be temporary extra-residential unions ending in abandonment of the coloured woman in preference for a spouse of the man's own class. Concubinage was thus often an alternative to marriage resorted to in cases of social incompatibility of the partners.[28] Admittedly, given the social stratification and economic system of Cuba at the time the social distance between whites and coloured people was extreme. Both R. T. Smith and Clarke, however, deal with predominantly negro communities in a post-slavery situation. Yet, as the analysis of elopement among free coloureds in Cuba has revealed, far from being a socially homogeneous group, it was wrought by acute conflicts over status, with similar effects on family organization as in the case of interracial relationships. It seems to me that all three, the two Smiths and Clarke, have not paid due attention to the possible gradations of status within the communities they studied.

Thus, as regards family forms and their organizational principle, my material tends to support M. G. Smith's thesis that it is the form of mating that determines the particular types of family obtaining in a society. I would add to this that the mating form is in turn determined by the relative social position of the partners to the union. It might be necessary to distinguish between matrifocality in R. T. Smith's sense originating from a union between low-class partners entered into with the intent of permanence but characterized by the gradual marginalization of the man, and extra-residential mating between socially unequal partners initiated without intent to marry. Although I would suggest that the latter has an effect on the former, this still leaves us to account for the predominance of one form of mating rather than another. Despite his initial reluctance to seek an explanation in extrinsic factors, in the end M. G. Smith resorts to them as well when he asserts that 'the persistence of high illegitimacy rates, unstable unions, and anomalous forms of domestic groups in the West Indies are all due to the same conditions. These conditions had their historical origin in slavery, especially in the mating organization of slaves.'[29]

My own work deals mainly with the social placing of the free coloureds in the Cuban slave society, which is undoubtedly determined in the last resort by the needs of the slave regime. Yet, while M. G. Smith regards the West Indian mating forms as the immediate product of slavery, in the Cuban case, and significantly while slavery still existed, it appears rather as a mediate result. The existence of slavery produced a social order which assigned to the coloured people, whether slaves or free, the lowest rank in the social hierarchy. In order to perpetuate this hierarchy it was essential to proscribe marriage between the dominant and the dominated groups. Yet, partly for demographic reasons, white men had to resort to the coloured community for women. By virtue of the hierarchical nature of the society these unions as a rule took on the form of sporadic or stable concubinage. Both the free and slave women acquiesced in this inferior form of mating because, due to the racial overtones of the system, it was a most effective means of social advance to them and particularly to their offspring. The principle of hypergenation applied as well to intraracial unions.

It is thus the hierarchical nature of the social order that in the final analysis produces the coloured woman's sexual marginalization, affects her forms of mating and expresses itself in the preponderance of con-cubinage and matrifocality. I would thus propose that, whenever the social order is rigidly stratified and group integrity is ultimately safe-guarded through its women, yet accompanied by an absence of consensus as to the legitimacy of the social order so that constant bids

are made by the lower ranks for social advancement, such a marginalization of the lower-class women obtains. The Spanish epigram quoted
above is pertinent. And in the *Romance de la Guirnalda* a girl who has lost
her honour at the hands of a gentleman tells her mother, 'it is better to
have a good friend than be badly married' (*que más vale buen amigo que
no ser mal maridada*). Moreover, as shown in the Cuban case, the low
social status of the coloured man is equally the consequence of this type
of social order. He does not become gradually marginalized throughout
the familial developmental cycle on account of his poor performance in
economic and status terms, but, according to the proverb 'rather mistress
of a white man than wife of a negro', has no chance from the start, and is
often already rejected in the struggle for social advancement at the
moment of mating.

Crucial in this debate is the evaluation of the different family forms by
the actors themselves. R. T. Smith maintains that there was no normative
distinction between marriage and concubinage, a view which is questioned
by M. G. Smith. My material again supports M. G. Smith's impression.
Also among the coloured people and despite its low frequency, marriage
enjoyed high esteem, that is marriage and concubinage were regarded
as actual alternatives. Hyman Rodman's concept of 'value stretch'[30]
appears useful to understand this apparent conflict between ideal and
practice. In this light marriage and concubinage are in the eyes of the
actors not two diametrically opposed norms: marriage is the preferred
form, yet due to the nature of the society concubinage is conceived as an
acceptable alternative. My cases of elopement among coloured people
contain regrettably little information on the socio-economic position of
the families involved, but it may be assumed that they belonged to the
most privileged stratum of the coloured community, which despite their
colour had achieved a certain social placing, and in order to legitimize
this position had, more than the lower strata, been subjected to the
dominant white sector's cultural hegemony, at the same time possessing
the means and the reasons to behave in accordance with their system of
values. That is to say, marriage was the ideal among both the upper and
the lower strata, yet the latter 'stretched' their values to include concubinage as well, to them as socially acceptable as marriage.

Rodman's concept of 'value stretch' was conceived as an alternative
to the view of those who approached the lower-class value system from
the middle- or upper-class perspective and thus characterized it as a
deviation from the norm and consequently as anomalous. While making
the point that the lower-class norms as exemplified in their family

forms are an alternative, Rodman, however, does not explain the sociological reasons for this 'stretching'.

Rivière and Campbell also point to the split between ideal and practice at the lower end of the social hierarchy, determined by the exigencies of the system: 'once a chink has appeared in the armour it gradually widens',[31] remarks Rivière, and Campbell states that 'certain of their number lose heart and are no longer concerned to act honourably'.[32]

Borah and Cook's statement,[33] to which Mörner also draws attention,[34] that in colonial Mexico 'although informal and irregular unions were a prominent feature of custom in the Spanish cities it should not be forgotten that most people did marry in accordance with church requirements',[35] would seem to contradict the above thesis, if one bears in mind the ethnic composition of colonial Mexico and the low socio-economic status of Indians and negroes. Yet it appears that, while in the ethnically homogeneous areas 'almost all Indians married early and in formal church ceremonies',[36] in those areas where there was racial mixture illegitimacy was high.[37] That is to say, in colonial Mexico also, in those areas where the social distance was marked, concubinage took the place of marriage and became an accepted form of conjugal union.

It is thus in the sociological factors deriving from the type of social order which prevailed in the colonial period, where the lower classes on account of their ethnic-cum-economic and social inferior status were sexually marginalized by the dominant sector, that one must seek the reasons for the family forms obtaining in the post-colonial period, and not so much in the labour relations characteristic of plantation systems productive of economic marginality or male absenteeism,[38] and much less even in Oscar Lewis' 'culture of poverty',[39] one of whose traits would be the informal and unstable nature of its conjugal unions, and the consequent matrifocality of the family.

### CASTE IN INDIA AND RACE IN AMERICA

The nature of the Cuban system of stratification can best be elucidated by a comparison with a social system markedly different from it in structural terms. Nineteenth-century Cuban society, though hierarchical, contained important egalitarian elements. Two alternative models of social stratification are a purely egalitarian or an exclusively hierarchical social system.

Dumont's model of hierarchy as presented in his recent study of the Hindu caste system would seem apposite for purposes of comparison.

## Conclusion: Some analytical comparisons

As Dumont himself suggests: 'the castes teach us a fundamental social principle, hierarchy. We, in our modern society, have adopted the principle contrary to it, but it is not without value for understanding the nature, limits and conditions of realization of the moral and political egalitarianism to which we are attached.'[40] Moreover, repeated attempts have been made in the past to draw parallels between American race relations and Hindu caste relations. Nineteenth-century Cuban society has never been analysed strictly in terms of caste. But, it seems to me, the difference between race relations in the Deep South and in Cuba is one of degree rather than of kind. The underlying principles of social organization are the same. Thus, any significant distinction that can be discovered between Cuban race relations and Hindu caste relations would be of relevance also for an understanding of race in the Deep South. A fruitful point of departure for such a comparison might be the respective systems of social classification.

Dumont attempts to prove the overall unity of India by abandoning the level of social action and focusing his attention on the 'spirit of the system'. He feels that one must seek the ultimate explanation of social action in the underlying operating principles, which in the Indian case he maintains are essentially hierarchical. Hence he concludes that hierarchy, being the primary principle governing the caste system, subsumes all other operating principles.

As he shows, in Hindu India the hierarchical distinctions can be reduced to one fundamental opposition which 'encompasses' all others, namely that of purity–impurity.[41] It is a dichotomic scheme. In the eyes of some sectors of Cuban society such a dichotomic scheme should be implemented in Cuba as well. One principle, the social division of labour, should systematically split society into two opposing groups, such as:

| | |
|---|---|
| slaves | *v.* free |
| coloureds | *v.* whites |
| Africans | *v.* Europeans |
| New Christians | *v.* Old Christians |
| manual workers | *v.* non-manual workers |
| poor | *v.* rich |
| plebeians | *v.* nobles (*hidalgos*) |
| illegitimates | *v.* legitimates |
| of impure blood | *v.* of pure blood |
| infamous | *v.* with honour |
| mixed | *v.* unmixed |

In all of Spanish America efforts were made to make these attributes coincide. As Solórzano, speaking of *mestizos* and mulattos said, 'generally they are born in adultery and in other illicit and ugly unions, because there are few Spaniards of honour who marry Indians or Negroes. This defect of their birth makes them infamous [to which are added] the stain of different colour and other vices',[42] thus equating racial mixture, illegitimacy and infamy. And again the Cabildo of Caracas in 1788 asserted that '*pardos*, mulattos and *zambos* ... have the infamous origin of slavery and the disgraceful one of illegitimacy'.[43] In this case slavery is equated with infamy and illegitimacy. Or inversely, as a member of the Council of the Indies remarked in 1806, 'it is reprehensible in the extreme that the sons or descendants of slaves known as such should sit and alternate with those who descend from the first Conquerors or from families that are noble, legitimate, white and devoid of any ugly stain'.[44] Nobility implied legitimacy, whiteness and purity. Similarly, it was pointed out in 1772 that 'foundlings are not only noble but also legitimate by virtue of the possible contingency that having been born within wedlock their *hidalgo* parents abandoned them at the door of a Church or other place'.[45] Here 'nobility' is presumably used in the sense of purity of blood which is equated with legitimacy. The Cabildo of Buenos Aires towards the end of the eighteenth century, when drawing up the *ordenanzas de gremios*, pointed out that several poor Spanish families 'do not apprentice their sons to trades so they they will not mix with those of another caste'.[46] And in 1805 mention is made of the 'general preoccupation of the genteel families [of New Spain] who choose to live in idleness and misery rather than take up any of those occupations [mechanical trades] which are generally reputed as infamous':[47] honourable families do not engage in manual skills to preserve their honour, for *oficios mecánicos* (mechanical trades) are infamous.

However, whereas in Hindu India 'there is one hierarchy and there can, therefore, be only one kind of status',[48] in Cuba in practice the hierarchy of social positions was not a 'simple gradation'[49] where exclusively one criterion determined its order. The lack of complete correspondence between the various sets of distinctions meant the open nature of Cuban society. There were, for instance, free coloureds, white manual workers, legitimate coloureds, rich coloureds. Although ascription, that is birth, was regarded as very important in determining an individual's place in society, personal achievement was approved of as a legitimate means of social advance. This interplay between ascriptive and achieved status criteria is exemplified most clearly by the process of mutual status compensation, where even 'racial' attributes could within limits be offset by economic attributes. An individual's social position did not derive from each factor independently, but was determined by the combination of all. All this applies to the free coloureds. Slaves, however, could neither be rich nor white nor of pure blood nor noble – the free coloureds could on occasion achieve some of these qualities by means of the so-called *gracias al sacar*.

As in India there was also in Cuba a fundamental principle of classification, namely the social division of labour, yet whereas the Indian distinction of the pure and the impure was generally approved of as being in the interest of the totality, in Cuba the division of labour was open to challenge.

However, more significant than the mere formal distinction between a simple and a synthetic gradation (where there is an interplay of attributes) is what this distinction says about the social consciousness behind it. In Cuba two alternative views of society obtained, one hierarchical which divided society into slaves and free, blacks and whites; but also an egalitarian one which declared 'all people equal before God'. As has been shown, secular interests as a rule prevailed over the mandates of religious doctrine. On the other hand, both as a result of the Enlightenment as well as for politico-economic reasons, egalitarianism gained some ground in the secular realm, so that a lieutenant governor could say approvingly in 1861 that 'the [white] proletariat treats the coloured class with the most perfect equality'.[50] It is in this ideological dualism that the explanation for the failure to enforce a dichotomic division of nineteenth-century Cuban society must be sought.

The fundamentally conflictive nature of nineteenth-century Cuban society as opposed to the high degree of consensus obtaining in Hindu caste society can be further elucidated through a comparison of marriage in the two contexts. According to Dumont, endogamy is no more than 'a corollary of hierarchy'[51] rather than vice-versa. On this basic premise Dumont then proceeds to analyse the deviations from the endogamic rule to show how rather than disrupting the integrity of the system, in the final analysis they partake of its very spirit.

There is the primary or principal marriage contracted between equals in caste status, which confers full caste membership and all rights and obligations this implies on the spouses and their offspring. But in some parts of India a secondary, subsidiary marriage is also permissible, which allows a great measure of freedom of choice of spouse. This latter marriage is of notably inferior status with regard to the first and so are its offspring.

This leads Dumont to conclude that rather than calling for as drastic a measure as excommunication, these secondary marriages are thus sanctioned by a degradation in status.[52] The consequence of this hierarchization of marriage itself is the existence within the endogamic unit of some measure of status gradation as well.

Another apparent exception to the endogamic pattern occurs in some parts of northern India, in the form of obligatory hypergamy, i.e. the union of a slightly inferior woman to a superior man at the time of the primary marriage, without this affecting the status of the offspring.[53] Dumont relates this type of marriage to the Brahmanic idea of the 'gift of a maiden' in order to show once more the interplay of statuses that takes place within the endogamic unit. Thus 'one gives a daughter and goods to a superior in exchange, not in this case for spiritual merits, but for something similar, namely the prestige or consideration which results from intermarriage with him'.[54] The hypothetical status decrease involved for a man in marrying an inferior woman is neutralized by the prestige he in turn derives from giving women to higher men. It appears that normally these hypergamic marriages take place between sub-castes, yet within the boundaries of the caste. There is then a degree of status differentiation between the sub-castes and between the individual families practising hypergamy which leads Dumont to assert that 'hierarchy, in the form of hypergamy, penetrates in the very core of the institutions of marriage and kinship'.[55] In the same way as endogamy is a concomitant of hierarchy, so is hypergamy, which is integrated into the system according to the same basic principle.

In the Cuban case intraracial marriage appears as the ideal form of marriage according to the norm that 'there cannot be marriage if there is no equality of lineage',[56] the ethnic groups being conceived as the basic endogamic units, the hereditary principle determining their membership and perpetuation. Yet already the legislation intended to enforce this endogamic norm and also its interpretation indicate a degree of ambiguity, which is further substantiated by the actual occurrence and official acceptance of, even if rare, intermarriage.

In India a hierarchization of marriage obtains. By providing an institutional framework in the form of the secondary marriage for those marriages that do not conform to the endogamic norm, they are accommodated within the system. In Cuba, however, there was no such thing as a principal and a secondary marriage in the Hindu sense. For a widow or widower it was just as important to make the right choice as it was when a first marriage was contracted. Attempts had been made in Spain by the secular powers to institute a secondary *alternative* form of marriage for unequal partners, of juridically inferior status. But, the Council of Trent had outlawed this so-called 'secret marriage' as incompatible with Christian doctrine. Only royalty had morganatic marriage available to them. Thus, and despite the Church's endeavours to implement marriage universally, unions between unequals were relegated to the realm of illegality with its concomitant disabilities. The consensual union became the institutionalized arrangement in cases of social incompatibility, accepted as a rule by the secular powers, yet necessarily rejected in principle by the Church. Because marriage meant equality, unequal marriage could not be institutionalized. In Cuba granting equal status to unequal marriages would have posed a serious threat to the social system. Conversely, instituting an inferior type of marriage for unequal partners was incompatible with religious doctrine. Dumont, however, for the sake of consistency must precisely posit hypergamy as a rule. If one of the characteristics of the Hindu caste system was consensus, then no exceptions could exist.

The institution of the elopement with a view to marriage probably reveals most cogently the fundamental ideological difference between the Cuban and the Hindu social systems. These couples, by rebelling against the prevalent secular view of society, disclose an element in their system of values which allowed such a rebellion. By asserting their individuality they claimed freedom of choice above and beyond the exigencies of the group and the social order at large. They appealed to the high regard for virginity as capable of swaying parents and the authorities to accept an unequal marriage. And they succeeded as long as the distance was not excessive, and necessarily so for the authorities were well aware of the need to prevent a devaluation of virginity as a central value of the system. But when the incompatibility between the partners to such a union was 'racial' the consensual union was the appropriate form of union in the secular view. The Church, however, obliged by its doctrine to enforce virginity, could not approve of this alternative, but had to take active steps to prevent its occurrence. Thus the Church did more than lend support to the value system. It not only admitted equality within the confines of the group, it proclaimed equality of all men before God, and virginity as a value to be enforced whatever the social status of the woman involved. In doing so it went beyond supporting the hierarchical system to challenge its very foundations.

It is this egalitarian element in secular ideology backed by religious doctrine which provided the framework for the couples who in the face of parental opposition resorted to the elopement to achieve marriage. In Dumont's model of hierarchy in Hindu India such a step would have been neither conceivable nor effective. Elopement presupposes the presence of such values as equality, individualism and freedom of choice. It is because these values existed that the slave regime was not regarded as the natural order of things, that the rebellion of the slaves as a real menace could inspire such widespread fears in nineteenth-century Cuba. A general consensus as to the legitimacy of the system did not exist. It was a system imposed by one sector on the other. And although the latter, often for lack of any other alternative, as a rule granted its active consent, aspirations to improve one's status by trespassing the boundaries of one's group were always latent.

This is particularly apparent in marriage. Group endogamy was pre-scribed by the dominant secular interest to perpetuate the hierarchical status quo. Yet, as the applications for interracial marriage licences showed, the endogamic principle was again and again defied. Whereas an Indian is born into a caste, and unless he opts out by choosing the life of a renouncer, also dies in it, in nineteenth-century Cuba a measure of social mobility within the society, precisely not corporate as in India where sub-castes can within limits modify their collective status, but individual, was tolerated. Interracial marriage, though as a rule frowned upon, did exceptionally occur, precisely because consensus as to the legitimacy of strict racial endogamy was absent. Besides, whereas corporate mobility would fundamentally have altered the social order, individual mobility provided a kind of safety-valve for the system.

As in Hindu India, in Cuba too group exogamy as a rule took the form of hypergamy. The reasons for the preference for hypergamy rather than hypogamy have already been set forth. Yet, as has been shown, because there was a feeling that any concessions in the field of marriage were 'against the *almost* fundamental order of the country, the dignity of its families and the acquiescence of the submissive serfs to their status',[57] hypergamy occurred only exceptionally. Dumont distinguishes between marriage and illegitimate unions. Equally, it is necessary to differentiate in the Cuban context between hypergamy, the union of an upper-class man with an inferior woman through marriage, and hypergamous free unions.

In racial terms, and those rejecting even sexual contact in the form of hypergamous free unions reveal an awareness of this, such unions would seem disruptive in their group boundary-blurring effect as well. Mulattos, the living symbols of miscegenation, were regarded with a special kind of unease by those asserting the discontinuity of the racial groups. In this light Cox's statement that 'hypergamy can never become a law in a biracial system, for the system will be doomed from the moment of its enactment'[58] would seem accurate. But in Cuba hypergamous free unions were tolerated and for that matter also in the United States, as the considerable number of mulattos there, despite their denomination as 'blacks', indicates.[59] Also, legal colour as a status-determining criterion was just as important as real colour in assessing a person's social position; as Pichardo's Dictionary said in 1836, '... there are some [mulattos] who are whiter than many of the white race'.[60] As has been pointed out earlier, the Cuban situation was thus not a 'racial' situation, if by race we mean phenotype. Legal colour shows that the basic criterion of social classification was social origin and not physical appearance, and that Cox is wrong in approaching hypergamy in purely 'racial' terms; and for that matter so too are all those who reduce the issue of whether the Hindu caste system is or is not fundamentally of the same nature as the American racial system to a contraposition of caste relations to 'race' relations, rather than class relations. Cox himself suggested that race relations were best studied as a form of class exploitation.[61]

The principle of social classification in both the caste system and race relations is the same, namely heredity. What distinguishes them, however, is the notion of *adelantar la familia* common in Cuba, which is analogous to that of 'passing' in the United States. That this method of social advancement should often be conceived by the people themselves in purely racial terms when they believe that a proportion of white 'blood' will guarantee higher status is no proof of Cox's interpretation: *legal* colour was important in Cuba, where a 'negro' could be whiter than a white. By conceiving of race as a criterion of social stratification in purely physical terms, the resulting groups are given a permanence they do not really possess. It is this reification of 'race' that has led scholars to equate race relations with caste relations.[62]

Also with regard to India a case has been made for explaining the caste system in 'racial' terms. The Indian population has its distant origin in two racially distinct groups, the local Dravidians purportedly of marked negroid features, and the invading Aryans of caucasian appearance. Some scholars argue that mild racism exists in India. Bouglé dismisses this view held by some late nineteenth-century anthropologists: 'the anthropometric measurements of individuals of different castes do not allow us to conclude that the caste hierarchy corresponds to a racial hierarchy'.[63] But he does so by drawing a distinction between the Brahmanic ideal of purity on the one hand, and actual social practice which finds its expression in total racial mixture on the other. He resolved the apparent paradox between the absence of a correlation between social and racial differences and the use of such proverbs as 'Méfiez-vous d'un Paria blanc et d'un Brahmane noir'[64] by maintaining that 'les prohibitions qui remplissent leur codes énoncent les *prétensions* des hautes castes à la pureté'.[65] According to Bouglé, race has become a means for the high castes to legitimate their claim to their place at the top, just as in Cuba, where when real racial differences were absent the dominant sector could resort to legal colour to maintain the status quo. Sixteenth- to eighteenth-century Spain and Nazi Germany are further instances of 'racism' without actual physical differences. By suggesting that in India 'racism' exists independently of actual physical distinctions, Bouglé supports our point that miscegenation does not mean a breakdown of the system as such.

Bouglé makes then two points: there is no 'parallelism between physical and social differences',[66] but there are 'claims to purity of the high castes'.[67] Dumont would, of course, agree that there is no parallelism between caste membership and phenotype, yet, there being general consensus as to the legitimacy of the Brahmans' precedence born of the essentially hierarchical spirit of the caste system, Dumont would disagree that they required *to claim* purity.[68] From Dumont's point of view race and caste are mutually exclusive concepts.

The constant efforts made in Cuba by the coloured sector to advance socially if not themselves at least their offspring by such means as hypergamous free unions and even marriage, and the partial acquiescence on the part of the dominant sector in these methods, reveals that the idea of social mobility existed and that consensus as to the legitimacy of the 'fundamental' nature of the social order was absent. As van den Berghe suggests, correctly at least for the American context: 'the principle involved in hypergenation is maximization of status. Hypergenation will tend to occur when it involves a gain of status for the woman and her children, and no commensurate loss of status for the male partner.'[69] By virtue of the class rather than racial nature of the Cuban social order, hypergamous marriage with its status-maximizing implications could not be approved of as a general rule, while hypergamous free unions, entailing no automatic loss of status by the white male but some social advancement on the part of the inferior woman and her offspring, could be tolerated. That hypergamous marriage did occasionally occur in Cuba was due to the penetration into the secular ideology of egalitarian elements. Yet it never became a rule as in parts of India. Hypergamy as the marriage rule in northern India occurred according to Dumont precisely for the opposite reason: because 'hierarchy, in the form of hypergamy, penetrates in the very core of the institutions of marriage and kinship',[70] and thus into the caste. Formally, hypergamy in Cuba and in India were identical; their meaning, however, was contrary in the two contexts. In Cuba, given that the rule was that like married like, hypergamous marriage meant equality. In northern India, hypergamous marriage being the rule, it meant hierarchy carried into the most intimate spheres of the system.

To return to the race *v.* caste controversy, it is, then, the absence of consensus in the system, born of the conflict between the secular hierarchical claims and the egalitarian and individualistic challenge, in which the essential difference between so-called race relations system and the caste system lies.[71]

## A LAST WORD ON MARRIAGE

In Dumont's model of the Hindu caste system, then, status is entirely ascriptive. In nineteenth-century Cuba the social position of an individual was determined in the first place by his family origin, but achievement could to an extent alter his ascriptive status. The marriage pattern in both contexts was seen to be a corollary of the social structure serving to regularize the inheritance of status. This interdependence between social structure and type of conjugal union – marriage or concubinage – means that a modification of the former should give rise to a corresponding transformation of the latter. Alexandra Kollontai, a militant Bolshevik, pointed out this interdependence when she argued in 1919 that in the new would-be egalitarian order the family ceases to be necessary. Legal marriage was a function of bourgeois society rendered necessary only by the importance attached to property relations. Wilhelm Reich made an attempt to explain the later reversal of family policy in the Soviet Union.[72] He attributed the paradoxical survival of what he called 'compulsive marriage', meaning conventional monogamous marriage, in spite of the abolition of private property and inheritance, to the effects of an authoritarian character structure thousands of years old. Though this explanation is dubious in many respects, Reich did point to an important problem, namely what the nature of a society in which bourgeois marriage and family would disappear is to be.

Another apparent paradox is offered by a country such as Sweden where, in spite of the preservation of private property and inheritance, bourgeois marriage and the conventional family seem to be losing ground rapidly. In recent years, free unions and the rate of illegitimacy have increased markedly, and instant divorce has recently been introduced. Without equality in distribution of production, a large degree of equality of opportunities has produced a sexual revolution in Sweden.

In view of the egalitarian outlook of the Cuban revolution, whose foremost objective is to abolish the old social inequalities, one would expect that marriage as the institution perpetuating the old order would take a central place in its social policy. In effect, measures were taken which, in the light of the foregoing analysis, appear contradictory. In the early years of the revolution, the revolutionary government was carrying out 'collective marriages', i.e. campaigns to marry those couples who had so far lived in concubinage (over one third of all unions, according to the 1953 census), thus following a trend already initiated by the 1940 Constitution which permitted those living in concubinage to have their unions declared legally equal to marriage in the courts.

It may be argued that the revolutionary government's early policy was born of middle-class discomfiture at lower-class morals. Yet Fidel Castro in March of 1968 ridiculed the rumour that the revolutionary government was about to put up the age of marriage in order to curtail the high birth rate by saying that in Cuba people had never needed to marry to have children.[73] I would think that this marriage policy – the 'collective marriages' campaign and the establishment of 'marriage palaces' where young couples can marry with all the luxury of a bourgeois wedding – was the product of a desire for social justice coupled with a misconception of the structural role of legal marriage. Being vaguely aware that the simultaneous existence of the consensual union and marriage was the result of social inequality, the revolutionary government opted for making available to the lower classes the status symbols formerly reserved to the upper classes, in this way depriving them of their status content. By doing so, they vindicated the lower classes and gave them a sense of equality, without, however, attacking the problem at its roots. Undoubtedly, above all the women who had so far lived in concubinage were in favour of 'collective marriages'. During my stay in a little village in the Sierra Maestra in 1968 women repeatedly approached me asking whether I formed part of the campaign and when would it come to the village. 'Collective marriages' have now been abandoned. This might be an indication that policy is changing. I have been told that my analysis of elopement and seduction in nineteenth-century Cuba has been published by the Ministry of the Interior for wide circulation.

## Conclusion: Some analytical comparisons

In the long run, in an egalitarian society legal marriage as an institution regularizing inheritance of status and property should become obsolete. In this light, those 'enemies of the people' who in 1968 were said to 'complain that socialism breaks up the family' would seem to be more perceptive in their assessment of truly egalitarian socialism than the official who countered this imputation by remarking that 'the efforts which were being made to legalize the consensual unions proved the contrary'.[74] Traditional values still persist. The incorporation of women into the work-force has been seized on by many as a basis for emancipation. But it has also been resented by many men who, as a Cuban journalist told Elizabeth Sutherland in 1969, 'wish they could put chastity belts on "their" women'.[75] A consequence of this conflict has been a marked rise in the divorce rate. Virginity is still valued. 'If I ever lost my morality I would want someone to shoot me', said a female member of one of the youth brigades doing agricultural work on the Isle of Pines in 1969.[76] But there is some indication that the elopement with a view to marriage is on the decrease.[77] Were it not for those 'collective marriages', one would expect the frequency of legal marriage itself to decrease and that of consensual unions to increase, and this for reasons strictly the opposite to those obtaining in nineteenth-century Cuba.

# APPENDIX

## THREE CUBAN GENEALOGIES

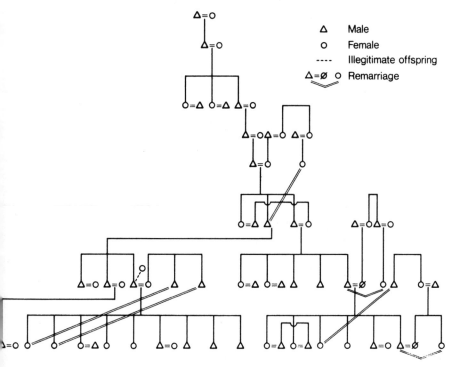

FIGURE 1. *Aquilera family*

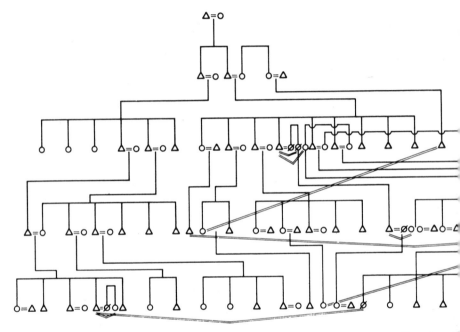

FIGURE 2. *L*

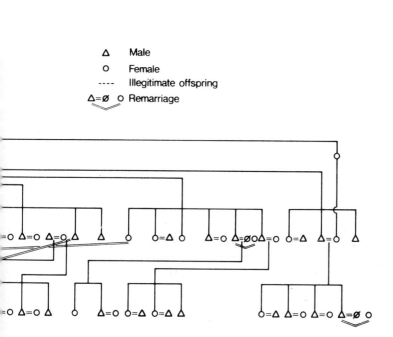

Δ      Male
O      Female
- - - -   Illegitimate offspring
Δ=∅  O   Remarriage

*riente family*

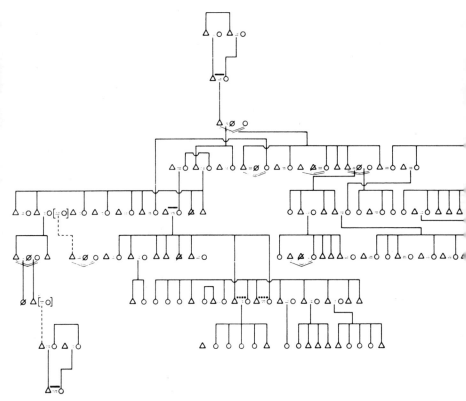

FIGURE

146

# Three Cuban Geneaologies

## Legend

- △  Male
- ○  Female
- [ ]  Concubine
- ----  Illegitimate offspring
- ○=∅ △  Remarriage
- ━━  Cousin marriage
- ▬▬  Uncle–niece marriage
  or aunt–nephew marriage

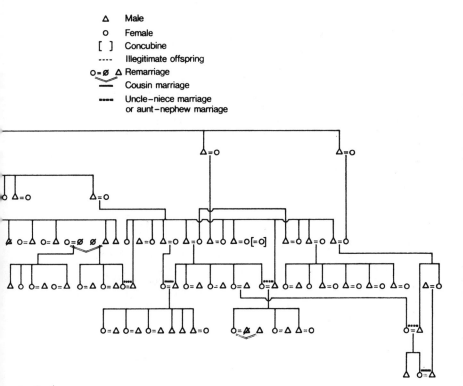

*ontalvo family*

147

# NOTES TO THE TEXT

### INTRODUCTION, pp. 1–7

1 J. G. Peristiany (ed.), *Honour and Shame: The Values of Mediterranean Society* (London, 1965); J. K. Campbell, *Honour, Family and Patronage* (Oxford, 1964); C. Lisón-Tolosana, *Belmonte de los Caballeros: A Sociological Study of a Spanish Town* (Oxford, 1966).

2 Major contributions to the study of family organization in the multiracial societies of the American South and the Caribbean are the following: E. Franklin Frazier, *The Negro Family in the United States* (Chicago Univ. Press, 1937); R. T. Smith, *The Negro Family in British Guiana. Family Structure and Social Status in the Villages* (London, 1956); E. Clarke, *My Mother Who Fathered Me* (London, 1957); M. G. Smith, *West Indian Family Structure* (Univ. of Washington Press, 1962).

3 F. Tannenbaum, *Slave and Citizen. The Negro in the Americas* (New York, 1947); S. M. Elkins, *Slavery: A Problem in American Institutional and Intellectual Life* (Chicago, 1959); H. Klein, *Slavery in the Americas: A Comparative Study of Virginia and Cuba* (London, 1967).

4 S. W. Mintz, Review of Elkins' *Slavery* in *American Anthropologist*, 63 (1961).

5 M. Moreno Fraginals, *El ingenio: el complejo económico-social cubano del azúcar* (Havana, 1964). This brilliant study has been of particular help to me.

6 Ibid. p. 6.

7 P. S. Foner, *A History of Cuba and its Relations with the United States* (New York, 1962), vol. 1.

8 Sources: the years 1774 and 1792 are taken from Ramón de la Sagra, *Historia económico-política y estadística de la Isla de Cuba* (Havana, 1831), p. 7; the remaining years are taken from the following censuses: *Cuadro estadístico de la siempre fiel Isla de Cuba, correspondiente al año de 1827* (Havana, 1829); *Cuadro estadístico de la siempre fiel Isla de Cuba, correspondiente al año de 1846* (Havana, 1847); *Noticias estadísticas de la Isla de Cuba en 1862* (Havana, 1864); *Censo de la población de España, 1877*, 2 vols. (Madrid, 1884); *Censo de la población de España en 1887* (Madrid, 1891); *Report of the Census of Cuba, 1899* (Washington, 1900).

9 Klein, p. 196.

10 F. W. Knight, 'The role of the free black and the free mulatto in Cuban slave society', unpublished paper presented at a symposium sponsored by the Department of History and the Institute of Southern History of the Johns Hopkins University, Baltimore, Maryland, April 1970, p. 12.

11 Klein, p. 84. Evidence is nowhere given to support this extraordinary statement. Hugh Thomas in his monumental history of Cuba does not mention the decree: H. Thomas, *Cuba or the Pursuit of Freedom* (London, 1971).

12 D. B. Davis, *The Problem of Slavery in Western Culture* (Cornell Univ. Press, 1966).

13 J. Ibarra, *Ideología Mambisa* (Havana, 1967).

14 W. D. Jordan, *White over Black: American Attitudes toward the Negro, 1550–1812* (Univ. of North Carolina Press, 1968).

15 E. D. Genovese addresses himself to this question in 'The American slave systems in world perspective' in *The World the Slaveholders Made. Two Essays in Interpretation* (London, 1970). This is also the best account of the controversy on the Anglo-American and Latin-American varieties of slavery.

16 H. Hoetink, *The Two Variants in Caribbean Race Relations* (Oxford, 1967); G. Freyre, *The Masters and the Slaves: A Study in the Development of Brazilian Civilization* (New York, 1946), pp. 11ff.

CHAPTER I, pp. 11–19

1 *CDFS*, III:1, pp. 406–13.

2 *CDFS*, III:1, pp. 438–42.

3 *CDFS*, III:2, p. 624.

4 *CDFS*, III:2, p. 695.

5 *CDFS*, III:2, p. 695.

6 José María Zamora y Coronado, *Biblioteca de legislación ultramarina en forma de diccionario alfabético* (Madrid, 1845). Real Cédula de 15 de octubre de 1805 acerca de los matrimonios que personas de conocida nobleza pretendan contraer con las de castas de negros y mulatos.

7 Ibid.

8 Ibid.

9 *CDFS*, III:2, p. 826.

10 Ibid. Auto de la Audiencia de Puerto-Príncipe de 9 de julio de 1806, en que para el mejor cumplimiento de la Real Cédula de 15 de octubre de 1805 de matrimonios entre personas desiguales, se adopta esta conclusión fiscal.

   Fernando Ortiz in *Los negros esclavos* (Havana, 1916) touches briefly on interracial marriage. He mentions the 15 October 1805 royal decree as well as the 9 July 1806 edict, which lead him to conclude wrongly that 'from this date onward marriage between whites and blacks was permitted, and little by little even the well-to-do families, in their proofs of purity of blood were able to omit the ethnic background of either of the marriage partners'.

11 My italics throughout. Joaquín Rodríguez San Pedro, *Legislación ultramarina, concordada y anotada* (Madrid, 1868), p. 531n. Also mentioned in the proceedings ANC, GSC, Leg. 932/32673, as enforceable in Cuba (Havana, 1875).

12 ANC, AP, Leg. 211/70.

13 I recorded a total of 199 applications for interracial marriage licences at the Cuban National Archives. They cover the period from 1810 to 1882. They are catalogued under the general heading 'marriage' and I recognized them either because their epigraph contained an explicit reference to the ethnic status of the candidates, or because one of the names lacked the appelative Don or Doña to which only whites were entitled. These would seem to be all the cases of interracial marriages kept at the Cuban National Archives.

   I also found further cases of interracial marriage at the Archivo de Indias of Seville referring only to the period from 1807 to 1825 (roughly fifty cases). A summary check showed, however, that this material does not alter the general impression gained from the Cuban evidence. I only recorded some of the more outstanding cases which I quote in the notes.

It is important to note that 80 per cent of the cases of parental dissent took place before the 1830s, and that of the 124 cases where the proceedings are directly initiated by the couple 34 occurred before 1830.

14 ANC, GSC, Leg. 894/30410.
15 ANC, GSC, Leg. 896/30630. D. Francisco Antonio García is slightly more specific; he insists that according to the law 16, book 10, title 2 of the *Novísima Recopilación*, marriage between whites and the castes is proscribed. This parent clearly does not know the 1805 decree. ANC, GSC, Leg. 901/30941.
16 ANC, GSC, Leg. 910/31527. Another mother in 1849 similarly alluded to the circumstances which produced these decrees. She argues that by wanting to marry a *parda* her son has 'disregarded the regulations which for political reasons, of which Y.E. is surely aware prohibit explicitly marriages between the white class and the castes of mulattos and people of colour'. ANC, GSC, Leg. 912/31658.
17 ANC, GSC, Leg. 895/30500.
18 ANC, GSC, Leg. 907/31334.
19 ANC, GSC, Leg. 888/29900.
20 ANC, GSC, Leg. 894/30371.
21 Antonio Domínguez Ortiz, *La sociedad española en el siglo XVIII* (Madrid, 1955), p. 233. And M. Martínez Alcubilla in *Diccionario de la administración española*, 5th ed. (Madrid, 1891) defines it as 'the quality of not having neither mixture nor race of Moors, Jews, heretics or convicts of the Inquisition' (vol. 7, pp. 890–1).
22 ANC, GSC, Leg. 920/32393.
23 ANC, GSC, Leg. 900/30920.
24 ANC, GSC, Leg. 888/29890.
25 ANC, GSC, Leg. 912/31658.
26 ANC, GSC, Leg. 914/31756.
27 ANC, GSC, Leg. 894/30434.
28 ANC, GSC, Leg. 893/30297.
29 ANC, GSC, Leg. 893/30312.
30 ANC, GSC, Leg. 901/30979.
31 ANC, GSC, Leg. 923/32229.
32 ANC, GSC, Leg. 923/32244.
33 ANC, GSC, Leg. 919/32011.
34 ANC, GSC, Leg. 888/29900.
35 Nevertheless, the authorities themselves would manipulate the principle of racial status assignment according to their own objectives. Thus an official of the central government in 1861 favoured a mixed marriage on the following grounds: 'Bearing in mind finally that the true interest of the white race consists in separating the future generations from their origin, an aim which in no way will be attained more successfully than by allowing marriage between the whites of the common estate and the free *pardas* for in this way a family will be created which *following the father's status* will be regarded as white and acquire all the interests and rights of such'. ANC, GSC, Leg. 923/32244 (my italics).
36 The royal decrees of 31 January 1835 and of 21 and 28 September 1836 did away with the need to supply evidence of purity of blood for most offices; and the law of 16 May 1865 at last abolished any remaining restrictions in this respect:

Martínez Alcubilla, vol. 7, pp. 890–1. According to Caro Baroja, the aristocratic characters of *La Gaviota* by Fernan Caballero, a novel published in 1849 and the action of which is only slightly earlier, talk of purity of blood and its loss through mixing with mulatto or Jewish blood as of something of some validity: J. Caro Baroja, *Los judíos en la España moderna y contemporanea* (Madrid, 1961), vol. 3, p. 173 n. 136.

37 ANC, GSC, Leg. 920/32393.

38 ANC, GSC, Leg. 888/29893.

39 ANC, GSC, Leg. 917/31906. Robert K. Merton in 'Intermarriage and the social structure: fact and theory', *Psychiatry*, 4 (1941), 361–74, makes the same point.

40 ANC, GSC, Leg. 893/30343.

41 ANC, GSC, Leg. 892/30199.

CHAPTER 2, pp. 20–41

1 ANC, GSC, Leg. 895/30509. In the cases of parental dissent where the final ruling is known, in eleven the dissent is overruled and in fourteen it is accepted and the marriage forbidden.

2 ANC, GSC, Leg. 889/29977.

3 Zamora y Coronado. Auto de la Audiencia de Puerto-Príncipe de 9 de julio de 1806, en que para el mejor cumplimiento de la Real Cedula de 15 de octubre de 1805 de matrimonios entre personas desiguales, se adopta esta conclusión fiscal.

4 AHNM, Ultramar, Cuba, Leg. 1603/57.

5 ANC, GSC, Leg. 891/30137. D. Alejandro Falcón, for instance, explicitly appeals to the lack of relatives as an extenuating circumstance: he wants to marry a 'freeborn *parda* . . . the legitimate daughter of parents who are equally freeborn . . . whose moral conduct is very satisfactory', he himself being 'a man of forty who by birth has no distinction whatsoever, and who does not have any relatives who could be degraded by this marriage in any way'. ANC, GSC, Leg. 896/30618.

6 ANC, GSC, Leg. 888/29871.

7 ANC, GSC, Leg. 888/29913.

8 ANC, GSC, Leg. 889/29969.

9 ANC, GSC, Leg. 888/29907.

10 ANC, GSC, Leg. 892/30219.

11 ANC, GSC, Leg. 926/32413. In the priest's words, 'the father upon being reprimanded by the undersigned for his so utterly obscene conduct, had the audacity to tell me that I should allow them to live in such a detestable state for he would never agree to a marriage with her'.

12 ANC, GSC, Leg. 894/30434, Leg. 901/30941 and Leg. 907/31334.

13 ANC, GSC, Leg. 916/31862.

14 ANC, GSC, Leg. 932/32673 (my italics).

15 ANC, GSC, Leg. 890/30044.

16 ANC, GSC, Leg. 893/30297.

17 A similar case is that of the young man of whom it is said that 'he is a person of no distinction [and] *has obscured himself* by his poverty and mixing in his occupation with persons of colour', whereas the coloured bride is recommended by her own and her family's reputation of honesty: ANC, GSC, Leg. 898/30813

(my italics). And in another instance the authorities believe that 'the fact that he is an artisan establishes equality between him and the *parda* whom he wishes to marry'. ANC, GSC, Leg. 917/31914.

18 ANC, GSC, Leg. 901/30941.
19 ANC, GSC, Leg. 912/31675.
20 ANC, GSC, Leg. 922/32167. On another occasion it is pointed out that 'the humble circumstances of the suitor . . . will make that the desired marriage pass unnoticed by the public': ANC, GSC, Leg. 922/32175. And in still another instance it was believed that 'the humble circumstances of the suitor remove any

*Type of occupation of applicants and their frequency as compared to percentage of coloured people in these occupations in 1862*

| Occupation | Frequency | Percentage of free coloured people in these occupations in 1862 |
|---|---|---|
| Artisan, craftsman | 7 | ... |
| Mule-driver | 2 | 32 |
| Mason | 3 | 56 |
| Barber | 2 | 52 |
| Stone-cutter | 1 | 30 |
| Carpenter | 5 | 48 |
| Cook | 2 | ... |
| Baker | 2 | 34 |
| Silversmith | 1 | 45 |
| Well-sinker | 1 | ... |
| Tailor | 5 | 58 |
| Cigar-maker | 3 | 28 |
| Shoemaker | 5 | 49 |
| Farm labourer | 12 | 32 |
| Peasant | 3 | 23 |
| In trade | 2 | 2 |
| Owner of boat engaged in coasting trade | 1 | — |
| Discharged soldier | 8 | — |
| City policeman | 1 | — |
| Soldier of militia | 2 | — |
| Lieutenant of infantry | 1 | — |
| Lieutenant constable | 1 | — |
| Captain constable | 1 | — |
| Grocer | 2 | ... |
| Clerk | 1 | — |
| Dancer | 1 | ... |

Source: *Noticias estadísticas de la Isla de Cuba – 1862.*

danger that the said marriage might have a bad effect on public opinion': Leg. 923/32242.

The occupations held by the white applicants for licences to marry coloured women are in the main humble occupations, occupations in which coloured people abounded, if not predominated. As one applicant said explicitly, he was 'of the class of workmen, being a tailor, which in this country markedly diminishes those whites who engage in these occupations': ANC, GSC, Leg. 895/30522; and another argued that 'by virtue of his poverty and mechanical trade he cannot [marry] anyone of his class': Leg. 895/30601. The table on p. 152 sums up the occupations as stated in the licence applications and their frequency and compares them with the percentage of coloured people engaged in them according to the 1862 census.

21 ANC, GSC, Leg. 889/29969.
22 ANC, GSC, Leg. 891/30118.
23 ANC, GSC, Leg. 907/31355.
24 ANC, GSC, Leg. 916/31839.
25 ANC, GSC, Leg. 935A/32860.
26 ANC, GSC, Leg. 893/30306.
27 ANC, GSC, Leg. 923/32229 (my italics).
28 ANC, GSC, Leg. 924/32284. Of another *parda* it is approvingly said that 'being sixteen years of age she is of good conduct and has an education that is superior to that common in her class. The unions between the *pardas* and the white generally encounter on the part of those of this privileged race the ill-will which due to custom, tradition, the anxieties and the disillusions of abandonments and frequent family disruptions they entail in society. Yet, if on account of their outstanding endowments some *pardas* were to be regarded as worthy of marrying a white man, surely none would be as worthy of this honour as Luisa Medina'. ANC, GSC, Leg. 924/32280.
29 ANC, GSC, Leg. 916/31862.
30 Ossowski calls this form of stratification defined by multiple criteria 'synthetic gradation': S. Ossowski, *Class Structure in the Social Consciousness* (London, 1963), pp. 44ff. Robert K. Merton in 'Intermarriage and the social structure' talks of 'mutual socio-economic compensation between the cross-caste mates'.

31

*Suitors and brides by colour and sex*

| | White | Pardo | Moreno | Colour unspecified | Total |
|---|---|---|---|---|---|
| Men | 170 | 24 | 2 | 3 | 199 |
| Women | 29 | 164 | 4 | 2 | 199 |

32 ANC, GSC, Leg. 908/31396, Leg. 912/31671, Leg. 924/32280 and Leg. 934/32745.
33 ANC, GSC, Leg. 888/29879. In 1818 another white man contends that 'he lacks the quality of nobility to which the royal decree of 1805 on such marriages refers': ANC, GSC, Leg. 893/30306.
34 ANC, GSC, Leg. 934/32756.

35 ANC, GSC, Leg. 924/32259.

36 ANC, GG, Leg. 335/16097.

37 ANC, GSC, Leg. 924/32284.

38 Slaves introduced illegally who were hired out by the government usually for seven years before gaining their freedom.

39 Miguel Estorch, *Apuntes para la historia sobre la administración del Marqués de la Pezuela en la Isla de Cuba desde 3 de diciembre de 1853 hasta 21 de setiembre de 1854* (Madrid, 1856), pp. 29–33.

40 Ibid. (italics in original).

41 It is interesting to note that the rumour is claimed to have been about marriages between blacks and *white women* which undoubtedly in the eyes of the 'respectable families' aggravated the matter even further.

42 Estorch. Porfirio Valiente, one of the delegates appointed to the Junta Informativa sent to Madrid in 1867, though recommending '[une] réforme demandée par les intérêts de l'humanité et de la civilisation, celle de la revocation de la loi qui prohibe le marriage entre les deux races, (p. 146), likewise had a clear perception that racial mixture was not for the like of him: 'Il est d'autant plus utile de favoriser le développement de ce penchant que la *classe inférieure de la race blanche* se mêle et se confond volontiers avec la race nègre dans plusiers actes de la vie, et qu'il n'est pas rare de voir dans des certains endroits des hommes blancs, même d'une certaine position sociale, vivant avec de femmes mêtisses et même avec de négresses: témoignages public de l'égalité dans la nature, qu'il est impossible de méconnaître dans l'absolu' (p. 142: my italics). P. Valiente, *Réformes dans les îles de Cuba et de Porto-Rico* (Paris, 1869).

43 'It has come to the attention of the Queen that a resolution is being talked about there in different versions, supposedly passed by the Archbishop of that Island relative to the marriage between whites and people of colour': AHNM, Ultramar, Cuba, Leg. 1696/134.

44 AHNM, Ultramar, Cuba, Leg. 4640/34.

45 ANC, GSC, Leg. 173/279.

46 ANC, GSC, Leg. 728/24329.

47 Stanley Urban in his article 'The Africanization of Cuba scare, 1853–5' gives a similar interpretation in which Great Britain, however, appears as the direct instigator of Pezuela's policy: 'A most significant fact is that in October 1853 England presented a series of demands upon Spain which anticipated the reform programme of Captain General Juan M. de la Pezuela. The latter precipitated the Africanization of Cuba scare on an international scale. The English Foreign Office justified these proposals on the ground that without them Spain could never honour its treaty obligations to suppress the slave trade. They contained two features of the subsequent Pezuela programme which most alarmed the wealthy classes of Cuba: the abolition of immunity of rural estates from search and seizure by the authorities of illegal slave entries and the registration of all slaves held on the island. The institution of these same measures a few months later by Pezuela shortly after assuming office can scarcely be regarded as coincidental' (pp. 32–3). Urban attributes to Pezuela also a measure permitting 'racial intermarriage' (p. 36). *Hispanic American Historical Review*, 37 (1957).

48 *Información sobre reformas en Cuba y Puerto Rico* (New York, 1867), vol. I, p. 161.

49 *Gaceta de la Habana*, 28 October 1854.

50 ANC, GSC, Leg. 729/24411.
51 ANC, GSC, Leg. 926/32413.
52 ANC, GSC, Leg. 926/32385.
53 ANC, AP, Leg. 228/1. Accordingly, an investigation into the advisability of enforcing in the overseas possessions the 20 June 1862 law on parental consent to marriage lowering the age of consent met with staunch resistance from Cuba, an attitude which was largely shared by the Consejo de Estado which resolved in 1866 that since 'the obstacles most difficult to overcome, the contradictions hardest to reconcile, created by the existence of slavery in these colonies, the scarce civilization in others, and the racial differences in all of them have made it that even those who are most in favour of the reform have proposed complicated modifications which denaturalize it entirely', one should refrain from aspiring to a legal symmetry between the mother country and its overseas possessions, more so in the case of Cuba, where 'one must take into account three types of marriages, i.e. those contracted between nobles or people of white race with others of colour, those between people of other race, and those between free people and slaves'. ACEM, Ultramar, Gracia y Justicia, Leg. 33/806 and 1376.
54 ANC, AP, Leg. 228/1.
55 ANC, GSC, Leg. 1148/43925.
56 For a summary discussion of the various interpretations see Foner, vol. 1, p. 217. Mario Hernández y Sánchez-Barba in 'David Turnbull y el problema de la esclavitud en Cuba', *Anuario de Estudios Americanos*, 14 (1957), shows quite convincingly that the conspiracy did take place.
57 The *hacendado rutinario*, as Saco called his enemy, Vazquez Queipo explained the Haitian revolution precisely as the work of the substantial mulatto population: José Antonio Saco, *Historia de la esclavitud de la raza africana en el Nuevo Mundo y en especial en los países Américo-Hispanos* (Havana, 1938 ed.). Prologue by Fernando Ortiz, vol. 1, p. xxxiv.
58 ANC, GSC, Leg. 922/32149.
59 ANC, GSC, Leg. 922/32175.
60 ANC, GSC, Leg. 925/32358.
61 ANC, GSC, Leg. 925/32358.
62 *Información sobre reformas en Cuba y Puerto Rico*, vol. 1, p. 159. Honorato Bernard de Chateausalins somewhat earlier attempted a similar apology of slavery: thus he argued that 'The Europeans and their American-born descendants cannot for long resist the burning heat of the tropics: the premature deaths of so many youths who come to America only to dig their graves offer sufficient proof of this lamentable fact. The African- or American-born negroes are the only ones who are able to support the constant fatigue under this burning climate that is similar to theirs; only they on account of the thickness of their skin and their complexion are accustomed to the equinoctial regions and to the rigours of all seasons.' Honorato Bernard de Chateausalins, *El vademecum de los hacendados cubanos* (Havana, 1854), p. vi.
63 A view held by Juan Perez de la Riva. I am particularly indebted to Juan Martinez-Alier for his assistance in making clear to me some of the intricacies of the economics of slavery.
64 Francisco de Arango y Parreño, 'Ideas sobre los medios de establecer el libre

comercio de Cuba y de realizar un empréstito de 20 millones de pesos' in *Obras*, vol. 2, pp. 306–7.

65 O'Donnell quoted by A. F. Corwin, *Spain and the Abolition of Slavery in Cuba, 1817–1886* (Univ. of Texas Press, 1967), p. 86.

66 In 1869 the Ministry of Overseas Affairs commented on rumours that the emigration of Africans to Sierra Leone was being considered in Havana and Puerto Rico, pointing out that the Sociedad Económica de Amigos del País de Puerto Rico thought it not a bad idea since the free negroes constituted an element so difficult to assimilate: *Emigración de Africanos de la Habana y Puerto Rico a Sierra Leona*, AHNM, Ultramar, Cuba, Gobierno, Leg. 4759/67. Already in 1845 a royal decree had been passed authorizing seventy-eight free blacks, probably victims of O'Donnell's persecutions, to leave Cuba for Africa: Juan Pérez de la Riva, 'Documentos para la historia de las gentes sin historia. Antiguos esclavos cubanos que regresan a Lagos', *Revista de la Biblioteca Nacional 'José Martí'*, 1 (1964), 34.

67 Saco, *Historia*, vol. 1, p. xxvii.

68 Ibid. pp. xxxiv–xxxvi.

69 Ibid. vol. 3, p. 157.

70 ANC, GSC, Leg. 924/32257.

71 ANC, GSC, Leg. 922/32175; also Leg. 922/32186 and Leg. 923/32244.

72 ANC, GSC, Leg. 911/31610; already in 1805 the Crown's ministers had spoken of the same need.

73 ANC, GSC, Leg. 924/32259.

74 Esteban Collantes, *Diario de sesiones de las Cortes*, 18 February 1873, quoted by Roberto Mesa, *El colonialismo en la crisis del XIX español* (Madrid, 1967), p. 149.

75 They were nationalists and therefore integrationists, *but also racists*. As Saco stressed when discussing the introduction of free labour, above all they should 'have a white face and know how to work honestly' (Saco, *Historia*, vol. 1, p. xxxiv), an attitude quite different from that of the *mambí* nationalists (the name given to the Cuban rebels).

76 ANC, GSC, Leg. 919/32011 (my italics).

77 ANC, Donativos y Remisiones, Leg. 473/2.

78 ANC, GSC, Leg. 931/32640.

79 ANC, Misc., Leg. 3046/Au.

80 The Law of Abolition of Slavery established an eight-year transition period of tutelage for the slaves to be freed. It was with regard to this new status that queries on marriage policy arose once again. Thus in 1882 a *Consulta de la Junta Patronos de la Habana acerca de los matrimonios de los patrocinados de Cuba con personas libres y sus consecuencias en la cesación del patronato* was resolved with a syllogism: 'The Council . . . taking into account this law which has not been abrogated by the *Recopilación de Indias* passed later, and bearing in mind that both jurisdiction and custom have always acknowledged it, declaring emancipated those who marrying a free person obtained their master's consent, rules that *patrocinados* may marry without obtaining their patron's consent; but in this case they will not become emancipated, contrary to the case when they demand and are given the said consent': that is to say, slaves marrying free persons become free when they succeed in obtaining their master's consent; but as *patrocinados* do not in principle require their *patron's* consent to marry even when the other partner is

free, neither do they become free by doing so. ACEM, Ultramar, Gobernación, Esclavos y Colonización, Leg. 38/40080.

Parents could still resort to dissent after 1881. By royal decree of 17 December 1883 a reform of the legislation on parental consent had been denied the island. Only upon the Archbishop's emphatic appeal that 'it is necessary to combat concubinage by easing legitimate unions, also in the cases of elopement where the seducer is sentenced to marrying the girl and the need to obtain parental consent hinders the speedy fulfilment of the sentence . . . [besides] the *hijos de familia* who by having reached twenty-five years of age and thus have become emancipated, are persons *sui juris* who after the enactment of the law of civil marriage are not held to obtain parental consent', was a modification of the law in this sense enacted in 1884, though with considerable reluctance on the part of the Spanish authorities. ACEM, Ultramar, Gracia y Justicia, Leg. 52/44735.

81 ANC, GC, Leg. 450/21942.

82 Thus in May 1882 the Governor of Sta. Clara inquired as to the policy to be followed in a case where a number of coloured people had filed a complaint because one of them had been banished from the public square on occasion of a public concert: ANC, CA, Leg. 76/7368. And on May of the previous year, D. Casimiro Bernabeau, a mulatto, and the president of the Spanish Casino of Havana for coloured people, arguing that 'H.M. does not go by colours but needs Spaniards who will defend integrity', had demanded that coloured people be treated with perfect equality also in restaurants and cafés. However, in both instances the authorities were reluctant to pass any general rules for 'the people of colour, who are already equal before the law, must trust time and the improving culture of their class to bring about the social equality to which they naturally aspire'. And as is pointed out in the Havana case, 'if a special decree were issued obliging these establishments to admit and serve coloured people, this would doubtless cause constant conflicts, and the whites attending these places would stop going there and many establishments of this kind would be shut down, for the coloured people could never maintain them, even if the whites were willing to serve, which cannot be expected of them; in the same way as a Casino has been created for coloured people, cafés and other establishments of this nature could be opened for coloured people': ANC, CA, Leg. 68/6799.

83 Ibarra, p. 52.

84 1912 saw a negro revolt put down at a cost, it appears, of some 3,000 lives. The memory of this massacre was still alive in Oriente in 1968.

## CHAPTER 3, pp. 42–56

1 *CDFS*, III:1, pp. 401–5. This type of marriage differed from the public church marriage in three respects: (*a*) it was registered in a special book kept by the Bishop and not accessible to the public; (*b*) the priest and all other persons involved in the ceremony were held to keep it secret; and (*c*) the parents' names were omitted in the offspring's baptism certificates.

Prior to the Council of Trent three types of marriage were practised in Spain: (*a*) marriage *in facie ecclesiae* called *matrimonio de bendición*, which was celebrated in public by a priest in church and in the presence of witnesses; (*b*) marriage *a furto*, i.e. secret, which had a civil rather than religious character for it consisted merely of an oath made by the couple in the presence of witnesses; and (*c*) the marriage called *a furto in manu clerici*, i.e. secret but with the intervention of a priest. Virginia Gutiérrez de Pineda, *La familia en Colombia* (Bogotá, 1963), p. 164.

2  *CDFS*, III:1, p. 404.

3  *CDFS*, III:1, p. 402.

4  *CDFS*, III:1, p. 404.

5  Thus in 1783 the Bishop of Cuba demanded of the Council of the Indies instructions as to how to proceed in those cases in which 'the Governor in charge of trials of parental dissent rules that despite the dissent being justified the marriage could take place by virtue of the reasons of conscience, the partners to the marriage undertaking to suffer the penalties decreed by the Royal Pragmatic': *CDFS*, III:2, p. 511.

6  *CDFS*, III:2, pp. 624–5.

7  *CDFS*, III:2, p. 763.

8  *CDFS*, III:2, p. 764.

9  *CDFS*, III:2, p. 766.

10  *CDFS*, III:2, p. 764.

11  *CDFS*, III:2, p. 795.

12  ANC, GSC, Leg. 921/32129.

13  ANC, GSC, Leg. 919/32011.

14  ANC, GSC, Leg. 922/32186. In the words of one official, 'it is bad that a white should marry a *parda*; but it is even worse that he should live dishonestly with her and of two evils the lesser one becomes a good thing': AGI, Capitanía General de la Isla de Cuba, Leg. 1697.

15  ANC, GSC, Leg. 916/31839.

16  ANC, GSC, Leg. 920/32055.

17  ANC, GSC, Leg. 926/32440.

18  ANC, GSC, Leg. 912/31675.

19  ANC, GSC, Leg. 934/32748.

20  Tannenbaum, Elkins, and most recently Klein, criticized by E. V. Goveia, 'Comment on Anglicanism, Catholicism, and the Negro slave', in L. Foner and E. D. Genovese (eds.), *Slavery in the New World. A Reader in Comparative History* (Englewood Cliffs, N.J., 1969) and by Gwendolyn Midlo Hall, *Social Control in Slave Plantation Societies. A Comparison of St. Domingue and Cuba* (Baltimore, 1971).

21  ANC, GSC, Leg. 905/31186; also Leg. 888/29900, Leg. 891/30137, Leg. 893/30356, Leg. 895/30507, Leg. 896/30595 and Leg. 9358/32963.

22  ANC, GSC, Leg. 888/29893.

23  ANC, GSC, Leg. 1148/43925. In 1865 one priest is said to have objected to a mixed marriage on the grounds that 'she was not of pure blood and of pure Caucasian race': ANC, GSC, Leg. 927/32466.

24  ANC, GSC, Leg. 924/32259.

25  ANC, GSC, Leg. 919/32011.

26  ANC, GSC, Leg. 934/32753.

27  ANC, GSC, Leg. 924/32259.

28  ANC, GSC, Leg. 1148/43925.

29  ANC, GSC, Leg. 919/32011.

30  ANC, GSC, Leg. 921/32118.

31 Diligencias practicadas para evacuar el informe pedido por el Exmo. Sor. Gob. Supremo Civil y Cap. Gral. de la Isla acerca de los matrimonios celebrados en esta jurisdicción de raza distinta. ANC, GSC, Leg. 916/31858.
32 Ibid.
33 AHNM, Ultramar, Cuba, Leg. 1662/81² and Leg. 1681/74.
34 ANC, GSC, Leg. 916/31858.
35 Ibid.
36 Ibid.
37 Ibid.
38 Bando de Gobernación y Policía de la Isla de Cuba expedido por el Exmo. Sr. Don Geronimo Valdés, Presidente, Gobernador y Capitan General, 1843. Instrucción de Pedáneos.
39 ANC, GSC, Leg. 916/31858.
40 Ibid. Cf. Raymond Carr, *Spain 1808–1939* (Oxford, 1966), p. 286, for a brief discussion of Claret y Clarà's role as the head of Catholic revival in Spain in the late 1850s.
41 AHNM, Ultramar, Cuba, Leg. 1662/81².
42 AHNM, Ultramar, Cuba, Leg. 1701/44. Sobre el atentado cometido en Holguín contra el Arzobispo de Cuba.
43 Emilio Bacardí y Moreau in his *Crónicas de Santiago de Cuba*, vol. 3, app. ii, dedicates a few pages to Archbishop Claret y Clara's tenure in Oriente province. He depicts him as a loyal agent of the Crown essentially interested in securing Spanish supremacy in Cuba. And the Marquis of Pezuela in his ardent defence of the Archbishop foresees dire consequences for 'religion, customs and *the legitimate and just domination of Spain in Cuba*' if he and his missionaries were hindered in their work: AHNM, Ultramar, Cuba, Leg. 1662/81² (my italics).
44 AHNM, Ultramar, Cuba, Leg. 1748/23.
45 Ibid.
46 Ibid.
47 Ibid. To give its ruling greater force and surely also to intimidate the indiscreet Bishop, the Consejo de Administración as a final warning cited article 403 of the Penal Code of 1848 which established the penalty of imprisonment and a fine of 50 to 500 *duros* for those clergymen who authorized marriages forbidden by civil law: *Código Penal* 1848, Chap. ii, Title xii, Celebración de matrimonios ilegales, art. 403.
48 AHNM, Ultramar, Cuba, Leg. 1755/102. Jacinto María Martínez y Saez, *Los voluntarios de Cuba y el Obispo de la Habana* (Madrid, 1871). Here he describes the whole conflict, without referring, however, to the earlier clash on interracial marriage.
49 In fact a reformist, the lawyer José Manuel Mestre, defended Abad Torres, who had attempted to assassinate the Archbishop in Holguín: Thomas, p. 233 n 7.
50 As Captain General Pezuela alleged, 'if the Government were to protect the interests of Cuba and keep her Spanish, it should increase the dioceses there and send to them bishops like the saintly Father Claret': P. Tomas L. Pujadas, C.M.F., *San Antonio María Claret, apóstol de nuestro tiempo* (Madrid, 1950).
51 Quoted by Thomas, p. 150.
52 When he was exhorted by the civil authorities to see to his clergy's morality first, he replied that 'he has had to keep the scandalous parish priest and sacristan

of Tunas because in the absence of a sufficient number of worthy priests he had put up with this evil': ANC, GSC, Leg. 916/31858.

53 Saco, *Historia*, vol. 4, pp. 326–7.
54 Klein, pp. 97–8.
55 *Cuadro estadístico de la siempre fiel Isla de Cuba, correspondiente al año 1846; Noticias estadísticas de la Isla de Cuba en 1862.*
56 Quoted by Midlo Hall, p. 46. This was not an isolated opinion. One of the reformist delegates to the Junta de Información of 1866, the Havana lawyer Rafael Ascárate, opposed the sending of missionaries to Cuba to evangelize the slaves on the grounds that, as he pointedly remarked, 'Bearing chiefly in mind the planters' interests when opposing such missions . . . he believed that religious teachings could either be in accord with the religion of Jesus Christ, and in this case being incompatible as it is with slavery it would arouse aspirations to freedom among the slaves and would be the cause of terrible disorders, or it would depart from true Christian doctrine out of fear of upsetting the social constitution of the Antilles, and in this case would gravely offend its exalted aims': Ibarra, pp. 19–20 n. 1.
57 *Noticias estadísticas de la Isla de Cuba en 1862.*

CHAPTER 4, pp. 57–70

1 I found 199 applications for interracial marriage at the Archivo Nacional de Cuba and about fifty at the Archivo General de Indias of Seville. Whether these are all the petitions filed throughout the century it is difficult to say.
2 ANC, GSC, Leg. 923/32244.
3 ANC, GSC, Leg. 916/31858.
4 ANC, GSC, Leg. 921/32129; see also Leg. 896/30601. The official who contended that 'the aspired marriage does not seem to be justified by the scarcity of white women in a country where they abound so much', was clearly falsifying the facts in the interest of racial segregation: ANC, GSC, Leg. 920/32055.
5 Jacobo de la Pezuela y Lobo, *Diccionario geográfico, estadístico, historico de la Isla de Cuba* (Madrid, 1863–6), vol. 3. Incidentally, the population figures given by Pezuela – omitting their source – differ from those given by the censuses which I used.
6 Ibid.
7 ANC, GSC, Leg. 916/31858.
8 AHNM, Ultramar, Cuba, Leg. 1748/23.
9 Richard H. Dana, Jr, *To Cuba and Back: A Vacation Voyage* (Boston, 1859), quoted by R. Freeman Smith (ed.), *Background to Revolution. The Development of Modern Cuba* (New York, 1966), p. 92.
10 Quoted by Angel Rosenblat, *La población indígena y el mestizaje en América* (Buenos Aires, 1954), vol. 2, p. 165.
11 ANC, GSC, Leg. 920/32052. The mother's objection was similarly 'the inequality between him and his concubine'; and another priest complained of a parishioner that 'for years [he] has lived publicly in this illicit society; he has rejected my charitable exhortations for more than six years . . . and has laughed at the recriminations by the local judges': ANC, GSC, Leg. 888/299907.
12 Martínez Alcubilla, vol. 1, p. 414.

13 AHNM, Ultramar, Leg. 1635/52, Leg. 1639/23, Leg. 1637/30, Leg. 1655/84, Leg. 1668/17, Leg. 1669/39, Leg. 1685/4, Leg. 1693/29, Leg. 1702/73, Leg. 1712/98 and Leg. 1763/20.

14 ANC, GSC, Leg. 896/30595.

15 In 84 of the total 199 cases the suitors themselves adduce one or more reasons which in their view justify, if not demand, marriage with a coloured woman.

16 ANC, GSC, Leg. 922/32143. Similarly, a white woman endeavoured to waive the authorities' opposition with the argument that 'it is true that in that village she has been reputed as white, but she is of the common estate and of the lowest class . . . her ancestors have never been anything but obscure whites and have never entered the ranks of those of absolute purity . . . [besides] her poverty is known'. As the suitor, although a *pardo*, is the legitimate son of free parents, they are granted the licence. ANC, GSC, Leg. 896/30595.

17 ANC, GSC, Leg. 934/32754; similarly Leg. 891/30091, Leg. 895/30555, Leg. 896/30618, Leg. 898/30813, Leg. 901/30941 and Leg. 935/32772.

18 ANC, GSC, Leg. 927/32478. Another white man argued that 'he found it unavoidably necessary to marry the *parda* Josefa Marcelina Sosa in order to repay in some way the affection and careful attention which she generously bestowed on him during his recent illness since he lacked the means to cover the expenses resulting from it': Leg. 9358/33000.

19 ANC, GSC, Leg. 892/30225.

20 ANC, GSC, Leg. 912/31673; similarly Leg. 924/32259, Leg. 923/32244, Leg. 935B/33000, Leg. 931/32640 and Leg. 890/30046.

21 ANC, GSC, Leg. 907/31363.

22 ANC, GSC, Leg. 917/31906; similarly Leg. 897/30724. Another white man, although at first emphasizing that the woman had 'all the circumstances and virtues that would recommend and make worthy of consideration any other of her sex', ends on a similarly practical note: 'she will not only give him peace of mind, but [this marriage] has the advantage as well of providing him with a person to take care of his domestic affairs and who would look upon and watch over what he may gain with his personal labour as if it were her own': ANC, GSC, Leg. 896/30618.

23 ANC, GSC, Leg. 919/32011.

24 ANC, GSC, Leg. 898/30764. One uncle told the authorities that despite his advice and recriminations and despite the stain that would fall on her, his niece intended to go ahead with the marriage 'blinded by a passion': ANC, GSC, Leg. 920/32393.

25 ANC, GSC, Leg. 923/32229.

26 ANC, GSC, Leg. 934/32745.

27 ANC, GSC, Leg. 894/30434. Another applicant says that 'even if the Hernández does not belong to the white race, this does not mean that there is a marked inequality between them; for as has been said earlier her appearance and manners place her in this category; on the other hand [he] does not have relations of any kind in this Island; he has come to America to make a fortune but lamentably things have turned out differently, for falling victim to a severe illness he spent the little he had earned, owing his life to the great care which the Hernández took in attending to him, a fact which . . . everybody knows in this municipality. As is natural, contact begot affection and the violence of passion made us go

astray, burdening our conscience with a fault which stains this girl's honour and which can only be repaired if the one who induced her to it gives her his name.' Earlier on, however, he had claimed that her baptism had been entered in the book for *pardos* and *morenos* by mistake. Leg. 924/32259.

28 ANC, GSC, Leg. 893/30356. In a number of proceedings the applicant specifies for how long he has lived in concubinage with the coloured woman and indicates the number of children had by her (see table below). Two conclusions may be

*Length of union and number of children born to couples by proceedings*

| ANC Leg. no.: | Length of concubinage, number of offspring |
| --- | --- |
| 888/29907 | many years, 2 children |
| 888/29879 | 10 years, 4 children |
| 889/29969 | 8 years |
| 891/30101 | 8 years, 5 children |
| 891/30103 | children |
| 892/20335 | 1 child |
| 892/30199 | 7 years |
| 892/30249 | several years, 5 children |
| 894/30408 | many years |
| 893/30356 | many years |
| 896/30595 | several years |
| 899/30879 | 2 children |
| 900/30884 | 1 child |
| 899/30829 | many years, 1 child |
| 907/31334 | several years |
| 913/31701 | more than 8 years |
| 914/31769 | several years |
| 920/32052 | 11 years |
| 935B/32963 | 17 years, 3 children |
| 923/32198 | 6 years |
| 921/32118 | 3 years, 1 child |
| 922/32186 | 1 child |
| 924/32259 | 4 years |
| 925/32323 | more than 30 years, 8 children |
| 926/32413 | several years, 1 child |
| 926/32440 | 2 children |
| 927/32461 | 1 child |
| 449/21865 | 1 child |
| 888/29890 | several years |
| 907/31363 | more than 40 years |
| 916/31862 | 11 years, 4 children; 13 years, 5 children |

drawn from this information: (*a*) these interracial concubinages were fairly stable, and (*b*) concubinage appeared to be an institutionalized alternative to marriage in the face of ethnic diversity of the partners.

29 ANC, GSC, Leg. 935B/32963.
30 ANC, GG, Leg. 421/20127.
31 ANC, GSC, Leg. 910/31509.
32 ANC, GSC, Leg. 924/32280; also Leg. 926/32440.
33 ANC, GSC, Leg. 926/32413.
34 As Domingo del Monte told Robert Richard Madden in 1838 upon his question whether the state of religion in the island was satisfactory: 'No, because few believe, and those who believe are superstitious, ignorant and corrupted'; 'indifference and incredulity could not be greater'. Saco, *Historia*, vol. 4, p. 327.
35 ANC, GSC, Leg. 907/31363.
36 AHNM, Ultramar, Cuba, Leg. 1747/111.
37 ANC, GSC, Leg. 888/29879.
38 ANC, GSC, Leg. 899/30879 and Leg. 900/30884.
39 ANC, GSC, Leg. 910/31509.
40 ANC, GSC, Leg. 888/29907.
41 ANC, GSC, Leg. 935B/32963.
42 ANC, GSC, Leg. 926/32440.

CHAPTER 5, pp. 71–81

1 *CDFS*, III:2, p. 625 (my italics).
2 Esteban Pichardo, *Pichardo Novísimo o Diccionario provincial casi razonado de voces y frases cubanas* (Havana, 1953), p. 660. The following case aptly illustrates the problem of social classification by physical appearance in a situation of racial mixture: 'As far as he can see the settlement of this case depends on Nicolás, the applicant's father, presenting himself, whom it appears Y.E. wants to see personally to deduce from his countenance whether he is *pardo* or not. Materially speaking colour is an accident, for as experience shows many individuals of the most distinguished and clear origin resemble and could be mistaken for *pardos* and conversely many of those whose grandparents on one or the other side have come in the hulk of a ship from the coast of Africa appear by their features, countenance and white skin to be of white origin. Thus although Nicolás Almanza, the father of the applicant, has a red colour, this does not mean that the applicant's grandmother, the *parda* Ana de Ayala, ceases to be his [the father's] mother, born, baptized and reputed as *parda* in the village of Guanabacoa . . . Even if his father has a white and pink skin, the kinky and rough hair and the coarse and thick nose along with other circumstances make him a true *pardo*.' AGI, Capitanía General de la Isla de Cuba, Leg. 1696.
3 ANC, GSC, Leg. 922/32149. Of another young woman it is said that 'although she says she is *mulatta* she is of light colour' (Leg. 893/30306), and of still another that 'although his bride is held to belong to the class of *parda* her appearance contradicts this' (Leg. 895/30522). Lastly, another young woman is described as being 'of those *pardas* who can in this village and even in other places pass for white' (Leg. 924/32259), and an official thought of another *parda* that 'she is of no bad appearance, of white colour' (Leg. 923/32229).

4 *CDFS*, III:2, p. 612.
5 *CDFS*, III:1, p. 392.
6 *CDFS*, III:2, p. 613.
7 *CDFS*, III:2, p. 614 (my italics).
8 *CDFS*, III:1, p. 392 (my italics).
9 *CDFS*, III:2, p. 787.
10 ANC, GSC, Leg. 924/32292.
11 ANC, GSC, Leg. 934/32748 (my italics).
12 ANC, GSC, Leg. 889/29969. In another case he is a foundling and thus registered as 'seemingly white'. Hence the authorities conclude: 'since the certificate of baptism of the applicant does not positively state that he is white; if the unfortunate beings living on public charity and protected by its kindness have an origin which will be eternally unknown, with more than sufficient reason this origin can be attributed as much to the highest as to the humblest source, to that resulting from the union of two beings of another than the white race, or descendants thereof in more or less remote degree. If this is so, Antonio Nazario Valdés cannot be regarded as white even if he appears as such, and less so if there is the slightest indication of the clandestine mixture of the races and if he himself states that "he is and wants to be regarded as pardo".' ANC, GSC, Leg. 932/32677.
13 Bacardí y Moreau, vol. 2, p. 459.
14 *CDFS*, III:2, p. 626.
15 ANC, GSC, Leg. 899/30891.
16 ANC, GSC, Leg. 910/31527; also Leg. 888/29900.
17 ANC, GSC, Leg. 898/30781.
18 ANC, GSC, Leg. 893/30297 (my italics).
19 ANC, GSC, Leg. 920/32393.
20 Cf. John Dollard, 'Hostility and fear in social life', *Social Forces*, 17 (1938), 15–26, quoted by Michael Banton, *Race Relations* (London, 1967), p. 294, on 'rational' and 'irrational' antagonisms.
21 ANC, GSC, Leg. 924/32284.
22 Juan Pérez de la Riva, 'Demografía de los culíes chinos en Cuba (1853–74)', *Revista de la Biblioteca Nacional 'José Martí'*, 4 (1966), 57–86.
23 ANC, GSC, Leg. 923/32226.
24 ANC, CA, Leg. 7/467.
25 ANC, GSC, Leg. 923/32226.
26 ANC, CA, Leg. 7/467.
27 ANC, GSC, Leg. 925/32318.
28 ANC, GSC, Leg. 925/32382.
29 ANC, CA, Leg. 7/487.
30 ANC, GSC, Leg. 930/32587.
31 ANC, CA, Leg. 7/487.
32 ANC, GSC, Leg. 923/32226.
33 ANC, GSC, Leg. 931/32620.
34 ANC, GG, Leg. 365/17461.
35 ANC, CA, Leg. 7/467.
36 An inquiry carried out in 1846 into the state and existence of Indians in the so-called *pueblos de indios* yielded rather contradictory results. The villages in question were Jiguaní, Jiguabos and El Caney, allegedly the last retreats of Indians in Cuba.

Yet most informants on that occasion shared the view that 'never have I known in this village any Indian who is really such, for I have always thought that they did not exist here, but only some natives, the descendants of those founders who due to their mixture with whites and *pardos*, have become removed from that race', and that 'few of the inhabitants of those villages preserve the physiognomy of Indians, this being due to the freedom with which from times immemorial Spaniards, *pardos* and *morenos* have settled there, which means that their population is composed almost entirely of *mestizos* and *zambos*, all of them enjoying indistinctly the right of natives': AHNM, Ultramar, Cuba, Leg. 1647/73.

37 Law 2, title 1, book 6 of the *Recopilación de Indias* declared Indian men and women equal to Spaniards with regard to marriage: quoted in ANC, GG, Leg. 345/16704.

38 ANC, GG, Leg. 345/16704.

39 ANC, GSC, Leg. 894/30417.

40 Richard Konetzke, 'La esclavitud de los indios como elemento de la estructuración social de Hispanoamérica', *Estudios de Historia Social de España* (Madrid, 1949), vol. 1, p. 479.

41 Bohumil Bad'ura, 'Algunos informes sobre la organización y las condiciones de investigación histórica en Cuba', *Ibero-Americana Pragensia*, Anuario del Centro de Estudios Ibero-Americanos de la Universidad Carolina de Praga, 2 (1968), p. 225.

42 Mary Douglas, *Purity and Danger. An Analysis of Concepts of Pollution and Taboo* (London, 1966), p. 139. With regard to the choice of clearly discernible physical attributes as criteria of social classification, it is interesting to note that the Jews of Spain were required to wear yellow patches as a distinguishing mark, and so were the German Jews. Also dress in general as a mark of class comes to mind, as for instance in the case of the crafts and trades.

43 By contrast, van den Berghe maintains for Mexico that 'Paradoxically, the very brutality with which the Spaniards annihilated indigenous civilization . . . the callousness with which they exerted their *droit de cuissage* over the conquered women, all contributed to the cultural and genetic homogenization of the population . . . [and] led in the long run to the relatively harmonious syncretism of modern Mexico': Pierre L. van den Berghe, *Race and Racism. A Comparative Perspective* (New York, 1967), p. 57. In nineteenth-century Cuba, however, it was precisely when the 'genetic homogenization' had advanced farthest that the atmosphere of the country was most segregationist, in the mid-nineteenth century. Some authors have argued that the Cuban free coloured population became progressively blacker throughout the nineteenth century due to the

| Year: | Ratio of mulattos to blacks |
|---|---|
| 1774 | 1.65 |
| 1792 | 1.67 |
| 1817 | 1.09 |
| 1827 | 1.18 |
| 1846 | 1.20 |

massive importation of Africans: Franklin W. Knight, *Slave Society in Cuba during the Nineteenth Century* (Univ. of Wisconsin Press, 1970). According to the censuses from 1774 to 1846 (the 1862 census unfortunately does not distinguish between free *pardos* and free *morenos*) the proportion of mulattos to blacks in the free coloured population is shown in the table on p. 165.

There is thus a sudden increase of blacks from 1792 to 1817 followed by a slow decrease up to 1846. Census figures for 1774 and 1792: de la Sagra, *Historia económico-política*; for 1817 and 1827: *Cuadro estadístico de la siempre fiel Isla de Cuba, correspondiente al año de 1827*; for 1846: *Cuadro estadístico de la siempre fiel Isla de Cuba, correspondiente al año de 1846.*

CHAPTER 6, pp. 82–99

1 ANC, GSC, Leg. 935A/32800.
2 I selected 92 petitions filed by white minors seeking supplementary marriage licences due to parental dissent of the roughly 2,500 cases kept at the National Archives of Cuba. The period covered begins in 1813 and ends in 1878. I selected every fifth year starting in 1814 and within each year I chose every tenth proceedings. This does not apply to 1859, however. When starting to work at the Archives I found reference to two sets of documents catalogued under the title 'correspondence on marriage' which turned out to be petitions for supplementary marriage licences for 1859. I recorded them all. In addition there are included a few proceedings pertaining to other years which at first sight seemed to refer to coloured people but then turned out to be of whites.

  In 64 out of the 92 cases of parental dissent recorded the grounds for opposition are stated. In addition I found a total 157 cases of elopement by whites, a device alternatively resorted to by the couple when faced with parental dissent. In 34 of the cases of elopement the grounds for parental opposition are specified.
3 ANC, Misc., Leg. 2285/T.
4 ANC, GSC, Leg. 935A/32881.
5 ANC, GSC, Leg. 921/32129.
6 ANC, GSC, Leg. 1148/43931; also Leg. 889/299979.
7 ANC, GSC, Leg. 923/32203.
8 ANC, GSC, Leg. 928/30467: the young man had been unable to produce his certificate of baptism and upon further investigation it turned out that in his baptism registration his mother's name had been omitted. ANC, GSC, Leg. 891/30132: the bride's father explains that 'he withheld the licence because [the suitor] was an unknown man since he had so far not been able to produce his certificate of baptism'. Also Leg. 921/32129.
9 One of the measures concerning the family taken by Charles III was the rehabilitation of illegitimates and foundlings for all legal purposes: Domínguez Ortiz, p. 54. The exclusion of illegitimate children from crafts and trades was lifted for the overseas possessions in 1784 in view of the large number of subjects that were prevented from practising the crafts on these grounds: *CDFS*, III:2, p. 540. Liberal professions and public offices, however, continued to be closed to them. In these cases the only way to overcome this impediment was through legitimation or dispensation of illegitimacy. The latter could be obtained through the *gracias al sacar*. In 1801 a new set of rates for such *gracias*, first introduced in

1795, was issued for the overseas possessions. It distinguished three categories of illegitimates, and the fees were graduated, as it were, in accordance with their respective degree of 'infamy': for the dispensation of illegitimacy of a 'natural' son, i.e. the offspring of parents who at the time of his birth were single and thus in a position to marry, 5,500 *reales de vellón* had to be paid, for that of a 'bastard', i.e. the child born to unmarried parents, or of a 'sacrilegious' son, i.e. that born to a priest, the fee was 33,000 *reales de vellón*; and for that of the offspring of an unmarried woman but a married man, 25,000 *reales de vellón*: *CDFS*, III:2, pp. 778–83. 1,000 *reales de vellón* were about 50 pesos, i.e. roughly five times the monthly wage of a domestic servant, and double that of an urban workman. In theory, legitimation meant the 'removal of all infamy, stain or defect', and from the legal point of view the 'restoration of all rights, liberties, exemptions, pre-eminences, prerogatives and immunities which are and should be enjoyed by the offspring of legitimate marriage': *CDFS*, III:2, p. 473.

Although the *gracias al sacar* permitted legitimation, even though at a considerable cost, such dispensations were rarely granted. As the authorities remark: 'It is necessary to put a stop to the corruption of manners even if it is painful to aggravate further the condition of adulterous offspring who bear no fault in it, and considering that it is in the public interest to reserve to marriage the civil prerogatives which all legal systems bestow on it and on the maintenance of which the well-being of the nations is so greatly dependent.' The applicant whose petition for legitimation was rejected in these terms appealed, quoting the case of one D. Angel Eduardo Laborde, the adulterous son of a general who had in fact been granted legitimation, upon which the official in charge of the case suggests that legitimation be conceded, but with a stipulation barring those legitimated from inheriting from their parent: AHNM, Ultramar, Cuba, Leg. 1619/86.

In another case, D. Carlos Mustelier, a natural son, was granted legitimation in 1834, whereas his sister, Da. Ma. de la Soledad, who had been born of the same woman but while her father's first wife was still alive, failed to obtain a modification of status: AHNM, Ultramar, Cuba, Leg. 1629/101. See also Leg. 1615/11, Leg. 1636/21 and Leg. 1737/15.

10 *CDFS*, III:2, p. 473.

11 *CDFS*, III:1, p. 335.

12 ANC, GSC, Leg. 923/32203. This is in 1859.

13 Quoted by Rosenblat, vol. 2, p. 165. In a document addressed to the King by the Cabildo of Caracas in 1788 and intended as a warning against allowing *pardos* to become priests it is argued: '*Pardos* are regarded here with great contempt, due to their origin and due to the taxes your Majesty's royal laws demand of them. They are descended of slaves, their filiation is illegitimate and they have their origin in the union of white men with negresses.' Carlos Siso, *La formación del pueblo venezolano* (Caracas, 1951), quoted by Rosenblat, vol. 2, p. 182. And in response to the royal decree on *gracias al sacar* the same Cabildo in 1796 reiterated once more its opinion that '*Pardos*, mulattos and *zambos*, the distinction between which is not commonly known, have the infamous origin of slavery and the disgraceful one of illegitimacy': Angel Grisanti, *El precursor Miranda y su familia* (Madrid, 1950), pp. 6–7, quoted by Rosenblat, ibid.

14 ANC, GSC, Leg. 927/32467.

15 The assumed legitimacy of foundlings dates from a Bull of Pope Gregory XIV issued in 1591 to the orphanage of Rome establishing that foundlings were to be regarded as legitimate and of pure blood. Yet the condition of foundlings continued to be a topic of discussion among scholars in Spain until the end of the eighteenth century when Charles III by royal decree of 19 February 1794 declared them legitimate by royal dispensation on the basis of the legalistic argument that 'illegitimacy entails infamy and it is not just that when there is any doubt a person should be regarded as infamous when as a rule in law a person is presumed innocent as long as there is no evidence to the contrary'. Tomas de Montalvo, *Práctica política y económica de expósitos* (Madrid 1756), pp. 241–80.

16 *CDFS*, III:2, p. 724.

17 *CDFS*, III:2, p. 818. This case refers to Guadalajara, Mexico.

18 ANC, GSC, Leg. 1148/43942.

19 ANC, GSC, Leg. 890/30042. This is in 1815. In eighteenth-century Spain some occupations (those of ironsmith, sheep-shearer, butcher and innkeeper) were regarded as particularly polluting. Domínguez Ortiz attributes the special discredit in which these occupations were held to the dealings with animals they involved: Domínguez Ortiz, p. 217. However, the official dealing with the case quoted above rejects the parent's objections as outdated for 'it is an error to say that the craft of butchery is vile and infamous and it is an even greater error to say that this vileness is transcendental to the sons of those who practise it; there have been many royal decrees on this and particularly one in which it is laid down that this craft and other similar ones confer vileness only on those who practice them and only while they are doing so'.

20 J. Vicens Vives (ed.), *Historia de España y América* (Barcelona, 1958–61), vol. 4, p. 126.

21 *CDFS*, III:2, p. 813.

22 *CDFS*, III:2, p. 834. *Pardos* were of mixed Indian and negro extraction but in Cuba of negro and Spanish. *Zambos* and *zambaigos* were both of mixed Indian and negro extraction. *Mestizos* were of mixed Spanish and Indian extraction. *Cuarterones* were quadroons, and *octavones* octoroons.

23 *Distribution of crafts and trades by colour in Cuba, 1846*

| Craft or trade | Number of whites in craft or trade | Number of free coloured in craft or trade |
| --- | --- | --- |
| Mason | 3,728 | 4,890 |
| Potter | 494 | 333 |
| Barber | 670 | 733 |
| Shopkeeper | 16,000 | 130 |
| Carpenter | 6,226 | 5,846 |
| Cigar dealer | 124 | 14 |
| Confectioner | 55 | 53 |
| Tanner | 76 | 31 |
| Shop-assistant | 15,285 | 40 |
| Cabinet-maker | 9 | 27 |

23 *contd.*

| Craft or trade | Number of whites in craft or trade | Number of free coloured in craft or trade |
|---|---|---|
| Founder | 57 | 26 |
| Ironsmith | 1,329 | 444 |
| Tinsmith | 149 | 95 |
| Silversmith | 183 | 151 |
| Musician | 298 | 618 |
| Comb-maker | 15 | 10 |
| House-painter | 228 | 188 |
| Baker | 521 | 273 |
| Tailor | 1,419 | 1,923 |
| Watch-maker | 50 | — |
| Saddler | 178 | 130 |
| Cooper | 323 | 240 |
| Weaver | 16 | 12 |
| Cigar-maker | 9,352 | 3,719 |
| Shoemaker | 3,226 | 3,719 |
| Butcher | 394 | 255 |

Source: *Cuadro estadístico de la siempre fiel Isla de Cuba, correspondiente al año de 1846.*

24 ANC, GSC, Leg. 895/30522.
25 Julio Caro Baroja, 'Honour and shame: a historical account of several conflicts' in Peristiany (ed.), *Honour and Shame*, p. 114.
26 ANC, GSC, Leg. 902/31051.
27 ANC, GSC, Leg. 1658/82813.
28 ANC, GSC, Leg. 926/32427.
29 Moreno Fraginals, *El ingenio*, p. 56.
30 Francisco de Arango y Parreño, *Notas al discurso sobre fomento de la agricultura*, quoted by Moreno Fraginals, ibid.
31 ANC, GSC, Leg. 906/31267. And conversely, an official advises against a marriage because 'the situation of the two families is unequal with respect to material possessions, for Casas is engaged in trading and simultaneously is a proprietor in the said village in which he owns several enterprises owing to which he is among the most well-to-do inhabitants [whereas the family] of Pérez possesses no more than the father's shop and a house': Leg. 921/32129.
32 ANC, GSC, Leg. 921/32129.
33 ANC, GSC, Leg. 923/32203.
34 *CDFS*, III:1, p. 73.
35 Still, in 1770 a Daniel Martínez, *judío de profesión* as he is described, was banished from Cuba. He is said to have entered the island 'under the pretext of converting to our Catholic religion', but the Council of the Indies rejected his demand because 'they [the Jews] are accustomed to feign good intentions as a pretext for

sinister purposes. The Hebrew Nation is a depraved, treacherous, ungrateful and fickle race ... and besides she is an irreconcilable enemy of the Christians whom they inwardly persecute and scorn.' *CDFS*, III:1, p. 376. And in 1780 a student was sent down from the University of Havana and was prevented from marrying because he was descended from Jews: *CDFS*, III:2, p. 469. But by the nineteenth century the preoccupation over the so-called New Christians had largely disappeared.

36 ANC, GSC, Leg. 890/30036. Marriage to 'unbelievers, Jews or Mohameddans' was forbidden to Catholics, for baptism being the prerequisite for all other sacraments, one could not receive the marriage sacrament without having been baptized first: Joaquín Escriche, *Diccionario razonado de legislación y jurisprudencia* (Madrid, 1876), vol. 4, p. 171.

37 ANC, GSC, Leg. 920/32063.

38 A number of well-to-do merchants and planters of peninsular origin having made their way from simple shop-assistants crowned their career by marrying into a prominent Cuban family. For instance, D. Luciano García Barbón, a wealthy merchant and owner of one of the most flourishing coffee plantations in Cuba, started out as a shop-assistant when he had first come from Asturias. Once he had managed to acquire some wealth he married the daughter of a rich Cuban tobacco dealer. Similarly, D. José Suárez Argudín, also from Asturias and at first shop-assistant in a textile shop, later advanced to become assistant of the rich *hacendado* (planter) Count of Lombillo with whose Cuban-born wife he is said to have had an affair until the Count died (it was rumoured at Argudín's hands) and he could marry her. Argudín became so prominent that in 1866 he was a member of the Junta Informativa sent to Madrid to report on the state of the island, on which occasion he staunchly defended the status quo. Another Asturian who made a similar career was Martínez Rico. Biblioteca Nacional, Madrid, Manuscritos de América, *Datos biográficos de varias personas visibles de Cuba como hacendados, comerciantes, abogados, laborantes*, 14.497[21].

39 ANC, GSC, Leg. 921/32129.

40 ANC, GSC, Leg. 921/32129.

41 Escriche: see heading *matrimonio canónico*, vol. 4.

42 AHNM, Ultramar, Cuba, Leg. 1717/73.

43 Thus the Council of Trent in its efforts to revitalize ecclesiastical authority made it a point of doctrine that 'no dispensations for marriage between kin be granted, or only very rarely and with good reason ... nor should dispensations be given in the case of kinship in the second degree unless pre-eminent Princes are involved': Escriche, vol. 4, p. 178; also mentioned in AHNM, Ultramar, Cuba, Leg. 1662/4[0]–81[2].

44 At the Council of Trent opinion was divided as to whether the faculty to grant dispensations for marriages among kin should be reserved to the Pope or be delegated on occasion to the local prelates. Pope Clement XIV in 1770 granted the bishops and archbishops of the Spanish overseas possessions this faculty for twenty years. In 1778 Pope Pius VI granted it for ten years, renewing it for another twenty years in 1789. Escriche, vol. 4, p. 173. In 1799 Mariano Luis de Urquijo, Minister to Charles IV, transferred the right to grant these dispensations to the Spanish bishops, as a regalist measure which would prevent the outflow of money: Luis Sierra, 'La restitución de las reservas pontificias sobre impedi-

mentos matrimoniales en la correspondencia Godoy-Azara', *Hispania*, 78 (1960).

45 It appears that subsequent Popes granted such faculties to the overseas prelates en bloc, but that the Cuban bishops either were not aware they enjoyed them or did not make use of them. Thus in a letter by the Papacy of 1858 referring to the problem of powers to dispense kinship in the case of Puerto Rico it was pointed out that 'this decree [of 1850 extending once more the powers granted by earlier Popes to the bishops of America] has been little known in America, where the Bishops have become used to apply individually to the Holy See for the said powers': AHNM, Ultramar, Cuba, Leg. 1717/73.

46 AHNM, Ultramar, Cuba, Leg. 1717/73. Note that there is no mention of cousin marriage.

47 AHNM, Ultramar, Cuba, Leg. 1717/73.

48 ACEM, Ultramar, Leg. 49/519.

49 As the Bishop of Havana complained in 1858, 'there are no more than ten [couples] a year who . . . apply to Rome for a dispensation', while most of those requiring this formality crossed over to the United States: AHNM, Ultramar, Cuba, Leg. 1717/73. No figures are available on marriages contracted by Cubans in the United States. Neither can one be certain that the 235 dispensations kept at the Archive of the Ministry of Overseas Affairs comprise the totality of those granted by the Pope to Cubans. This figure provides a lower limit. If we compare these 235 dispensations granted over a period of seventy years with an average of 2,478 marriages celebrated among whites per year in the 1840s (*Cuadro estadístico de la siempre fiel Isla de Cuba, correspondiente al año de 1846*), the number is indeed low. However, if we take the Bishop of Havana's assertion that there were more than ten marriages among kin in his diocese per year, i.e. more than 0.5 per cent of the number of marriages among whites, this type of marriage appears more common.

50 Francisco Xavier de Sta. Cruz y Mallen, Conde de Jaruco, *Historia de la familias cubanas*, 6 vols. (Havana, 1940–50).

51        *Types of intra-kin marriage and their frequency, from male ego's point of view*

| | |
|---|---|
| With WS | 124 instances |
| WS = cousin | 5 |
| WS = BD | 3 |
| WS = BW | 1 |
| WS = BW | 1 |
| BW | 8 |
| | 142 |
| BD or SD | 78 |
| BD = FBDD | 1 |
| SD = MBSD | 1 |
| | 80 |
| FS or MS | 5 |
| WSD = goddaughter | 1 |
| goddaughter | 1 |
| | 7 |

| Type of kinship relation not stated | 7 |
|---|---|
| Total dispensations | 236 |

The instances where people are twice related are evidence that intra-skin marriage was resorted to generation after generation.

52 For example, AHNM, Ultramar, Cuba, Leg. 1723/18. In forty-three cases it is the concern for the wife's sister's circumstances that is alleged and in fifty-three it is the anxiety over the children's well-being; frequently, however, both reasons are given simultaneously; and often none are given at all.

53 AHNM, Ultramar, Cuba, Leg. 1715/37 and Leg. 1626/54. In those instances where the exact age is stated, it oscillates between twenty-four and forty-two.

54 Escriche, vol. 4, p. 177.

55 AHNM, Ultramar, Cuba, Leg. 1671/97.

56 AHNM, Ultramar, Cuba, Leg. 1671/97; in canon law this circumstance was called *pro indotada*; a slight variant of it is what was termed *ob incompetentiam dotis*, in which case it is alleged that the woman in question does not have a sufficiently large dowry to enable her to marry a man of her station: Escriche, vol. 4, p. 177.

57 It is interesting in this context that a royal decree of 1760 on the prohibition of marriages by military officers without royal consent, established for a junior officer intending to marry a woman whose father was not an officer that she be of a family of at least equal circumstances to his, and that she possess means of her own equal to his pay: *CDFS*, III:1, p. 294. Apparently this regulation raised a number of queries on the exact amount of the dowry required, for in 1789 a further decree was passed fixing it at 3,000 pesos fuertes regardless of whether the bride belonged to the noble or common estate and whether her father was an officer: *CDFS*, III:2, pp. 652–3. The 1760 decree gives a clue to the considerations behind this requirement of a dowry: it was conceived as a device to prevent junior officers from getting themselves through a mésalliance into a situation that would not allow them to live with the 'decency' that their station demanded.

Foundlings were upon their marriage given a dowry of 500 pesos, presumably to make them more attractive as spouses and rid the State of the duty to provide for them: AHNM, Ultramar, Cuba, Leg. 1607/30.

58 AHNM, Ultramar, Cuba, Leg. 1671/97.

59 AHNM, Ultramar, Cuba, Leg. 1626/46.

60 AHNM, Ultramar, Cuba, Leg. 1701/39.

61 AHNM, Ultramar, Cuba, Leg. 1737/11. This circumstance is termed *ab infamiam*: Escriche, vol. 4, p. 178.

S. Wolfram when discussing the debates over marriage with deceased wife's sister in nineteenth-century England shows that the arguments used by the advocates of the bill intended to abrogate this affinal prohibition ran very much along the same lines as those used by the Cubans: that a woman should care for a deceased sister's children, and that extra-marital sex relations between a man and his deceased wife's sister were undesirable: S. Wolfram, 'The explanation of prohibitions and preferences of marriage between kin', unpublished D.Phil. thesis, Oxford, 1956, p. 570.

62 Occasionally a man wants to marry his deceased brother's wife. According to law 4, title 2, book 10 of the *Novísima Recopilación*, widows could remarry freely a year after their husband's death. The reason given is the need to provide for the brother's children.

63 When a reason is stated it is the need either to provide for the niece or to safeguard her reputation.

64 Escriche points out that uncle–niece marriage had become so common that dispensations could be obtained with great ease: Escriche, vol. 4, p. 175.

65 AHNM, Ultramar, Cuba, Leg. $1662/4^0$–$81^2$.

66 AHNM, Ultramar, Cuba, Leg. 1717/73.

67 AHNM, Ultramar, Cuba, Leg. 1753/35.

68 Cf. Gutierrez de Pineda, vol. 1, p. 161.

69 Escriche, vol. 4, p. 175.

70 AHNM, Ultramar, Cuba, Leg. $1662/4^0$–$81^2$.

71 A systematic analysis of the roughly six hundred families recorded in this genealogy of prominent Cuban families would be a fruitful piece of research. The effective frequency of the different forms of intra-kin marriage could be ascertained; but also such matters as birth rate, age of marriage, frequency of marriage and of remarriage could be determined over time. Furthermore, light could be shed on such questions as the continuity of the Cuban élites, and the depth of regional cleavages, i.e. whether for instance families of Oriente intermarried with families of Occidente. Thus the Betancourt of Puerto Príncipe, from whose ranks a number of the men prominent in the struggle for independence emerged, married with few exceptions with local families. Also, on the political cleavages obtaining, i.e. whether independist families intermarried with families loyal to Spain; on the degree to which the newly arrived merchants attempted to and succeeded in consolidating their recently attained economic power by marrying into the old-established families, and to what extent these latter accepted these nouveaux riches; how far these successful merchants identified with the country of their choice and settled there for good, or returned to Spain once they had made good. The Zuluetas, a dynasty founded by the famous slave trader, who made a fortune out of the trade and received a title of nobility for it, went regularly to die in Europe. By contrast the Aldamas, who also went to Cuba at the beginning of the nineteenth century, married into well-established Cuban families – for instance the Alonso – and stayed there for good. Second-generation Aldamas were more or less active in the independence movement. And, finally, light could be thrown on the depth of the alleged split between *peninsulares* and *criollos*; whether this division was as clearcut as it is sometimes assumed to have been, and which types of families accepted intermarriage. This is not an exhaustive plan of study but a beginning could be made along these lines. It would no doubt be a time-consuming enterprise. Such a study could be supplemented by using the two other works on Cuban families available: Conde de Vallellano, *Nobiliario cubano*, 2 vols. (Madrid, n.d.) and Rafael Nieto y Cortadellas, *Dignidades nobiliarias en Cuba* (Madrid, 1954). The Conde de Jaruco's work is by far the most comprehensive one.

72 *CDFS*, III:1, p. 408.

73 *CDFS*, III:1, p. 439.

74 *CDFS*, III:2, p. 794. M. Mörner and A. Rosenblat failed to realize that parental

consent to marriage became a formal requirement also for coloured people: M. Mörner, *Race Mixture in the History of Latin America* (Boston, 1967), p. 39; Rosenblat, vol. 2.

75 *Auto de la Audiencia de Puerto Príncipe de 9 de julio de 1806 en que para el mejor cumplimiento de la Real Cédula de 15 de octubre de 1805 de matrimonios entre personas desiguales, se adopta esta conclusión fiscal.* Rodríguez San Pedro (1868).

76 Diego Mejía Bejarano had obtained such a *gracia* and in this way been allowed to attend the University of Caracas. He then asked for this dispensation of his condition of *pardo* to be made extensive to his sons. This was rejected by the Council of the Indies 'so that the *pardos* will not attempt to generalize these *gracias* and under their protection, believing themselves equal to the whites without any other distinction than the accidental one of colour, think themselves qualified for all employments and offices, even the higher ones, of the church, the military, civil and political, and to become related by marriage to any legitimate and unmixed family'. *CDFS*, III:2, p. 822. Bernardo Ramirez in 1783 suffered a similar fate; his request to be dispensed of the 'infection he suffered' having some *pardas* in his ancestry was refused on account of the ill-feeling and discord such a dispensation might create among the 'notorious Spaniards and Americans of distinction'. *CDFS*, III:2, p. 535.

77 *CDFS*, III:2, p. 828.

78 *CDFS*, III:2, p. 826. In 1806 a member of the Council of the Indies gave a lucid explanation of the social function exercised by the complex hierarchy arising from the coupled criteria of purity of blood and occupation: 'In the overseas possessions the firm idea of the stained origin or birth of those bearing such a stigma has persisted, so that people may refrain from communicating with those suffering from this disability, and from admitting them to certain acts and offices. Since it is undeniable that the diverse hierarchies and spheres are of utmost importance for the preservation and good government of a monarchy, because the obedience and respect of the lowest subject for the sovereign's authority is achieved and maintained by their gradual and linked dependence and subordination, in America this system is all the more necessary, on account of the greater distance from the Throne as well as in view of the great number of this kind of people whose vitiated extraction and nature makes them inferior to the common estates in Spain. It is therefore extremely objectionable that the sons or descendants of slaves, known as such, should sit down and associate with those descending from the first conquerors, or of nobles, legitimate and white families, who are free of any ugly stain.' *CDFS*, III:2, p. 825.

79 ANC, GSC, *matrimonio*, José Anselmo Cárdenas solicitando matrimonio con Juana de la Caridad Reyes, 1816.

I recorded 107 proceedings arising from parental dissent to marriage among coloured people at the Archivo Nacional de Cuba. They refer to the period from 1813 to 1866. I do not know why there are no such cases after 1866.

Not all proceedings are complete. Only occasionally are explicit reasons for opposition given. The table below (p. 175) lists them in order of frequency.

80 ANC, GSC, Leg. 923/3223.

81 ANC, GSC, Leg. 894/30452.

82 ANC, GSC, Leg. 896/30583. *Negro* is the pejorative term for a black person.

83 ANC, GSC, Leg. 906/31312.

*Reasons for parental dissent to marriage among coloured people*

| | | |
|---|---:|---:|
| Inequality | | 29 |
| (a) on account of 'colour' | 16 | |
| (b) on account of *condición* | 12 | |
| (c) not specified | 1 | |
| Bad reputation | | 15 |
| (a) of her | 7 | |
| (b) of him | 8 | |
| Youth, lack of occupation and means | | 13 |
| Other | | 4 |
| Total | | 61 |

84 ANC, GSC, Leg. 906/31312.
85 ANC, GSC, Leg. 893/30329.
86 ANC, GSC, Leg. 924/32284.
87 ANC, GSC, Leg. 913/31686.
88 ANC, GSC, Leg. 920/32080.
89 ANC, GSC, Leg. 909/31057. As one official remarks: 'The woman who breaks the laws of modesty by virtue of the tenderness felt, only rarely decides to clear herself of the guilt of that instant of love by leading an exemplary life'.
90 ANC, Misc., Leg. 2512/An.
91       *Distribution of coloured population of Cuba by shade and legal status, 1774–1846*

| | Free coloureds | | Slaves | |
|---|---|---|---|---|
| Year: | Mulattos | Negroes | Mulattos | Negroes |
| 1774 | 19,207 | 11,640 | 5,724 | 38,609 |
| 1792 | 33,886 | 20,266 | 12,135 | 72,455 |
| 1817 | 59,682 | 54,376 | 32,302 | 166,843 |
| 1827[a] | 57,514 | 48,980 | ... | ... |
| 1846[b] | 81,664 | 67,562 | 12,791 | 310,968 |

Sources: 1774–1817: de la Sagra, *Historia económico-política*; 1827–46: *Cuadro estadístico de la siempre fiel Isla de Cuba.*

(a) In this year the division of slaves into mulattos and negroes is not made.

(b) In later censuses the coloured population is no longer divided by shade.

92 ANC, Misc., Leg. 2165/A.
93 In fifty-four instances the occupation of the suitor is stated.

*Occupations of suitors and their frequency*

| | |
|---|---|
| Member of the *pardo* militias | 5 |
| 1 captain, 1 sergeant, 1 corporal, 2 soldiers | |
| Member of the *moreno* militias | 5 |
| 2 corporals, 1 sergeant, 2 soldiers | |
| Painter | 2 |
| Ironsmith (master) | 1 |
| Shoemaker | 4 |
| Musician | 2 |
| Barber | 2 |
| Tailor | 4 |
| Driver of a calash | 1 |
| Turner | 1 |
| Cooper | 1 |
| Carpenter | 8 |
| Silversmith | 2 |
| Cigar-maker | 6 |
| Mason | 2 |
| Artisan | 2 |
| Vendor of textiles | 1 |
| Sailor | 1 |
| Peasant | 3 |
| Shepherd | 1 |

94 Pedro Deschamps Chapeaux, 'Historia de la gente sin historia. El Negro en la economía habanera del siglo XIX. El funerario Felix Barbosa y la burguesía de color', *Revista de la Biblioteca Nacional 'José Martí'*, 4 (1966), 87–96.
95 Ibid. p. 88.
96 Pedro Deschamps Chapeaux, *El Negro en la economía habanera del siglo XIX* (Havana, 1971), pp. 84–5.
97 ANC, Escribanía de José Agustín Rodriguez, Leg. 148/21.
98 Deschamps Chapeaux, 'El funerario Felix Barbosa', p. 89.
99 Quoted by Deschamps Chapeaux, *El Negro en la economía habanera*, p. 24.

CHAPTER 7, pp. 103–119

1 *CDFS*, III:2, p. 465.
2 Rine Leal, 'Qué viva la tierra que produce la caña', *Cuba* (October 1968), p. 23. In Cirilo Villaverde's novel *Cecilia Valdés* there is also an account of an elopement. The daughter of an overseer runs away with her suitor in order to be able to marry him. At first her father is very annoyed, but later becomes reconciled with the couple at the instigations of the plantation owner's sister, and gives his consent to the marriage. Cirilo Villaverde, *Cecilia Valdés o la Loma del Angel* (New York, 1882), p. 221.
3 *CDFS*, III:2, p. 468.

4 The data used here are derived from criminal proceedings on elopement and seduction held at the Archivo Nacional de Cuba. I extracted 231 cases of elopement and 71 cases of seduction; and found reference to a further 131 cases of one or the other in the nineteenth century which, however, I was not able to extract for lack of time. The cases recorded are spread out fairly evenly over the whole of the nineteenth century. I could trace no earlier instances, probably because they are either kept in other archives or have been lost. There are also many instances referring to the twentieth century in the court archives and in the publications of the Supreme Court of Cuba. The proceedings which served as a basis for this study consist, on the one hand, of the depositions of the parties concerned, which were presumably taken down very much as they were made; on the other, there are the court officials' comments, résumés of the events and of the court verdicts. Not all the proceedings are complete, nor do they follow a uniform pattern. At times there is no way of knowing how the affair ended. Therefore, quantification poses some problems. The distribution of the cases by colour and type of offence is as follows:

*Distribution of court cases on elopement and seduction by colour*

| Type of offence: | Colour of parties involved | | | |
|---|---|---|---|---|
| | Both white | White and coloured | Both coloured | Total |
| Elopement | 157 | 32 | 42 | 231 |
| Seduction | 54 | 13 | 4 | 71 |
| Total | 211 | 45 | 46 | 302 |

Criminal statistics are available for a number of years. They show that the cases recorded do not cover all the actions brought to the courts for elopement or seduction in nineteenth-century Cuba, even if one includes the 131 cases which I did not extract.

*Court cases brought for elopement and seduction in Cuba, 1841–73*

| Year: | Elopement | | | Seduction | | | Grand total |
|---|---|---|---|---|---|---|---|
| | Occidente | Oriente | Total | Occidente | Oriente | Total | |
| 1841 | ... | ... | ... | ... | ... | ... | 18 |
| 1842 | ... | ... | 54 | ... | ... | 21 | 75 |
| 1843 | ... | ... | 21 | ... | ... | 21 | 42 |
| 1844 | ... | ... | 8 | ... | ... | 18 | 26 |
| 1848 | ... | ... | ... | ... | ... | 124 | 124 |
| 1849 | ... | ... | 22 | ... | ... | 95 | 117 |
| 1851 | ... | ... | 2 | ... | ... | 109 | 111 |
| 1852 | ... | ... | 11 | ... | ... | 57 | 68 |
| 1853 | ... | ... | 27 | ... | ... | 45 | 72 |
| 1854 | 45 | 11 | 56 | 25 | 14 | 39 | 95 |

| Year: | Elopment Occidente | Oriente | Total | Seduction Occidente | Oriente | Total | Grand total |
|-------|---------|---------|-------|---------|---------|-------|-------|
| 1855 | — | — | — | 10 | 2 | 12 | 12 |
| 1856 | 36 | 8 | 44 | 34 | 6 | 40 | 84 |
| 1857 | ... | ... | 51 | ... | ... | 39 | 90 |
| 1858 | 22 | 10 | 32 | 25 | 7 | 32 | 64 |
| 1860 | 35 | 14 | 49 | 23 | 6 | 29 | 78 |
| 1863 | 17 | 6 | 23 | 11 | 10 | 21 | 44 |
| 1865 | 25 | 9 | 34 | 15 | 17 | 32 | 66 |
| 1866 | 20 | 3 | 23 | 9 | 4 | 13 | 36 |
| 1868 | 4 | 8 | 12 | 6 | 4 | 10 | 22 |
| 1869 | 6 | — | 6 | 7 | — | 7 | 13 |
| 1871 | 21 | 10 | 31 | 18 | 18 | 36 | 67 |
| 1872 | 19 | 6 | 25 | 55 | 3 | 58 | 83 |
| 1873 | ... | ... | 20 | ... | ... | 28 | 48 |

Source: AHNM, Ultramar, Cuba, Leg. 1630/1, Leg. 1635/52, Leg. 1637/30, Leg. 1639/23, Leg. 1655/84, Leg. 1668/17, Leg. 1669/39, Leg. 1685/4, Leg. 1693/29, Leg. 1704/95, Leg. 1715/46, Leg. 1734, Leg. 1742/25, Leg. 1745/28, Leg. 1754/81, Leg. 1756/2, and Leg. 1763/20.

5 As one parent says: 'he [the daughter's suitor] filled me with bitterness eloping with and thus destroying my daughter's honour; I tried to discover the place where they had gone to, and at last D. Secundino himself and his brother D. Rafael came to me begging me not to take any steps with the authorities in this matter, promising once more that the marriage would take place presently . . . So that the necessary steps were taken I talked to D. Secundino's father and did not meet any opposition from him until at last I realized to my dismay that I had been deceived once again; the criminal has again disappeared leaving his promise unfulfilled, betraying his victim . . . a fact that has induced me to resort to the authority of this court to place my complaint'. ANC, Misc., Leg. 1331/Z; see also Leg. 1300/Ad., Leg. 2543/H, Leg. 2580/8m and GSC, Leg. 1039/36145.

6 ANC, Misc., Leg. 2548/D.

7 Francisco Figueras, *Cuba y su evolución colonial* (Havana, 1907), pp. 276–7. Remy Bastien in a discussion of present day Haitian rural family describes a similar institution. Couples who for financial reasons are not able to formalize their union in church enter into a stable concubinage called *plasaj*. As soon as their financial resources allow they have a religious ceremony and give a wedding party. Remy Bastien, 'Haitian rural family organization', *Social and Economic Studies*, 10 (1961), no. 4, 504. In one of the cases recorded in Cuba the young man states that he had been *aplazado* with his girl with a view to marriage: ANC, GSC, Leg. 912/31671. The term *aplazarse* is still used today in the eastern part of Cuba for free unions entered into with the intention of marrying at some later date. According to Bastien, *plasé* means to establish oneself with a view to marriage. *Aplazarse* in Cuba may mean two things: to establish oneself but also

to postpone marriage. In view of the similarity of the term and its meaning, and the substantial immigration from Haiti to the eastern part of Cuba, it is possible that the Cuban term *aplazarse* had its origin in the Haitian *plasaj*. But the same kind of concubinage also exists in the western part of Cuba, where it is called *arrimarse*.

8  D. Domingo Cueto in 1844 filed a complaint alleging that the excessive fee of 29 pesos and six sheets of stamped paper had been demanded of him by the ecclesiastical authorities for his marriage: ANC, GSC, Leg. 908/31413. Doubtless more evidence could be found of such abuses.

9  ANC, GSC, Leg. 910/31495.

10  ANC, Misc., Leg. 2390/N.

11  ANC, Misc., Leg. 2445/Q.

12  For instance, ANC, GSC, Leg. 911/31550: the mother declared 'when at the beginning she became aware of this affair she reprimanded him and since he offered to marry her daughter . . . she allowed him to visit her home for a few days'.

13  ANC, Misc., Leg. 1333/F; also Leg. 1198/K and GSC, Leg. 912/31504.

14  In 91 proceedings of the 157 cases of elopement between whites, a reason for the elopement is given by either the girl or the young man. In 56 cases it is said to have been provoked primarily by parental opposition to the marriage and in 35 by ill-treatment by parents.

15  ANC, Misc., Leg. 2298/F.

16  ANC, GSC, Leg. 909/31484.

17  ANC, Misc., Leg. 3641/Bb.

18  ANC, GSC, Leg. 908/31405.

19  ANC, GSC, Leg. 927/32451.

20  ANC, GSC, Leg. 927/32496; see also Leg. 1148/43944.

21  ANC, Misc., Leg. 1248/L.

22  ANC, Misc., Leg. 2500/M. Or as another mother laments, '[the elopement causes] the ruin of my family who knows no other patrimony but its intact honour': ANC, Misc., Leg. 1228/W.

23  J. A. Pitt-Rivers coined the concepts of honour-precedence and honour-virtue in his essay 'Honour and social status' in Persistiany (ed.), *Honour and Shame*.

24  In several cases endowment is agreed upon as a solution. In one instance the girl is to receive 'in the way of indemnity for the damage she might have suffered in her wealth and possessions . . . 4 *caballerías* of land . . . free of mortgage': ANC, GSC, Leg. 909/31480. Virginity had a price. The amount of the indemnity was fixed in accordance with the girl's 'class and fortune': ANC, Misc., Leg. 2683/Cb and Leg. 3641/Bs. In thirteen instances the actual amount of the endowment is given. It ranges from 300 to 5,000 pesos. As a clue as to what these sums amounted to it is worth noting that a domestic servant earned 10 pesos a month at the time, and the average price for a young male slave in mid-century Cuba was 600 pesos: Deschamps Chapeaux, 'El funerario Felix Barbosa', p. 91.

25  ANC, GSC, Leg. 912/31504. But occasionally the suspicion of defloration was enough to intimidate parents. Until 1875 in theory a man could be prosecuted for elopement only if the prior virginity of the girl was attested. Two sentences of the Spanish Supreme Court of 1875 and 1881 respectively contain a legal definition of virginity: 'The *doncellez* [virginity] to which the law refers is that

consisting of the state of respectability and the concept of such enjoyed by any young girl while she has not been dishonoured in the eyes of society by an act that injures her respectability and constitutes an offence against custom and public morals.' ANC, Misc., Leg. 2314/M. No explicit mention of actual physical integrity is made. Da. Gumercinda Valdés y Carranza, a widow, describes well what is socially regarded as a disreputable woman. 'Although she knew Da. Caridad Valdés who lived with Da. Francisca Valdés', she says, 'she could not guarantee her respectability, neither did she consider her reputable when [the girl] ran off with her fiancé D. Perfecto Alvarez because she frequently saw her going out alone, staying outside for long periods of time, this not being the modest behaviour a young maiden should observe.' ANC, Misc., Leg. 2314/M. In effect, no conclusive proof of actual loss of virginity was thus required for a young woman to lose her virtue. It was assumed that women on their own were helpless in the face of the perils of the world. They did not possess the moral strength to control their own impulses nor successfully to resist the enticements of men. Therefore they must never be left unprotected. Thus, even if a girl technically continued a virgin, the unchaperoned absence from the home could be sufficient to put pressure on parents to seek marriage. 'Whatever Raina's circumstances', argues one official, 'the irregular conduct of the bride . . . has made [marriage] imperative in the interest of her family's reputation, for although one does not suppose that Raina took advantage of the opportunity provided by Da. Isabel, public opinion is far from believing him . . . who knows whether this view does not come close to the truth.' ANC, GSC, Leg. 923/32203.

26  ANC, Misc., Leg. 1179/A.
27  ANC, Misc., Leg. 2619/G.
28  ANC, Misc., Leg. 1333/B.
29  ANC, Misc., Leg. 2751/F. Da. Magdalena Alvarez's case is a particularly striking instance of this strategy. She had been courting with D. Felipe Pérez for the last two years. There had been repeated attempts at eloping which had always been frustrated by D. Magdalen's uncle with whom she lived. But at last the young couple manage to get away. Her uncle goes to the police and they are found at the sugar mill of the young man's father. The girl states that he had been the first man she had known, that her relatives had been opposed to their liaison and that as a consequence they had decided to go off together. He, however, alleges that she had admitted to an earlier affair with another man. A letter that is said to be by her but which turns out to have been forged by the young man is produced. Here she begs him to forgive her 'for not having been able to present [him] with the chastity of a virgin which [he] had hoped to find in [her]'. At this point a number of letters by him are discovered. In one of them he says: 'If it is true that you love me, if your love is disinterested and sincere, as you have sworn me so often, you must place my tranquillity and well-being above the wicked aims of your family . . . what does your family want? Your family, and you yourself have told told me this, wants me to marry you even though I might abandon you in the very instant the . . . ridiculous church ceremony is over. What does this show? It shows, listen well, that it is not your happiness which they are concerned with (which consists in living with me, in any way, doesn't it?) but a desire which reaches to the point of fury to see their self-respect satisfied.' ANC, Misc., Leg. 2445/E.

30 Two points, however, need to be made with regard to women's passivity or submissiveness. First, contrary to the general pattern, in a few cases of elopement the initiative to run away seemed to stem from the girl rather than the young man. Rather than viewing these cases as exceptions I would argue that they are in perfect accord with elopement as the manifestation of a rejection of the traditional order in favour of the assertion of individual freedom of choice both for men *and* women. Second, and related to the first point, since woman's submissiveness is largely socially and not physiologically determined, when she is given the chance she will often use it to become what is then negatively qualified as a 'virile' woman. In sum, there is a constant latent conflict between the socially defined male and female roles. While women attempt to assert their independence, men are structurally obliged to repress this drive for freedom.

31 ANC, GSC, Leg. 914/31756.

32 ANC, Misc., Leg. 2434/D.

33 ANC, Misc., Leg. 1272/A.

34 As has already been perceptively shown by Lisón in his study of a Spanish town, p. 85.

35 ANC, GSC, Leg. 900/30878.

36 ANC, Misc., Leg. 2165/A.

37 ANC, Misc., Leg. 2733/B.

38 ANC, GSC, Leg. 935A/32851.

39 ANC, GSC, Leg. 889/29955.

40 ANC, GSC, Leg. 914/31756. Another father 'has refused and continues to refuse his approval . . . because [the suitor] has always been held to be a doubtful person as regards his quality and purity of blood': ANC, GSC, Leg. 915/31819. In the majority of cases of persistent dissent, it is the girl who is white. In view of the generally colour hypergamous pattern of interracial unions, this is surprising at first sight. But the fact that more colour hypogamous couples should resort to elopement to persuade the white parents to accept the marriage might indicate that in fact parental opposition was fiercer to such unions, i.e. that greater care was taken with a daughter's than with a son's marriage.

41 *CDFS*, III:2, p. 533.

42 AGI, Capitanía General de la Isla de Cuba, Leg. 1697. In another instance a father demanded that the daughter's seducer be prosecuted for '[he] is a known mulatto as evidenced by his certificate of baptism while my daughter is recognizedly white and free of any bad race': AGI, Capitanía General de la Isla de Cuba, Leg. 1697.

43 ANC, Escribanía de Vergel, Leg. 73/14.

44 ANC, GSC, Leg. 903/31065.

45 ANC, GSC, Leg. 888/29884.

46 *Informe de la Sección sobre el Reglamento formado para atenuar los efectos de la prostitución*, 1863: ANC, CA, Leg. 6/394. According to a census of the brothels of Havana of 1869 it seems, however, that the majority of prostitutes were white. The comparatively low number of coloured prostitutes might be due to the fact that white men were both unwilling and had also no need to pay a coloured woman for her sexual services (see table on p. 182).

47 Villaverde, p. 358.

48 *Memoria de la Real Sociedad Económica, sobre la fuente de desmoralización de las personas libres de color, con indicaciones sobre su reforma. Leida por el Sr. Bachiller y*

*Census of brothels and prostitutes therein by colour in Havana, 1869*

| | No. of brothels | 'Madams' | Whites | Prostitutes *Pardas* | *Negras* | Total |
|---|---|---|---|---|---|---|
| 1st district | 121 | 121 | 189 | 8 | 15 | 333 |
| 2nd district | 64 | 64 | 65 | 10 | 12 | 151 |
| 3rd district | 3 | 3 | 10 | 1 | — | 14 |

Source: Biblioteca Nacional, Madrid, Manuscritos de América, *Ordenes sobre mujeres públicas*, Leg. 20,138. *Estado demostrativo de las casa de prostitución existentes en este Distrito, con expresión de barrios, calles en que están situadas, nombres de las dueñas, pupilas y raza a que pertenecen estas.*

*Morales en Junta celebrada el 7 de octubre de 1864*, Biblioteca Nacional 'José Martí', Havana.

49 See Part I above.

50 As one official argues, 'Marimón it seems is a white man and therefore since a coloured person cannot bring action for seduction against a white person, even if the offence in question has been proved' he cannot be prosecuted: ANC, Misc., Leg. 1141/W.

51 ANC, Misc., Leg. 2301/A.

52 ANC, Misc., Leg. 2733/B.

53 AHNM, Ultramar, Cuba, Leg. 1748/23.

54 See Chapter 4 above.

55 Martínez Alcubilla, vol. 1, p. 176 (my italics). Cf. José María Ots Capdequí *Instituciones sociales de la América Española en el período colonial* (La Plata, 1934), p. 250. Nur Yalman 'On the purity of women in the castes of Ceylon and Malabar', *Journal of the Royal Anthropological Institute of Great Britain and Ireland*, 93 (1963), no. 1, 25–58, explains the emphasis on purity of women there in similar terms.

56 ANC, GSC, Leg. 912/31671.

57 ANC, GSC, Leg. 920/32052.

58 In a report by the Council of the Indies of 1788 one of the ways used by slave women to earn the means to buy their freedom is well illustrated: 'the methods slave women availed themselves of to obtain the means they needed for their *coartación* were not always the most licit and respectable ones; it frequently happened that imbued with the desire to obtain their freedom and in view of the possibility of achieving this aim little by little by means of the *coartación*, this opportunity . . . became a pretext and even the stimulus for occasionally making use of wicked and sinful ways and means . . in evident detriment of the conscience of the slave women themselves and of their accomplices in sin'. *CDFS*, III:2, p. 634.

59 ANC, Misc., Leg. 2669/An. Eldridge Cleaver's account of how he became a

rapist of white women is relevant here: Eldridge Cleaver, *Soul on Ice* (London, 1969).

60 Knight in *Slave Society in Cuba during the Nineteenth Century* also points to the increasing tensions between the races in nineteenth-century Cuba deriving from the expansion of the sugar industry which demanded the introduction of ever-growing number of slaves.

CHAPTER 8, pp. 120–141

1 Peristiany (ed.), Campbell, Lisón.

2 J. K. Campbell, 'Honour and the Devil' in Peristiany (ed.), *Honour and Shame*; Pitt-Rivers, 'Honour and social status' in ibid. In these works rather more prominence is given to the male aspect of honour, in contrast with the present study. While this differing emphasis may be partly due to the kind of evidence I used, I would suggest that there may be a deeper reason. Lisón has already pointed out the complementarity of both aspects of honour. But while these authors seem to propose that male honour demands female honour, I would invert the relationship. The hierarchical social order depends importantly on the value attached to female honour which in its turn is supported by male honour. The relative overtness of the two aspects is related to the spheres in which they are implemented but does not necessarily reflect on their respective sociological relevance.

3 Campbell, *Honour, Family and Patronage.*

4 Lisón-Tolosana, *Belmonte de los Caballeros.*

5 Pitt-Rivers, 'Honour and social status'.

6 Peristiany (ed.), *Honour and Shame.*

7 Ibid. p. 11.

8 Pitt-Rivers, 'Honour and social status'. It seems pertinent here to point out the probable origin of this proverb. Honour here implies purity of blood. It was alleged that the only social class that could justifiably claim an ancestry free from contamination with Jewish blood were plebeians, who had neither the social status nor the wealth that could have attracted the New Christians (converted Jews) to intermarry with them in their struggle for social recognition. Therefore a time came when the only true guarantee of a person's purity of blood consisted in his being plebeian. Cf. Caro Baroja, 'Honour and shame' in Peristiany (ed.), *Honour and Shame*, p. 107, and H. Kamen, *The Spanish Inquisition* (London, 1965), p. 10. Pitt-Rivers' use of the proverb is thus a slight misrepresentation. The honour of the village derives not from its size but precisely from the placing of the villagers within the total social structure.

9 Campbell, *Honour, Family and Patronage*, p. 266.

10 Campbell, 'Honour and the Devil', p. 144.

11 Pitt-Rivers, 'Honour and social status', p. 49.

12 Lisón, p. 84.

13 Béteille, significantly an Indologist, also finds that although 'From these studies [on the Mediterranean] we do not always get a clear picture as to how these concepts [of honour and shame] are related to the social hierarchy ... such a relationship is implicit': André Béteille, 'The decline of social inequality' in Béteille (ed.), *Social Inequality* (Penguin Books, 1969), p. 373. It may be pointed out here that there are indications that in Brazil similar values and principles

operate. Thus Zimmerman states in a study of the Sertão that 'it is still true that the most important attributes for upper-class membership is family background or, as the people of Monte Serrat put it, *antecedentes*... One of the reasons, in fact, that a Negro can never truly be upper-class in the community is because he does not have a "family"'. B. Zimmerman, 'Race relations in the Arid Sertão' in Charles Wagley (ed.), *Race and Class in Rural Brazil* (Unesco, 1952), p. 86.

14  P. G. Rivière, 'The honour of Sánchez', *MAN*, 2 (1967).

15  Yalman, 'On the purity of women', p. 40.

16  For the various forms of control over choice of spouse see W. J. Goode, 'The theoretical importance of love', *American Sociological Review*, 24 (1959), 38–47.

17  For a discussion of the definition of race relations as class relations rather than caste relations see  p. 130.

18  Caro Baroja, 'Honour and shame', p. 120.

19  AHNM, Ultramar, Cuba, Leg. 1748/23.

20  J. Melville and F. S. Herskovits, *Trinidad Village* (New York, 1947).

21  Frazier, *The Negro Family*.

22  R. T. Smith, *Negro Family*; Clarke, *My Mother Who Fathered Me*.

23  Clarke, p. 21.

24  R. T. Smith, *Negro Family*, p. 221.

25  M. G. Smith, *Introduction to Clarke*, 2nd ed. (London, 1966).

26  Ibid. p. xv.

27  M. G. Smith, *West Indian Family Structure*.

28  It is worth noting here that M. G. Smith in his study of *Stratification in Grenada* (London, 1965) makes precisely this point when he stresses the emphasis on class endogamy within the élite and its concomitants: 'Elite regard marriage as a permanent association, sacralized by religion, sanctioned by social groups as well as by law, and involving coresidence of spouses and offspring. Matings between élite males and folk women lack these conditions... Normally the illegitimate issue of an élite male live with the mother apart from the father' (p. 186).

29  M. G. Smith, *West Indian Family Structure*, p. 260.

30  Hyman Rodman, 'Illegitimacy in the Caribbean social structure: a reconsideration', *American Sociological Review*, 31 (1966), no. 5, 673–83.

31  Rivière, p. 578. In this article Rivière attempts to give some specificity to the 'face-to-face' *v.* 'anonymous' hypothesis by approaching the concepts of honour and shame from the male angle. He takes up Pitt-Rivers' assertion that 'honour has gone to the village', and suggests that in the Mexican context a 'correlation between the absence of (successful) *machismo* and a face-to-face community may have more meaning than any distinction between urban and rural environment', as proposed by Oscar Lewis (Rivière, p. 578). He argues that, whereas in the small-scale community anonymity is non-existent and consequently an individual's family background is common knowledge and the rigorous scrutiny by his fellow villagers demands of him a conduct in accordance with it, in the anonymous context of the urban setting the individual is no longer the protagonist of his family or group and is therefore free from sanctions imposed by the regard for his family reputation, but at the same time lacks also the status derived from its membership. Thus, to return to female honour, in the face-to-face community it is paramount to the family honour, and male aggressiveness, though needed at the level of ideals, is proportionately unsuccessful at the level of action. In the

urban context status may be achieved solely through the individual's performance. This demands a higher degree of aggressiveness, *machismo*, of a man. This in turn affects the viability of virginity, which although still the ideal becomes largely inoperative.

32 Campbell, *Honour, Family and Patronage*, p. 266.
33 W. Borah and S. F. Cook, 'Marriage and legitimacy in Mexican culture: Mexico and California', *California Law Review*, 54 (1966), no. 2.
34 Mörner, *Race Mixture*, p. 67.
35 Borah and Cook, p. 962.
36 Ibid. p. 963.
37 Ibid. pp. 963–4.
38 Nancie L. Solien de Gonzalez in her article 'Family organization in five types of migratory wage Labour', *American Anthropologist*, 6 (1961), 1264–80, concludes that different forms of migration have different effects on social organization, 'recurrent migration' clearly acting disintegratingly on the family. Yet it must be taken into account that those who resort to migratory wage labour belong to the lowest stratum of society. In other words, I would suggest that family instability is not the consequence of recurrent migration, but that both are parallel and mutually reinforcing products of the position of this sector of the population within the social structure.
39 Oscar Lewis, *Five Families: Mexican Case Studies in the Culture of Poverty* (New York, 1959); the list of traits of the 'culture of poverty' appears in *Children of Sánchez: Autobiography of a Mexican Family* (New York, 1961). For critical assessments of the concept of 'culture of poverty' see Eleonor Burke Leacock (ed.), *The Culture of Poverty: A Critique* (New York, 1971) and Charles A. Valentine, *Culture of Poverty: Critique and Counter-Proposals* (Univ. of Chicago Press, 1968).
40 Louis Dumont, *Homo Hierarchicus. The Caste System and its Implications* (London, 1972; first published in French, 1966), p. 36.
41 Louis Dumont, 'Caste: a phenomenon of social structure or an aspect of Indian culture?' in A. de Reuck and J. Knight (eds.), *Caste and Race: Comparative Approaches* (London, 1967), p. 35.
42 Quoted by Rosenblat, vol. 2, p. 165.
43 Angel Grisanti, *El precursor Miranda y su familia* (Madrid, 1950), pp. 6–7, quoted by Rosenblat, vol. 2, p. 183.
44 Richard Konetzke, 'Las ordenanzas de gremios como documentos para la historia social de Hispano-américa durante la época colonial', *Revista Internacional de Sociología*, 5 (1947), p. 520.
45 *CDFS*, III:2, p. 825.
46 *CDFS*, II:1, p. 391.
47 *CDFS*, III:2, p. 813.
48 'A. M. Hocart on caste – religion and power', *Contributions to Indian Sociology*, 2 (1958), 54.
49 Ossowski, pp. 41–4.
50 ANC, GSC, Leg. 924/32257.
51 Dumont, *Homo Hierarchicus*, p. 156.
52 Ibid. p. 155.
53 Ibid. p. 160.

54 Ibid. pp. 159–60.
55 Ibid. p. 167.
56 ANC, Misc., Leg. 2285/T.
57 ANC, CA, Leg. 12/1316 (my italics).
58 O. C. Cox, 'Race and caste: a distinction', *American Journal of Sociology*, 50 (1944–5), 366–7. This notion appears to have a history for Kingsley Davis had already maintained in 1941 that hypergamy is disfunctional in a racial context: 'In racio-caste systems . . . the institution of hypergamy becomes totally incompatible with the very basis of the stratification. When race is made the basis, there is a double sense in which marriage is relevant to caste: first as the institutional mechanism through which descent and socialization are regulated, second as the genetic mechanism through which biological identity is maintained.' 'Intermarriage in caste-society', *American Anthropologist*, 43 (1941), 393.
59 Pierre L. van der Berghe thus states that 'In the United States, only an estimated 22 per cent of American Negroes are of pure African ancestry according to Herskovits, and this estimate does not include the many light-skinned mulattoes who have in fact "passed" into the white group.' 'Hypergamy, hypergenation, and miscegenation', *Human Relations*, 13 (1960), 86.
60 Esteban Pichardo, *Diccionario provincial*, p. 660.
61 Cox, 'Race and caste', p. 360. There are also those who regard the caste system as basically a particularly rigid form of class exploitation and in this way establish a continuity between the two systems: e.g. F. G. Bailey, *Caste and the Economic Frontier. A Village in Highland Orissa* (Manchester Univ. Press, 1957). Bailey here asserts: 'There was a high coincidence between politico-economic rank and the ritual ranking of caste. This is a reflection of the general rule that those who achieve wealth and political power tend to rise in the ritual scheme of ranking. It is what is meant by saying that the ranking system of caste-groups was validated by differential control over the productive resources of the village. But the correlation is not perfect, since at each end of the scale there is a peculiar rigidity in the system of caste . . . in between these two extremes, [their] ritual rank tends to follow their economic rank in the village community' (pp. 266–7). And in *Tribe, Caste and Nation* (Manchester Univ. Press, 1960) he professes the view that also in India it is the control of productive resources which is the source of status. A lengthy debate has been sustained between D. Pocock and L. Dumont on the one hand and F. G. Bailey on the other, on whether 'un système d'idées et de valeurs' or the distribution of politico-economic power constitute the basic organizing principle of the caste-system. 'For a sociology of India', *Contributions to Indian Sociology*, 1 (1957), 7–22; 3 (1959), 88–101.
62 Van den Berghe goes even further: he distinguishes ethnic groups from racial groups depending on whether they are physically or only culturally different and asserts that 'racial stratification . . . results in a nearly impermeable caste system more easily than ethnic stratification; race . . . represents an extreme case of ascribed status and lack of social mobility'. *Race and Racism*, p. 22. However, by restricting the concept of race relations to those situations where actual visible physical distinctions obtain, the very problem of 'racism' is defined away.
63 C. Bouglé, *Essais sur le régime des castes* (Paris, 1908), pp. 155–6.
64 Ibid. p. 140.
65 Ibid. p. 144 (my italics).

66 Ibid. p. 145.

67 Ibid. p. 144.

68 As he writes: it is 'In a universe in which men are conceived no longer as hierarchically ranked in various social or cultural species, but as essentially equal and identical, [that] the difference of nature and status between communities is sometimes reaffirmed in a disastrous way: it is then conceived as proceeding from somatic characteristics – which is racism'. Dumont, *Homo Hierarchicus*, p. 51.

69 Van den Berghe, 'Hypergamy', p. 84. Van den Berghe subsumes under his 'maximization of status' hypothesis of hypergamy also the 'hindu type case of hypergamy'. This is not surprising if one bears in mind that in an earlier article he had conceived of caste 'as a closed endogamous group which has relations of subordination or superordination to other similar groups in the same society' and had expressed his disagreement with Cox: 'The dynamics of racial prejudice: an ideal-type dichotomy', *Social Forces*, 37 (1958), 139 n. 4.

70 Dumont, *Homo Hierarchicus*, p. 167.

71 Some scholars argue, however, that also the Indian caste system exhibits some measure of conflict over ranking. Thus Berreman holds that 'Consensus is not lacking between castes . . . but it is a distinctly limited consensus. People largely agree to the facts of the behavioural and interactional hierarchy . . . Where they disagree is on subjective and ideological matters: on the legitimacy of the hierarchy or, more commonly, *on the place their group has been accorded in it*.' G. D. Berreman, 'Stratification, caste and race. Comparative approaches' in de Reuck and Knight (eds.), *Caste and Race*, p. 55 (my italics). Yet, as pointed out by Dumont, caste mobility does not directly interfere with the hierarchy of groups as such, it merely produces a modification of the ranking without challenging the hierarchy itself.

72 Wilhelm Reich, *The Sexual Revolution*, 4th ed. (New York, 1969).

73 Speech of 13 March 1968.

74 *Granma*, 15 January 1968, p. 3.

75 E. Sutherland, *The Youngest Revolution* (New York, 1969), p. 175.

76 Ibid. p. 244.

77 *Granma*, Weekly Review, 11 May 1969.

# BIBLIOGRAPHY

## I ARCHIVAL SOURCES

Archivo Nacional de Cuba, Havana

*Fondo de Gobierno Superior Civil*
*Fondo de Gobierno General*
*Fondo de Asuntos Políticos*
*Fondo de Consejo de Administración*

These sections are catalogued by subject matter. The heading *matrimonio*, particularly of the Fondo de Gobierno Superior Civil, holds the bulk of the material on parental dissent to marriage by minors and on interracial marriage.

*Fondo de Miscelánea*

Uncatalogued, but an inventory exists. Most of the material on elopement and seduction is contained in this section.

*Fondo de la Sociedad Económica de Amigos del País*

Catalogued. Under the headings *esclavos*, *población*, *vagancia* data on economic and political implications of slavery were found.

Archivo Histórico Nacional, Madrid

*Sección de Ultramar. Cuba. Gracia y Justicia*

Uncatalogued. Holds data on kinship dispensations in marriage and on legitimation as well as on the dispute between Church and State over marriage.

Archivo del Consejo de Estado, Madrid

*Sección de Ultramar. Gracia y Justicia*

The section *preces, bulas y rescriptos* contains further material on kinship dispensations.

*Sección de Ultramar. Gobernación*

The section *esclavos y colonización* holds material on slavery and the introduction of indentured labourers.

Archivo General de Indias, Seville

*Sección XI. Capitanía General de la Isla de Cuba*

These documents are listed in an inventory published in Joaquín Llaverías, *Historia*

# Bibliography

*de los Archivos de Cuba* (Havana, 1949). This inventory has several headings *matrimonio* referring to proceedings on cases of parental dissent to marriage by minors, interracial marriage and elopement.

## 2 DOCUMENTARY AND LEGAL COLLECTIONS, CENSUSES AND DICTIONARIES

*Censo de la población de España, 1877.* 2 vols. Madrid, 1884.

*Censo de la población de España – 1887.* Madrid, 1891.

*Cuadro estadístico de la siempre fiel Isla de Cuba, correspondiente al año de 1827.* Havana, 1829.

*Cuadro estadístico de la siempre fiel Isla de Cuba, correspondiente al año de 1846.* Havana, 1847.

Erenchun, Felix. *Anales de la Isla de Cuba; diccionario administrative, económico, estadístico y legislativo.* 5 vols. Havana, 1861–5.

Escriche, Joaquín. *Diccionario razonado de legislación y jurisprudencia.* 4 vols. Madrid, 1876.

García de Arboleya, José. *Manual de la Isla de Cuba; compendio de su historia, geografía, estadística y administración.* Havana, 1852.

*Información sobre reformas en Cuba y Puerto Rico.* 2 vols. New York, 1867.

Konetzke, Richard (ed.). *Colección de documentos para la historia de la formación social de Hispanoamérica, 1493–1810.* 3 vols. Madrid, 1953–62.

Martinez Alcubilla, Marcelo. *Diccionario de la administración española.* 5th ed. 9 vols. Madrid, 1886.

*Memorias de la Sociedad Económica de Amigos del País.* Biblioteca Nacional 'José Martí', Havana.

de Montalvo, Tomás. *Práctica política y económica de expósitos.* Madrid, 1756.

Nieto y Cortadellas, Rafael. *Dignidades nobiliarias en Cuba.* Madrid 1954.

*Noticias estadísticas de la Isla de Cuba en 1862.* Havana, 1864.

Ots Capdequí, José María. *El derecho de familia en la legislación de Indias.* Madrid, 1921.

*Instituciones sociales de la América Española en el período colonial.* La Plata, 1934.

Pacheco, Joaquín Francisco. *El código penal. concordado y comentado.* 3 vols. Madrid, 1848.

de la Pezuela y Lobo, Jacobo. *Diccionario geográfico, estadístico, histórico de la Isla de Cuba.* 4 vols. Madrid, 1863–6.

Pichardo, Esteban. *Pichardo Novísimo o Diccionario provincial casi razonado de voces y frases cubanas.* Havana, 1953; first publ. 1836.

*Report of the Census of Cuba, 1899.* Washington, 1900.

Rodríguez San Pedro, Joaquín. *Legislación ultramarina, concordada y anotada.* 12 vols. Madrid, 1868.

de la Sagra, Ramón *Historia económico-política y estadística de la Isla de Cuba.* Havana, 1831.

*Historia física, política y natural de la Isla de Cuba.* 12 vols. Paris, 1842–61.

de Sta. Cruz y Mallen, Francisco Xavier, Conde de Jaruco. *Historia de las familias cubanas.* 6 vols. Havana, 1940–50.

Vallellano, Conde de. *Nobiliario cubano.* 2 vols. Madrid, n.d.

# Bibliography

Zamora y Coronado, José María. *Biblioteca de legislación ultramarina en forma de diccionario alfabético.* 6 vols. Madrid, 1844–6.


### 3 BOOKS AND ARTICLES

Abou-Zeid, Ahmed. 'Honour and shame among the Bedouins of Egypt' in Peristiany (ed.), *Honour and Shame.*
Acosta Saignes, Miguel. *Vida de los esclavos negros en Venezuela.* Caracas, 1967.
Aimes, H. H. S. *A History of Slavery in Cuba, 1511–1868.* New York and London, 1907.
Ames, David W. 'Negro family types in a Cuban solar', *Phylon*, 2 (1950).
Amigó, Gustavo. 'La iglesia católica en Cuba', *Revista Javeriana*, 28 (1947).
de Arango y Parreño, Francisco. *Obras.* 2 vols. Havana, 1888–9.
Arredondo, Antonio. *El Negro en Cuba.* Havana, 1939.
Atkins, Edwin F. *Sixty Years in Cuba.* Cambridge, Mass., 1926.
Bacardí y Moreau, Emilio. *Crónicas de Santiago de Cuba*, 3 vols. Santiago de Cuba, 1925.
Bad'ura, Bohumil. 'Algunos informes sobre la organización y las condiciones de investigación histórica en Cuba', *Ibero-Americana Pragensia* Anuario del Centro de Estudios Ibero-Americanos de la Universidad Carolina de Praga, 2 (1968).
Bailey, F. G. *Caste and the Economic Frontier. A Village in Highland Orissa.* Manchester Univ. Press, 1957.
*Tribe, Caste and Nation.* Manchester Univ. Press, 1960.
Banton, Michael. *Race Relations.* London, 1967.
Barnet, Miguel. *Biografía de un cimarrón.* Havana, 1966.
de las Barras y Pardo, Antonio. *La Habana a mediados del siglo XIX.* Madrid, 1925.
Barrera y Domingo, Francisco. *Reflexiones histórico físico naturales médico quirúrgicas.* Havana, 1798.
Bastide, Roger. *Les Amériques Noires. Les civilisations africaines dans le nouveau monde.* Paris, 1967.
'Color, racism and Christianity', *Daedalus* (Spring 1967).
Bastien, Remy. 'Haitian rural family organization', *Social and Economic Studies*, 10 (1961), no. 4.
'The dynamics of racial prejudice: an ideal-type dichotomy', *Social Forces*, 37 (1958).
'Hypergamy, hypergenation, and miscegenation', *Human Relations*, 13 (1960).
Béteille, André (ed.). *Social Inequality.* Penguin Books, 1969.
'The decline of social inequality' in Béteille (ed.), *Social Inequality.*
Blake, Judith, Mayone Stycos, J. and Davis, Kingsley. *Family Structure in Jamaica: The Social Context of Reproduction.* New York, 1961.
Blanco, T. *El prejudicio racial en Puerto Rico.* San Juan, 1942.
Borah, W. and Cook, S. F. 'Marriage and legitimacy in Mexican culture: Mexico and California', *California Law Review*, 54 (1966), no. 2.
Bouglé, Celestin. *Essai sur le régime des castes.* Paris, 1908.
Boxer, C. R. *Race Relations in the Portuguese Colonial Empire, 1415–1825.* Oxford, 1963.
Braithwaite, L. 'Social stratification in Trinidad. A preliminary analysis', *Social and Economic Studies*, 3 (1953).

# Bibliography

Brown, Gerardo. *Cuba Colonial*. Havana, 1925.

Bustamante, José Angel. *Raíces psicológicas del Cubano*. Havana, 1960.

Caballero, José Agustín. 'En defensa del esclavo (a los nobilísimos cosecheros de azúcar, señores amos de ingenios, mis predilectos paisanos)' in *Escritos Varios*, Havana, 1956, vol. 1.

Cabrera, Lydia. *Cuentos negros de Cuba*. Havana, 1940.

Campbell, J. K. *Honour, Family and Patronage*. Oxford, 1964.

'Honour and the Devil' in Peristiany (ed.), *Honour and Shame*.

Cardoso, Fernando Henrique and Ianni, Octavio. *Côr e mobilidade social em Florianapolis: aspectos das relações entre negros e brancos numa comunidade do Brasil meridional*. São Paulo, 1960.

Caro Baroja, Julio. *Los judíos en la España moderna y contemporánea*. 3 vols. Madrid, 1961.

'Honour and shame: a historical account of several conflicts' in Peristiany (ed.), *Honour and Shame*.

Carr, Raymond. *Spain 1808–1939*. Oxford, 1966.

Castro, Américo. *The Structure of Spanish History*. Princeton Univ. Press, 1954.

Cepero Bonilla, Raul. *Azúcar y Abolición*. Havana, 1948. 2nd ed. in *Obra Histórica*, Havana, 1963.

Chailloux Cardona, Juan M. *Síntesis histórica de la vivienda popular. Los horrores del solar habanero*. Havana, 1945.

de Chateausalins, Honorato Bernard. *El vademecum de los hacendados cubanos*. Havana, 1854.

Clarke, Edith, *My Mother Who Fathered Me*. London, 1957.

Cleaver, Eldridge. *Soul on Ice*. London, 1969.

*Contributions to Indian Sociology*, vols. 1–10, 1957–66.

Corwin, Arthur F. *Spain and the Abolition of Slavery in Cuba, 1817–1886*. Univ. of Texas Press, 1967.

Coulthard, G. R. *Race and Colour in Caribbean Literature*. Oxford, 1962.

Cox, Oliver C. *Caste, Class and Race*. New York, 1959.

'Race and caste: a distinction', *American Journal of Sociology*, 50 (1944–5).

Cumper, G. E. 'Household and occupation in Barbados', *Social and Economic Studies*, 4 (1961).

Dana, Richard H. Jr. *To Cuba and Back: A Vacation Voyage*. Boston, 1859.

Davenport, W. 'The family system of Jamaica', *Social and Economic Studies*, 4 (1961).

Davis, D. Brion. *The Problem of Slavery in Western Culture*. Cornell Univ. Press, 1966.

Davis, J. 'Honour and politics in Pisticci', *Proceedings of the Royal Anthropological Institute of Great Britain and Ireland* (1969).

Davis, Kingsley. 'Intermarriage in caste-society', *American Anthropologist*, 43 (1941).

Deschamps Chapeaux, Pedro. *El Negro en la economía habanera del siglo XIX*. Havana, 1971.

'Historia de la gente sin historia. El Negro en la economía habanera del siglo XIX. El funerario Felix Barbosa y la burguesía de color', *Revista de la Biblioteca Nacional 'José Martí'*, 4 (1966).

'Historia de la gente sin historia. El Negro en la economía habanera del siglo XIX. Augustín Ceballos, capataz de muelle', *Revista de la Biblioteca Nacional 'José Martí'*, 1 (1968).

# Bibliography

Domínguez Ortiz, Antonio. *La sociedad Española en el siglo XVIII*. Madrid, 1955.

Douglas, Mary. *Purity and Danger. An Analysis of Concepts of Pollution and Taboo*. London, 1966.

Dumont, Louis. *Homo Hierarchicus. The Caste System and its Implications*. London, 1972; first published in French, 1966).

'Hierarchy and marriage alliance in South Indian kinship', *Occasional Papers*, 12, Royal Anthropological Institute, 1957.

'Marriage in India. The present state of the question. Postscript to Part One', *Contributions to Indian Sociology*, vol. 7 (1964).

Elkins, Stanley M. *Slavery: A Problem in American Institutional and Intellectual Life*. Chicago, 1959.

Entralgo, Elias José. 'Un forum sobre los prejuicios étnicos en Cuba', *Nuestro Tiempo* (1959).

Epstein, T. Scarlett. *Economic Development and Social Change in South India*. Manchester Univ. Press, 1962.

d'Estefano Pisani, Miguel. *El rapto. Su doctrina y evolución en el derecho positivo cubano*. Havana, 1945.

Estorch, Miguel. *Apuntes para la historia sobre la administración del Marqués de la Pezuela en la Isla de Cuba desde 3 de diciembre de 1853 hasta 21 de setiembre de 1854*. Madrid, 1856.

Fernandes, Florestan. *A integração do negro na sociedade de classes*. São Paulo, 1965.

Fernandez, Cristobal, C. M. F. *El Beato Padre Antonio María Claret. Historia documentada de su vida y empresas*. Madrid, 1941.

Figueras, Francisco. *Cuba y su evolución colonial*. Havana, 1907.

Firth, Raymond (ed.). *Two Studies of Kinship in London*. L.S.E. Monographs in Social Anthropology, 15. London, 1956.

Foner, Laura and Genovese, Eugene D. (eds.). *Slavery in the New World. A Reader in Comparative History*. Englewood Cliffs, N.J., 1969.

Foner, Philip S. *A History of Cuba and its Relations with the United States*. 2 vols. New York, 1962.

Frazier, E. Franklin. *The Negro Family in the United States*. Chicago Univ. Press, 1937.

Freyre, Gilberto. *The Masters and the Slaves: A Study in the Development of Brazilian Civilization*. New York, 1946.

Genovese, Eugene D. *The World the Slaveholders Made. Two Essays in Interpretation*. London, 1970.

Goode, W. J. *World Revolution and Family Patterns*. New York, 1963.

'The theoretical importance of love', *American Sociological Review*, 24 (1959).

Goveia, Elsa V. 'Comment on "Anglicanism, Catholicism, and the Negro slave"' in Foner and Genovese, *Slavery in the New World*.

Greenfield, Sidney M. 'Socio-economic factors and family form', *Social and Economic Studies*, 1 (1961).

'Household, families and kinship systems in the West Indies', *Anthropological Quarterly*, 3 (1962).

'Culture-historical and structural functional orientations and the analysis of the West Indian family', *Proceedings of the First Conference on the Family in the Caribbean*, Inst. of Caribbean Studies, Univ. of Puerto Rico, Rio Piedras, Puerto Rico, 1968.

# Bibliography

Guerra y Sanchez, R. *Manual de historia de Cuba: económica social y política*. Havana, 1938.

et al. *Historia de la Nación Cubana*. 10 vols. Havana, 1952.

Gutiérrez de Pineda, Virginia. *La familia en Colombia*. Bogotá, 1963. vol. 1.

*Familia y cultura en Colombia*. Bogotá, 1968. vol. 2.

Hall, Gwendolyn Midlo. *Social Control in Slave Plantation Societies. A Comparison of St. Domingue and Cuba*. Baltimore, 1971.

Henriques, Fernando. *Family and Colour in Jamaica*. London (1963).

'West Indian family organization', *Caribbean Quarterly* (1952).

Hernández y Sánchez-Barba, M. 'David Turnbull y el problema de la esclavitud en Cuba', *Anuario de Estudios Americanos*, 14 (1957).

'A. M. Hocart on caste – religion and power', *Contributions to Indian Sociology*, vol. 2 (1958).

Hoetink, H. *The Two Variants of Caribbean Race Relations*. Oxford, 1967.

Ianni, Octavio. *As Metamorfoses do Escravo*. São Paulo, 1962.

Ibarra, Jorge. *Ideología Mambisa*. Havana, 1967.

Jayawardena, G. 'Marital stability in two Guianese sugar estate communities', *Social and Economic Studies*, 1 (1960).

Jerez Villareal, Juan. *Oriente: biografía de una provincia*. Havana, 1960.

Jordan, Winthrop D. *White over Black: American Attitudes toward the Negro, 1550–1812*. Univ. of North Carolina Press, 1968.

Kamen, Henry. *The Spanish Inquisition*. London, 1965.

Klein, Herbert. *Slavery in the Americas: A Comparative Study of Virginia and Cuba*. London, 1967.

Knight, Franklin W. *Slave Society in Cuba during the Nineteenth Century*. Univ. of Winconsin Press, Madison, 1970.

'The role of the free black and the free mulatto in Cuban slave society'. Unpublished paper presented at a symposium sponsored by the Department of History and the Institute of Southern History of the Johns Hopkins University, Baltimore, Maryland, April, 1970.

Konetzke, Richard. 'La emigración de mujeres españoles a América durante la época colonial', *Revista Internacional de Sociología*, 3 (1945).

'Las ordenanzas de gremios como documentos para la historia social de Hispanoamérica durante la época colonial', *Revista Internacional de Sociología*, 5 (1947).

'La esclavitud de los indios como elemento de la estructuración social de Hispanoamérica', *Estudios de Historia Social de España*, Madrid, 1949, vol. 1.

Leach, Edmund R. (ed.). *Aspects of Caste in South India, Ceylon and North-West Pakistan*. Cambridge Univ. Press, 1960.

*Pul Eliya. A Village in Ceylon. A Study of Land Tenure and Kinship*. Cambridge Univ. Press, 1961.

Leacock, Eleonor Burke (ed.). *The Culture of Poverty: A Critique*. New York, 1971.

Leiseca, Juan Martin, *Apuntes para la historia eclesiástica de Cuba*. Havana, 1938.

LeRiverend, Eduardo. *Matrimonio anómalo*. Havana, 1942.

LeRiverend, Julio. *La Habana: biografía de una provincia*. Havana, 1960.

Lewis, Oscar. *Five Families: Mexican Case Studies in the Culture of Poverty*. New York, 1959.

*Children of Sánchez: Autobiography of a Mexican Family*. New York, 1961.

*La Vida. A Puerto Rican Family in the Culture of Poverty – San Juan and New York*. London, 1967.

# Bibliography

Lisón-Tolosana, C. *Belmonte de los Caballeros: A Sociological Study of a Spanish Town*. Oxford, 1966.

Mair, Lucy. *Marriage*. Pelican Books, 1971.

Maluquer de Motes, Jorge. 'El problema de la esclavitud y la Revolución de 1868', *Hispania*, 31 (1971).

Martin, Juan Luis. *Esquema elemental de temas sobre la caña de azúcar como factor topoclimático de la geografía social de Cuba*. Havana, 1944.

Martinez-Alier, Juan and Verena. *Cuba: economía y sociedad*. Paris, 1972.

Martinez-Alier, Verena. 'Color, clase y matrimonio en Cuba en el siglo XIX', *Revista de la Biblioteca Nacional 'José Martí'* (1968).

'Elopement and seduction in nineteenth-century Cuba', *Past and Present*, 55 (1972).

Martínez y Saez, Jacinto María. *Los voluntarios de Cuba y el Obispo de la Habana. Historia de ciertos sucesos por el mismo Obispo, Senador del Reino*. Madrid, 1871.

Melville, J. and Herskovits, Frances S. *Trinidad Village*. New York, 1947.

Merton, Robert. 'Intermarriage and the social structure: fact and theory', *Psychiatry*, 4 (1941).

Mesa, Roberto. *El colonialismo en la crisis de XIX español*. Madrid, 1967.

Mintz, Sidney W. 'Review of *Slavery* by Stanley M. Elkins', *American Anthropologist*, 63 (1961).

'The Caribbean as a socio-cultural area', *Cahiers d'Histoire Mondiale*, 4 (1966).

Moreno, Francisco. *Cuba y su gente: apuntes para la historia*. Madrid, 1887.

Moreno Fraginals, Manuel. *José Antonio Saco. Estudio y bibliografía*. Univ. Central de Las Villas, 1960.

*El ingenio: el complejo económico-social cubano del azúcar*. Havana, 1964.

Mörner, Magnus. *Race Mixture in the History of Latin America*. Boston, 1967.

'The history of race relations in Latin America: some comments on the state of research', *Latin American Research Review*, 3 (1966).

Nogueira, Oracy. 'Skin color and social class' in *Plantation Systems of the New World*, Pan American Union, Social Science Monograph 7, Washington, 1959.

Ortiz, Fernando. *Los negros esclavos*. Havana, 1916.

*Cuban Counterpoint: Tobacco and Sugar*. New York, 1947.

'Origen geográfico de los afrocubanos', *Revista Bimestre Cubana*, 1 (1957).

Ossowski, Stanislaw. *Class Structure in the Social Consciousness*. London, 1963.

Otterbein, K. F. 'Caribbean family organization: a comparative analysis', *American Anthropologist*, 1 (1965).

Pérez de la Riva, Francisco. 'Una familia de color en Cuba. El pintor Vicente Escobar', *Trimestre* (1947).

Pérez de la Riva, Juan. *Correspondencia reservada del General Tacón*. Havana, 1964.

'Documentos para la historia de las gentes sin historia. Antiguos esclavos cubanos que regresan a Lagos', *Revista de la Biblioteca Nacional 'José Martí'*, 1 (1964).

'Demografía de los culies chinos en Cuba (1853–74), *Revista de la Biblioteca Nacional 'José Martí'*, 4 (1966).

'La contradicción fundamental de la sociedad colonial cubana: trabajo esclavo contra trabajo libre', *Economía y Desarrollo*, 2 (1970).

Peristiany, J. G. (ed.). *Honour and Shame: The Values of Mediterranean Society*. London, 1965.

Pitt-Rivers, J. A. 'Honour and social status' in Peristiany (ed.), *Honour and Shame*.

# Bibliography

Pujadas, P. Tomas L., C. M. F. *San Antonio María Claret, apóstol de nuestro tiempo*. Madrid, 1950.

Reich, Wilhelm. *The Sexual Revolution*. 4th ed. New York, 1969.

de Reuck, A. and Knight, J. (eds.). *Caste and Race: Comparative Approaches*. London, 1967.

Rivière, Peter G. 'The honour of Sánchez', *MAN*, 2 (1967).

Rodman, Hyman. 'On understanding lower class behaviour', *Social and Economic Studies*, 4 (1959).

'Illegitimacy in the Caribbean social structure: a reconsideration', *American Sociological Review*, 31 (1966), no. 5.

Rosenblat, Angel. *La población indígena y el mestizaje en América*. Buenos Aires, 1954. 2 vols.

Saco, José Antonio. *Colección de papeles científicos, históricos, políticos y de otros ramos sobre la isla de Cuba ya publicados, ya inéditos*. Paris, 1858-9.

*Historia de la esclavitud de la raza africana en el Nuevo Mundo y en especial en los países Américo-Hispanos*. 4 vols. Havana, 1938.

Santa Cruz y Montalvo, Maria de las Mercedes, Condesa de Merlin. *Mis doce primeros años*. Havana, 1922.

Siegel, Morris. 'Race attitudes in Puerto Rico', *Phylon* (1953).

Sierra, Luis. 'La restitución de las reservas pontificias sobre impedimentos matrimoniales en la correspondencia Godoy-Azara', *Hispania*, 78 (1960).

Smith, M. G. *West Indian Family Structure*. Univ. of Washington Press, 1962.

*The Plural Society in the British West Indies*. Univ. of California Press, 1965.

*Stratification in Grenada*. London, 1965.

Smith, R. Freeman (ed.). *Background to Revolution. The Development of Modern Cuba*. New York, 1966.

Smith, R. T. *The Negro Family in British Guiana. Family Structure and Social Status in the Villages*. London, 1956.

'Family structure and plantation systems in the New World' in *Plantation Systems of the New World*, Pan American Union, Social Science Monograph 7, Washington, 1959.

Solien de Gonzalez, Nancie L. 'Family organization in five types of migratory wage labour', *American Anthropologist*, 6 (1961).

Srinivas, M. N. *Religion and Society among the Coorgs of South India*. Oxford, 1952.

Sutherland, Elizabeth. *The Youngest Revolution*. New York, 1969.

Sylvian-Comhaire, S. 'Courtship, marriage and plasaj at Kenscoff, Haiti', *Social and Economic Studies*, 4 (1958).

Tannenbaum, F. *Slave and Citizen. The Negro in the Americas*. New York, 1947.

Tejera, Diego V. *El rapto*. Matanzas, 1921.

Thomas, H. *Cuba or the Pursuit of Freedom*. London, 1971.

Urban, C. Stanley. 'The Africanization of Cuba scare, 1853-1855', *Hispanic American Historical Review*, 37 (1957).

Valentine, Charles A. *Culture of Poverty: Critique and Counter-Proposals*. Univ. of Chicago Press, 1968.

Valiente, Porfirio. *Réformes dans les îles de Cuba et Porto-Rico*. Paris, 1869.

van der Berghe, Pierre L., *Race and Racism. A Comparative Perspective*. New York, 1967.

Vial Correa, Gonzalo. 'Los prejuicios sociales en Chile al terminar el siglo XVIII', *Boletin de la Academia Chilena de Historia*, 73 (1965).

# Bibliography

Vicens Vives, J. (ed.). *Historia de España y América*. 5 vols. Barcelona, 1958–61.

Villaverde, Cirilo. *Cecilia Valdés o la Loma del Angel*. New York, 1882.

Wagley, Charles (ed.). *Race and Class in Rural Brazil*. Unesco, 1952.

Wilson, Peter J. 'Household and family in Providencia', *Social and Economic Studies*, 4 (1961).

'Reputation and respectability – a suggestion for Caribbean ethnology', *MAN*, 2 (1969).

Wolfram, S. 'The explanation of prohibitions and preferences of marriage between kin'. Unpublished D.Phil. thesis. Oxford, 1956.

Yalman, Nur. 'On the purity of women in the castes of Ceylon and Malabar', *Journal of the Royal Anthropological Institute of Great Britain and Ireland*, 93 (1963), no. 1.

'De Tocqueville in India: an essay on the caste system', *MAN*, 2 (1969).

Young, M. and Wilmott, P. *Family and Kinship in East London*. London, 1957.

# INDEX

# Index

# Index

Marriage *(cont.)*
and status ascription, 122, 123, 139
Marriage, types of
isogamic among coloureds, 13, 62, 91–9
isogamic among whites, 13, 57–60, 62, 70, 82–91
between whites and negroes, 13, 24, 32, 64, 118
between whites and mulattos, 11, 12, 14, 15, 17, 19, 21, 24, 25, 26, 31, 34, 37, 40, 57, 62, 65–6, 67
between whites and Chinese, 77
between whites and Indians, 64
between Chinese and mulattos, 76, 77
between negroes and mulattos, 21, 93, 112
among slaves, 2, 93–4
Martí, José, 41
Martínez Alcubilla, M., 150n., 151n., 160n., 182n.
Martínez y Saez, Jacinto María, 53, 54, 55, 63, 159n.
*(see also* Havana, Bishop of)
Mating systems
and status systems, 127–8
Matrifocality, 124–30
and the family cycle, 126
and mating options, 127–8
and socio-economic structure, 125–7, 129
and status ascription, 126
*(see also* Sexual marginalization; Concubinage)
Mediterranean, 2, 120
Merchants, 33, 34–5, 38, 54
Merton, R. K., 151n., 153n.
Mesa, Roberto, 156n.
Mexico, 130
Viceroy of, 13
Militias, of coloureds, 28, 33, 92, 98
Mintz, S. W., 2, 148n.
Miscegenation, 6, 136
and demography, 81
Montalvo, Tomás de, 168n.
Morality, 19, 45, 53, 68, 87, 105, 119
double standard of, 67, 115–16, 117, 121
*(see also* Norms; Virginity; Religion)

Moreno Fraginals, M., 3, 34, 85, 148n., 169n.
Mörner, M., 130, 173n,, 185n.
Morúa Delgado, Martin, 41

Nieto y Cortadellas, Rafael, 173n.
Norms, 1, 4, 6, 7, 14, 15, 57, 71, 85–6, 92, 103, 106, 129, 134
conflict on the level of, 1, 7, 45, 66, 85, 111, 114, 119, 120, 122, 132–3, 135–6, 138, 181n.
and the entrepreneurial class, 85–6
and social organization, 7, 119, 122, 135–6

O'Donnell, General, 35, 99, 156n.
Oriente, 30, 39, 50, 51, 64, 68, 79, 80, 90, 91, 157n., 159n.
Ortiz, Fernando, 149n., 155n., 178n.
Ossowski, S., 5, 153n., 185n.
Ots Capdequí, José María, 182n.

Parental opposition to marriage, 1, 7, 11, 14, 15, 16, 19, 26, 44, 82–7, 103–4, 117, 118, 135–6 *(see also* Family honour)
action taken against, *see* Elopement; Female honour; Family honour
appeals against, *see* Civil authorities, as court of appeal
coloureds against whites, 96
coloureds against coloureds, 93–8
coloureds against Chinese, 79
whites against whites, 82, 106–9
whites against coloureds, 14, 15–19, 40, 113
*(see also* Family honour; Marriage, interracial)
*peninsulares* (Spaniards), 4, 30, 56
Pérez de la Riva, Juan, 155n., 156n., 164n.
Peristiany, J. G., 121, 148n., 169n., 183n.
Petty bourgeoisie
coloured, 32, 98–9 *(see also* Parental opposition, coloureds against coloureds)
Pezuela y Lobo, Jacobo de la, 28–31, 53, 55, 154n., 159n., 160n.
Pichardo, Esteban, 71, 137, 163n., 186n.

# Index

Pitt-Rivers, J., 120, 121, 122, 123, 179n., 183n.

Pocock, D., 186n.

Portugal
colonies of, 2

Pozos Dulces, Conde de, 34, 35

Prejudice
racial, 2, 6, 75, 80, 99
(*see also* Race; Purity of blood)

Puerto Príncipe, Audiencia of, 13

Pujadas, P. Tomas L., 159n.

Purity of blood, 6, 12, 13, 15–19, 21, 52, 72, 75, 80, 82, 119, 181n.
(*see also* Spain, cultural tradition of; Race, and pollution ideas)

Race
anomalous status and danger, 76
classification and anomaly, 71, 76, 78, 80–1 (*see also* Dichotomous classificatory schemas)
difficulties in the identification of, 71, 73–4
factors compensating for, 22–6, 65, 76, 95, 133
fraudulent registration of, 83
legal and real colour, 71, 73–4, 76–80, 137
political effect of separation, 35, 36, 37, 38, 39, 53, 54 (*see also* Civil authorities, political influences upon their decisions)
and pollution ideas, 14, 15, 16, 17–19, 80, 113, 131–2 (*also see* Purity of blood)
and social organization, 2, 5, 6, 16, 39, 71, 75–6, 80, 119
and the solidarity of the oppressed, 39, 53, 92, 96–7
as a symbol of social cleavage, 5, 6, 16, 49, 72, 74–6, 79, 80–1, 124, 137–8

'Reasons of conscience', 11, 22, 43, 46

Regla, 62, 96–7

Reich, Wilhelm, 139, 187n.

Religion, 7, 43, 46, 68, 69, 86, 119, 120, 122, 133

as a factor in interracial marriages, 7, 46, 68, 69, 86, 119, 120, 122, 133
and slavery, 53, 55

Reuck, A. de, 185n., 187n.

Revolution of 1959, 6, 7, 140

Rivière, P. G., 123, 130, 184n.

Rodman, Hyman, 129, 130, 184n.

Rodríguez San Pedro, Joaquín, 149n.

Rosenblat, Angel, 160n., 167n., 173n., 185n.

Saco, José Antonio, 35, 36, 37, 155n., 156n., 160n., 163n.

Sagra, Ramón de la, 148n., 166n., 175n.

Sta. Cruz y Mallén, Conde de Jaruco, Francisco Xavier de, 88, 91, 171n., 173n.

Sta. María del Rosario, 60–2, 96–7

Santiago de Cuba, Archbishop of, 26, 28, 40, 49–52, 158n., 159n. (*see also* Claret y Clarà)

Sarakatsani, 120, 122, 124

Secession, War of, 31, 33

Secularization, 55
of the State, 4 (*see also* Catholic Church, its relationship with the State)

Seduction, 44, 114, 121, 172n., 178n.
coloureds by whites, 116–17, 182n.
whites by coloureds, 113, 114
whites by whites, 107, 109–12

Serra, Rafael, 41

Sexual marginalization, 128–30

Sharecropping, 34, 35

Siso, Carlos, 167n.

Slave dealers, 4, 28, 30, 33, 38 (*see also* Sugar planters, and slave dealers; Slavery, and slave trading)

Slavery, 2, 3, 4, 5, 28, 33–8, 40, 55–6, 82, 94, 119, 128
abolition of, 4, 5, 33, 34, 36, 39, 40, 82
and economic developments, 2, 33, 34, 78
and international relations, 30
and the significance of race in everyday life, 2, 5, 6, 14, 16, 25, 75, 80 (*see also* Race, as symbol of social cleavage; Marriage, and legal status)